THEORIES OF DISTINCTION

Cultural Memory

in

the

Present

Mieke Bal and Hent de Vries, Editors

THEORIES OF DISTINCTION

Redescribing the Descriptions of Modernity

Niklas Luhmann

Edited and introduced

by William Rasch

Translations by Joseph O'Neil,
Elliott Schreiber, Kerstin Behnke,
and William Whobrey

STANFORD UNIVERSITY PRESS

STANFORD, CALIFORNIA

2002

Stanford University Press
Stanford, California

Printed in the United States of America on acid-free, archival-quality paper

Library of Congress Cataloging-in-Publication Data

Luhmann, Niklas.
    Theories of distinction : redescribing the descriptions of modernity /
Niklas Luhmann ; edited and introduced by William Rasch ; translations by
Joseph O'Neil . . . [et al.].
        p. cm. — (Cultural memory in the present)
    Includes bibliographical references and index.
    ISBN 0-8047-4122-0 (alk. paper)—ISBN 0-8047-4123-9 (pbk.)
        1. Sociology—Philosophy. 2. Social sciences—Philosophy. 3. Participant
observation—Philosophy. 4. Knowledge, Sociology of. I. Rasch, William, 1949–
II. Title. III. Series.

HM585 .L84 2002
301'.01—dc21

                                                            2001049220

Original Printing 2002

Last figure below indicates year of this printing:
11   10   09   08   07   06   05   04   03   02

Typeset by G & S Typesetters in 11/13.5 Adobe Garamond.

Contents

Preface

In an interview conducted in 1994, Niklas Luhmann freely acknowledged his "addiction to theory." The essays collected in this volume give ample evidence of this addiction. Luhmann the theory addict found pleasure solving intellectual problems in the way an engineer or a carpenter finds pleasure in solving practical ones. In an earlier time one would have called it "thinking for its own sake," and would not have been embarrassed to do so.

Four of the nine essays—"The Modern Sciences and Phenomenology" (Chapter 1) "Identity—What or How?" (Chapter 5), "What Is Communication?" (Chapter 7), and "I See Something You Don't See" (Chapter 9)—were translated especially for this volume by Joseph O'Neil and Elliott Schreiber. Two essays—"The Paradox of Observing Systems" (Chapter 3) and "Deconstruction as Second-Order Observing" (Chapter 4)—were written originally in English, and the remainder were translated by those identified below. Whatever modifications may have been made to these latter translations were adopted to regularize usage and vocabulary across the volume.

I would like to acknowledge the following publishers for granting permission to translate or to publish existing translations:

Picus Verlag in Vienna, Austria, for allowing us to translate *Die neuzeitlichen Wissenschaften und die Phänomenologie* (1996) (Chapter 1).

Westdeutscher Verlag in Opladen, Germany, for allowing us to translate, or publish existing translations of, the following:

"Identität—was oder wie?" (Chapter 5), "Das Erkenntnisprogramm des Konstruktivismus und die unbekannt bleibende Realität" (Chapter 6), "Was ist Kommunikation?" (Chapter 7), "Wie ist Bewußtsein an Kommunikation beteiligt?" (Chapter 8), and "Ich sehe was, was du nicht siehst"

(Chapter 9). The German originals can be found in Niklas Luhmann, *Soziologische Aufklärung*, volumes 5 (1990) and 6 (1995).

We would also like to express our gratitude to the following publishers for kindly granting us permission to reprint these essays:

"The Modernity of Science," trans. Kerstin Behnke, *New German Critique* 61 (1994): 9–23. Reprinted by permission of Telos Press (Chapter 2).

"The Paradox of Observing Systems," *Cultural Critique* 31 (1995): 37–53. Reprinted by permission of the University of Minnesota Press (Chapter 3).

"Deconstruction as Second-Order Observing," *New Literary History* 24 (1993): 763–82. Copyright, University of Virginia. Reprinted by permission of the Johns Hopkins University Press (Chapter 4).

"The Cognitive Program of Constructivism and the Reality That Remains Unknown," in *Selforganization: Portrait of a Scientific Revolution*, ed. W. Krohn et al. (Dordrecht, Holland: Kluwer Academic Publishers), 64–85. Reprinted by permission of Kluwer Academic Publishers (Chapter 6). (Selected papers in this volume were translated, without specific attribution, by Peter Germain, Jonathan Harrow, and John Bednarz.)

"How Can the Mind Participate in Communication?" in *Materialities of Communication*, ed. Hans Ulrich Gumbrecht and K. Ludwig Pfeiffer, trans. William Whobrey (Stanford, Calif.: Stanford University Press, 1994), 371–87. Reprinted by permission of Stanford University Press (Chapter 8).

Before writing the introduction to the present volume, I convened a small group, including the two primary translators, to read the essays included in this volume. I wish to thank Hossein Mehdizadeh, Joseph O'Neil, Elliott Schreiber, Sharon Wailes, and Wilfried Wilms for their comments and insights. In particular, I wish to acknowledge the help of Mr. Mehdizadeh, who subsequently read with me some of the formal logic and mathematical texts dealt with in the introduction. All and sundry are absolved from any responsibility for the ideas expressed therein.

THEORIES OF DISTINCTION

Introduction: The Self-Positing Society

William Rasch

It is the peculiar goal of the Western philosophical tradition, the tradition of first philosophy, to attain a global, rational understanding of the cosmos, and thereby discover the purpose and meaning of human life. The aim of this knowledge is to be total and valid for all times, and the ability to attain this knowledge depends upon the use of unblemished reason. Reason, it is said, raises us above partiality—above both historical and cultural limitation and the occluded vision that comes with interest—to afford us a comprehension of the whole. The greatest modern representative of this Greek ideal, Leo Strauss, is absolutely clear on the role that true philosophy should serve:

Philosophy, as quest for wisdom, is quest for universal knowledge, for knowledge of the whole. . . . Instead of "the whole" the philosophers also say "all things": the whole is not a pure ether or an unrelieved darkness in which one cannot distinguish one part from the other, or in which one cannot discern anything. Quest for knowledge of "all things" means quest for knowledge of God, the world, and man—or rather quest for knowledge of the natures of all things: the natures in their totality are "the whole." (Strauss 1988, 11)

Knowledge of "the whole" or of "all things" may never be achieved, but, according to Strauss, its fundamental possibility must be affirmed. The ground for this possibility is the discovery of nature, or rather, the discovery of the distinction between nature (natural right) and ancestral or conventional authority. "Philosophy appeals from the ancestral to the good, to that which is good intrinsically, to that which is good by nature," and "the human faculty that, with the help of sense perception, discovers nature is reason or understanding" (Strauss 1953, 91, 92). Reason thus serves as the common bond between human nature and the nature of the cosmos. To deny reason is to set the individual and the species adrift on a sea of incomprehensibility.

The hallmark of modernity, to be contemplated with dismay or equanimity, is the loss of this faith in the continuum of reason that links the human with a rationally ordered universe. The vision of all things, once guaranteed by reason's elevation, expires as the whole disappears beyond an infinite horizon and classical reason turns into scientific rationality. Contemplating the modern "world picture," we no longer feel embedded in the whole; rather, we "forget" it (we forget "Being") and cross-examine what remains, as if it were a system susceptible to scientific interrogation.[1] The German idealist tradition attempts to regain the ability to view the whole, but only in the form of a transcendental or historical (and/or historical-materialist) project. The whole serves as a mythical origin and a utopian telos, but it remains invisible. The view of the whole transforms itself into a temporalized desire. No longer an individual pursuit, the quest becomes a historical mission.

As a philosophical project, this mission exhausts itself in the twentieth century. True, Edmund Husserl could still maintain in the mid-1930s that European humanity, born with the Greeks, is equivalent to universal humanity; that "philosophical reason represents a new stage of human nature"; and that this "stage of human existence [under] ideal norms for infinite tasks, the stage of existence *sub specie aeterni*, is possible only through absolute universality, precisely the universality contained from the start in the ideal of philosophy" (Husserl 1970b, 273). But he had to concede that this view was mightily under siege, challenged by a variety of "skeptical philosophies" (Husserl 1970a, 15). It is perhaps a fitting irony that if Husserl begot Heidegger, and Heidegger begot both Gadamer and Derrida, then the skeptical "nonphilosophies" (15) that Husserl feared seem not only to have carried the day but also, perversely, to have issued from his own more fundamental aspirations. At any rate, what has dominated in both the philosophical and the social-theoretical projects of the past one hundred years has been an intense concentration on the immanence of the posited world. The whole may be the transcendent or transcendental condition of possibility for this immanent world, but as such it can never be perceived. In Husserl's own terminology, the world, as horizon, cannot become a theme. Consequently, the immanent, partial, and severed world, the posited world, gradually achieves autonomy and takes center stage. What was once "the whole" or the nature of "all things" that could be seized in an instant and for all time as a totality now becomes an immanent field of observations, descriptions, and communications, a "totality of facts," as Wittgenstein wrote (see below), that must contend with the uncomfortable situation that any observation of a fact is itself a fact that can be observed. The whole that is modernity is the whole that strains to see itself and thus a whole that forever divides itself with every observation into more and more "facts." The whole we now deal with is a self-referential whole, thus an inescapably paradoxical one. Accordingly, we are no longer in the realm of a foundationalist "first" philosophy but rather in the realm of a "second-order" philosophy of observations of the observations of self and other.

As you will read in the essays contained in this volume, the notion of second-order observation—that is, the observation of observations, including one's own—constitutes a major epistemological principle that structures Niklas Luhmann's general social theory. The idea, of course, is not new. As Luhmann recognizes, it informs the major intellectual developments of the modern era, including, but not restricted to, the critique of ideology derived from Marx and the psychoanalysis of Freud. In the orthodox renditions of both Marxism and psychoanalysis, the purpose of the observation of others' observations is to locate "latencies" (class interest, traumatic experience) that account for error (ideology, pathological behavior). To the extent that utopic hope attaches to these orthodoxies, these disturbing latencies can be "cured" (made transparent and thus harmless) by sociopolitical or individual "therapies" of a necessarily violent or ideally nonviolent nature. Again, to the extent that the hunt for latencies is embedded in a form of enlightenment orthodoxy, the observation of observation is guided by some functional equivalent of a substantive notion of reason—the therapeutic dialog, the class consciousness of the proletariat, or discursively achieved consensus, to name a few. Deviant observation will be identified and corrected by "true" observation—true because rational, and normative (i.e., having the authority of law) because true. The loss of metaphysical reason, in other words, is compensated for by a gain in "communicative" or morally normative rationalities. However, in the wake of Nietzsche and Max Weber, and in the continuing turbulence of the major "non-philosophies" of the late twentieth century—pragmatism, hermeneutics, and poststructuralism—such trust in the therapeutic effects of reason and its substitutes has all but vanished. In its stead, Luhmann offers a thoroughgoing radicalization of the observation of latencies by locating latencies in *all* observations, including his own—latencies that simply cannot be finally and fundamentally accounted for. What is needed, then, is a theory that can account for this lack of accountability. Luhmann's Herculean (or should one say "Hegelian"?) attempt to provide us with such a theory culminated in 1997 with the publication of his monumental *Die Gesellschaft der Gesellschaft* (The society of society). The essays collected in the present volume, all originally published in the decade prior to the 1997 publication of Luhmann's 1,164-page *magnum opus*, are a series of *Vorstudien*, preliminary studies that explore the implications of fully acknowledging the radically ungrounded nature of observation. The aim of this introduction is to weave an intellectual narrative incorporating tales of self-reference, paradox, and the partiality of observation that have intrigued twentieth-century practitioners of science, logic, philosophy, and social theory. That is, this introduction is more concerned with offering a genealogy of Luhmannian motifs than with a direct paraphrase of specific positions and utterances. I hope readers will then be able to insert Luhmann into this narrative as they make their way through the essays.

Self and Not-Self

The problem of self-consciousness, as the German idealists well knew, is the problem of paradox. How can the self refer to itself without making of itself something other than itself, something that can be referred to, pointed to, as if it were not what was doing the pointing? In Fichte's *Science of Knowledge*, for instance, we have a clear articulation of the puzzle, along with a proposed solution.

For pure consciousness to be conscious of itself, it must be conscious of itself as other; thus it must split itself in two. It must, that is, posit itself as a self-positing subject and as a reflected object. The self-positing of the self must also posit its own negation, the not-self. Such positing and counter-positing have a common origin (the self) and occur simultaneously. The not-self is no afterthought; rather, it emerges with the logically presup-posed self. We therefore have a logical contradiction — or, at least, a conflict that Fichte structures logically. In its mode of self-positing, the self can be captured logically as identity: $A = A$; in its coterminous mode of counter-positing (of the not-self), the self loses its identity, so to speak: $A = \text{not-}A$. Logically, then, positing should preclude counterpositing, as the latter would cancel the former. Instead, a middle that ought to be excluded is in-cluded: A is both A and not-A. Fichte specifically utters this contradiction as a paradoxical result of the two principles — positing and counterposit-ing — with which he starts. "Insofar as the not-self is posited, the self is not posited," he writes, "for the not-self completely nullifies the self." However, "the not-self can be posited only insofar as a self *is* posited in the self (in the identical consciousness), to which it (the non-self) can be opposed." There-fore, the principle of counterpositing nullifies itself. "But it nullifies itself only insofar as the posited is annulled by the counterposited, which is to say, insofar as it is itself valid. . . . Thus it does not annul itself. The second principle [counterpositing] annuls itself; and it also does not annul itself" (Fichte 1982, 106–7).[2]

The paradox is resolved by introducing the notion of quantity and the finitude of space. "How can A and $-A$, being and nonbeing, reality and negation, be thought together without mutual elimination and destruc-tion?" Fichte asks. "They will mutually *limit* one another" (Fichte 1982, 108). Self and not-self occupy finite and partial areas of space, each serving as the limit of the other. Thus the self and not-self become divisible — in-deed, they define that very notion. One is tempted to say that self and not-self emerge as limit functions of each other. Reference to self becomes ref-erence to a double negation, for if reference to the other is reference to a not-self, then reference to self becomes reference to a not not-self. But with this resolution of the paradox, a second paradoxical distinction arises, one that must be resolved in a different manner from the first. The posited self that is limited by its not-self is no longer the absolute self that initiated all positing and counterpositing. As a quantifiably determinate self, limited and reflected by its other, the posited self stands in opposition to or contra-distinction from the absolute self. *That* self still remains — and must re-main — invisible and without predicate if it is to serve as the undivided ground for the unity of the difference between self and not-self. The ab-solute self is "equal to itself" and "posited as indivisible; whereas the self to which the not-self is opposed is posited as divisible. Hence, insofar as there is a not-self opposed to it, the self is itself in opposition to the absolute self" (109). Thus, with one stroke, the initial act of self-positing effects two cuts—the one severing self from not-self in a limited space of mutual determination, and the other severing the absolute self from that limited space of the (now) empirical self and its indispensable partner, the not-self. We witness, then, the paradox of a self that alienates itself from itself in the very act of self-positing.

Now, ever since Adam and Eve discovered naked self-observation, a perceived alienation has automatically provoked a longing for reconciliation. The legacies of both the German idealist and the German Marxist traditions are no different in this regard. Whereas the former might stress the ethical overtones of what is essentially described as a logical problem, the latter imaginatively correlates the antinomies of thought—subject and object, intuition and concept, theory and practice—with the contradictions of social relations brought about by the capitalist economic order. Accordingly, the reconciliation in one sphere presupposes revolutionary action in the other; yet the correct revolutionary action presupposes simultaneous imaginative reconciliation. Correct theory, in other words, presupposes correct practice, which in turn is based on correct theory. The "dialectical" effort of "critical" theory, then, has been to move society through its self-alienated state to a higher unity consciously articulated as the realization of autonomy and justice. Revolutionary transformation of society both presupposes and brings about the desired harmonious state of affairs. Though temporally the movement is always conceived to be a progression of history, logically the movement moves backward, retracing the steps of paradox in order to erase them.

We, however, may wish to look upon Fichte's creation narrative not as a fall from grace in need of world-spiritual compensation but as a headlong plunge into irreversible complexification. And we may wish to look at this complexification as the unfolding of the social world in which we find ourselves. And we may *not* wish to consider this unfolding of the social world, whether we care for it or not, as a sinful one. Were we to view "alienation" in this more neutral light, we would direct our attention not to the absolute that is *prior* to distinction but to the absolute *of* distinction and thus to the productivity of paradoxes. Unlike those, then, who see the task of social theory to be the construction of "counterfactual" utopian projections, we may find ourselves quite content to remain in the fallen and limited state of distinctions in order to see how the social world, which determines itself by positing the difference between *A* and not-*A*, builds its forms. We may not like these forms. We may not like their consequences. But we would have to realize that every effort to scramble back "up" and out of the world of forms toward an impossible, primary unity leads us further "down" into the world that we cannot escape because it is the world that we continually make. What Fichte would have given us, therefore, is *not* a projection of human freedom as "our highest practical goal" (Fichte 1982, 115) but rather, more modestly, a rudimentary calculus of self-reference based on Aristotelian logic. Fichte may have interpreted it for consciousness, but it could just as well be interpreted for a variety of other self-referential machines or systems.

We could, for instance, have given the following narrative twist to the basic Fichtean scheme:

Let us then consider, for a moment, the world as described by the physicist. It consists of a number of fundamental particles which, if shot through their own space, appear as waves, and are thus . . . of the same laminated structure as pearls or onions, and other wave forms called electromagnetic which it is convenient, by Occam's razor, to consider as traveling through space with a standard velocity. All these appear bound by certain natural laws which indicate the form of their relationship.

Now the physicist himself, who describes all this, is, in his own account, himself constructed of it. He is, in short, made of a conglomeration of the very particles he describes, no more, no less, bound together by and obeying such general laws as he himself has managed to find and to record.

Thus we cannot escape the fact that the world we know is constructed in order (and thus in such a way as to be able) to see itself.

This is indeed amazing.

Not so much in view of what it sees, although this may appear fantastic enough, but in respect of the fact that it *can* see *at all*.

But *in order* to do so, evidently it must first cut itself up into at least one state which sees, and at least one other state which is seen. In this severed and mutilated condition, whatever it sees is *only partially* itself. We may take it that the world undoubtedly is itself (i.e. is indistinct from itself), but, in any attempt to see itself as an object, it must, equally undoubtedly, act so as to make itself distinct from, and therefore false to, itself. In this condition it will always partially elude itself.

It seems hard to find an acceptable answer to the question of how or why the world conceives a desire, and discovers an ability, to see itself, and appears to suffer the process. That it does so is sometimes called the original mystery. Perhaps, in view of *the form* in which *we* presently *take* ourselves *to exist*, the mystery *arises from* our insistence on *framing* a question where there is, in reality, *nothing* to question. However it may appear, if such desire, ability, and sufferance be granted, the state or condition that arises as an outcome is, according to the laws here formulated [i.e., Spencer Brown's "laws of form"], absolutely unavoidable. In this respect, at least, there is no mystery. We, as universal representatives, *can* record universal law far enough to say

> and so on, and so on you will eventually construct the universe, in every detail and potentiality, as you know it now; but then, again, what you construct will not be all, for by the time you will have reached what now is, the universe will have expanded into a new order to contain what will then be.
>
> In this sense, in respect of its own information, the universe *must* expand to escape the telescopes through which we, who are it, are trying to capture it, which is us. The snake eats itself, the dog chases its tail. (Spencer Brown 1979, 104–6)

This lengthy passage comes from an explanatory note to chapter 12 of George Spencer Brown's *Laws of Form*. We will have occasion below to examine what these purported laws allow us to see, or, more accurately, what they allow Luhmann to see, but for now, as a fast introduction to the notion of self-reference that plays such an important role in Luhmann's thought, I simply wish to examine some of the implications of this passage.

We see that what Fichte called consciousness, Spencer Brown calls the "world" or the "universe"—with observation enabled by physical, not mental, devices. Though physical, observation is nonetheless still self-observation. The self-positing self becomes the self-examining universe that uses physical elements (e.g., humans and telescopes) to explore its own physical nature. In so doing, it must "posit" itself as divisible. It "cuts" itself up into self ("one state which sees") and not-self ("one other state which is seen"). What sees is no disembodied mind but "a conglomeration of the very particles" it describes; thus, what sees, sees itself, but "*only partially* itself."

We also understand, however, that Spencer Brown's observation of the self-observation of the world is enmeshed in its own paradox, for Spencer Brown's description takes on the form of a total description. It is as if his observation hovered over and above the world, as if that world were projected onto a two-dimensional plane, like a map. It seems, in other words, that the thesis that all observation is partial is itself not partial, as if its description of the world's description of itself as partial could encompass both the primal unity of the universe and the fallen, "post-cut" state. But if all observation and description is partial, then so must be the observation that makes this description. It, too, must operate by the same rules, the same necessity to "cut" and the same limitation this necessity brings about. Thus, the unity described as "the world" must be a unity presupposed, not a unity observed. Indeed, Spencer Brown merely *assumes* that there is such a unity that undergoes this operation ("*We may take it* that the world undoubtedly is itself" [emphasis added]), but he never claims to "see" it. The thesis that all descriptions are partial needs to presuppose the fiction of totality against which the notion of partiality can be understood. But the world (or absolute self) remains an inconceivable and inaccessible horizon. Any "project" to recuperate or reunite the totality only pushes it beyond further horizons as the universe grows in response to the telescopes constructed to encompass it. Thus, not only can one not get back to the original unity, one can never really perceive the first cut. All cuts are already made in a divisible and cut world. The primary cut disappears beyond the horizon along with the primal unity. In fact, that horizon is itself already a limit, a cut, a distinction, one that cannot be gotten beyond, precisely because it serves as the presupposition or "ground" for all subsequent cuts, even the "first" cut that severs what "sees" from what "is seen." In the terms of the natural laws *of* the physicist that must also account *for* the physicist, observation requires a nonequilibrium state—the difference between negentropy and entropy. As Lawrence Sklar notes:

In order for there to be sustained, complex organisms (like ourselves) that could perform observations, there must be energy flows. Only these can counteract the normal process of equilibration and keep a highly structured active organism, like a life-form, in operation. But such energy flows presuppose a nonequilibrium situation. So if there are to be observers at all, they must be found in the small, deviant, nonequilibrium portions of the universe.[3]

This, then, would be Spencer Brown's "original mystery," the differentiation of order—a highly improbable defiance of the second law of thermodynamics—that makes the "desire, ability, and sufferance" of observation possible.

And our observation of Spencer Brown is no different. Any reference to the world is self-reference, and any self-reference requires external reference, a not-self against which it can be distinguished. The "unity" of self-reference and external reference—which is to say, the ineluctable linkage and reciprocal necessity of the two—requires the difference of unity and distinction that is marked by the horizon beyond which we cannot go. The "first" cut that marks the emergence of self and external reference is made in a space that has already been cut, a cut space that allows further cuts to be made.

It is against this background, then, that we can understand Luhmann's repeated claim that social theory is a form of social self-observation. Just as one can think consciousness only from within consciousness and see the world only from within the world, one can observe society only from within society and thus observe it only partially. Banal sounding, the claim is at once matter-of-fact and polemical. The reality it purports to describe aggressively displays the limits of self-observation, and any attempt to view society normatively, as if from the outside, is greeted with bewilderment. Norms, too, are socially embedded, not transcendently given. Society, as an informationally closed system, defined by communication and internally differentiated into function systems, is, to use Spencer Brown's hyperbolic phrase, "severed and mutilated." This condition is seen to be one of the inescapable "facts" of modern society. Luhmann neither longs for the view of "the whole" nor bemoans its absence. Jeremiads against reification, rationalization, neutralization, or alienation are no more part of his repertoire than demands for communal participation or discursively achieved consensus. We live in a "severed" state, and our observation is possible precisely because it is partial. Society's lack of universal normativity, of consensus and integration, simply reminds us that we inhabit a universe that insistently exceeds the power of its own telescopes. Yet the contention that society can be seen only from within society and only partially is a total observation, a total observation about the impossibility of total observations. It therefore cannot help but fall victim to paradox. Paradox, however, is not the perplexing dead end of a false path but every path's point of origin. Consequently, a theory of society must above all account for this paradox and the limits that it exposes—not in order to overcome or evade paradox but to include it as a constituent moment of the universe that theory describes.

Completeness and Paradox

When Strauss gives voice to the Greek notion of "the whole" or of the nature of "all things," he utters a qualitative—not quantitative—statement about the unity of the Good, the True, and the Beautiful. Unlike scientific rationality, which decomposes reality into potentially infinite constituent parts, the classical concept of reason affords direct access to qualitative essences that give order and meaning to social and political structures. Similarly, any unmediated and transparent consciousness of the Fichtean absolute self, were it possible, would be an instantaneous (if infinitely deferred) quality of mind, an act of pure freedom, and not an empirical gathering of the shards of existence. When, however, we post-idealist moderns speak of the whole, "all things" tend to become countable. The whole we seek is the posited whole, and we think—or once hoped—that that whole can be completely accounted for. Wittgenstein, for instance, famously speaks of the world as a "logical space" comprising a "totality of facts." "The world is determined by the facts, and by their being *all* the facts."[4] Or, more succinctly, the world is the *set* of all facts. What cannot be linguistically articulated as a member of this logically ordered set simply recedes from view. Meaning and value are not facts of the world, but must lie outside it. Ethics and aesthetics are also "transcendental" (Wittgenstein 1974, 6.421). The will can change only the boundaries of the world, not its facts. And death simply marks the end or limit of the world; it cannot be experienced as an event (6.43–6.4311). The world simply is, and the true experience of the world, Wittgenstein believes, does not consist of imagining the qualitative merging of the world with its transcendent conditions of possibility. Rather, "to view the world sub specie aeterni is to view it as a whole—a limited whole. Feeling the world as a limited whole—it is this that is mystical" (6.45). This mystical feeling is achieved by excluding one more element from the world—the subject. Like death, the subject is the limit of the world. It allows for the vision of the limited whole precisely because it is not included within that limited whole. The subject is the eye that sees the world, but it cannot see itself doing so (5.632–5.6331).

But is the contemplation of the world as a limited whole possible? Is this set of facts complete? Is, for instance, the statement that describes the world as the "totality of facts" itself a fact of the world, made from within the same "logical space" of which the world is composed? In other words, is "The world is the totality of facts" a fact of the world? One can hardly imagine that it is not. The fact that the world consists of all the facts in logical space would seem to be one of the facts of this space; thus the statement that the world is the set of all the facts must be a statement that is included in the set it describes. And this, it seems, can be indefinitely extended, for what about the statement that immediately precedes the question I am currently writing? Is it, too, a fact of the world, and does it therefore also belong to the set of all facts? That is, does the world contain not only the "facts" of the world but also the description of these facts, and the description of this description as well? What of Wittgenstein's sense of the world contemplated *sub specie aeterni*? Does Wittgenstein's contemplation of the world occur within the world? If so, how can he contemplate the world, in which he is included, "sub specie aeterni"? If the statement is uttered from within the circumscribed world, where do we find the limits that give us our ordered and complete whole? Does the exclusion of the subject, the "seeing eye," give us these limits? But if the description of this "mystical" feeling is not made from within the world, if it occupies the margin or hovers one level higher, so to speak, how are words found to express it, for as Wittgenstein also, and quite famously, tells us: "*The limits of my language* mean the limits of my world" (Wittgenstein 1974, 5.6).

We are entering ambiguous, fascinating, and, by now, well-known territory. A limited, bounded totality is sought to contain the aporias of infinity, yet the very act of describing such a totality destroys it, since every description "increases" the totality it describes, necessitating a new, more comprehensive description. Thus the attempt to contain infinity seemingly produces it instead. Nevertheless, at the beginning of the twentieth century, containment remained the goal. Writing in 1901, with a confidence that was to be greatly qualified later, Bertrand Russell made the following exuberant claim:

There is a greatest of all infinite numbers, which is the number of things altogether, of every sort and kind. It is obvious that there cannot be a greater number than this, because, if everything has been taken, there is nothing left to add. Cantor has a proof that there is no greatest number, and if this proof were valid, the contradictions of infinity would reappear in a sublimated form. But in this one point, the master has been guilty of a very subtle fallacy, which I hope to explain in some future work. (Russell 1981, 69)

What Russell eventually had to explain, however, was not the fallacy of Cantor's proof but the consequences of its validity.[5] Georg Cantor's theory of infinite sets and transfinite numbers, developed in the late nineteenth century, contradicted mathematical orthodoxy and the philosophical tradition in a number of ways. For instance, he defined infinite sets as actually existing sets, not as potential or analytically convenient ones. Cantor, in other words, no longer thought of infinity simply as the hypothetical ability to add the number "1" to any highest thinkable number; rather, he thought of infinity in the plural, as actual sets that could be compared to one another. Thus, by defining an infinite set as a set that could be placed into a one-to-one correspondence with a proper subset of itself, he produced counterintuitive results, including, to use a common example, the fact that the set of positive even numbers is the same size as the set of all positive integers:

$\{1, 2, 3, 4, \ldots\}$
$\{2, 4, 6, 8, \ldots\}.$

He also advanced the notion that there are greater and lesser infinities. If we have two infinite sets, A and B, we can say that B is larger than A if we can place A in a one-to-one correspondence with a subset of B but cannot place B in a one-to-one correspondence with a subset of A. Transfinite numbers are the numbers one assigns to progressively larger infinite sets. Thus the set of natural numbers and all infinite sets equal to it in size are assigned the number aleph_0; the next largest infinite set would be designated by the number aleph_1; and so on. Most interestingly for our purposes, he noted that every infinite set could generate a larger infinity from within itself, a so-called power set consisting of all the original set's subsets. To use a finite example, the set $\{1, 2, 3\}$ has three elements. Its power set, however, has eight elements (including the null set): $\{\emptyset, \{1,2,3\}, \{1\}, \{2\}, \{3\}, \{1,2\}, \{1,3\}, \{2,3\}\}$. Accordingly, no set can be the largest set or set of all sets, since any "largest" set could always spawn a set larger than itself. The problem can be phrased as a paradox. The set of all sets generates a power set of itself that is larger than the set of all sets. But since the smaller set is the set of all sets, it must include its power set as part of itself. Paradoxically, a smaller infinity contains a larger infinity within itself. Thus, there is no set of all sets.

The problems produced by his notions of infinity did not much bother Cantor because they conformed to his religious beliefs. Writing to his fellow mathematician, Richard Dedekind, Cantor noted the following: "A collection [*Vielheit*] can be so constituted that the assumption of a 'unification' of *all* its elements into a whole leads to a contradiction, so that it is impossible to conceive of the collection as a unity, as a 'completed object.' Such collections I call *absolute infinite* or *inconsistent* collections" (qtd. in Dauben 1990, 245). Cantor's biographer, Joseph Warren Dauben, emphasizes that not only Cantor the mathematician but also Cantor the devout Catholic was interested in absolute infinite sets because they provided him with a suitable image for the incomprehensibility of God:

The set of all transfinite numbers, like the absolute itself, could be acknowledged, but it could never be completely understood. The mystical-religious implications were all a part of Cantor's conceptualization of the infinite, and of his *Transfinitum* in particular. He always regarded the absolutely infinite succession of transfinite numbers as a thoroughly appropriate symbol for the Absolute. . . . By recognizing the connections Cantor drew between his transfinite numbers and the Absolute, it is easier to understand why the paradoxes of set theory did not upset him as they did so many mathematicians at the turn of the century. Essentially, he had recognized the impossibility of subjecting the entire succession of transfinite numbers to exact mathematical analysis. The nature of their existence as a unity in the mind of God constituted a different sort of perfection, and Cantor was not disturbed that it was beyond his means to comprehend it precisely. In fact, the inaccessibility of the Absolute to any maximal transfinite determination seemed both fitting and appropriate. (Dauben 1990, 245–46)

Russell's God, however, was not the incomprehensible infinite, but logic. The paradoxes of self-reference and infinity that arose from set theory presented a grave challenge to him, as they did to others who worked on the total axiomatization of mathematics. Formalists such as David Hilbert and logicists such as Gottlob Frege and Russell saw as their task the rigorous formalization of mathematics using nothing but logical rules of inference.[6] The object was to create of the entire field of mathematics a complete and consistent system. Consistency requires that no contradictory theorems can be derived from the system's postulates (e.g., that from the same set of postulates one cannot prove both A and not-A). Completeness requires that all true statements be provable by use of the axioms of the system, such that there are no undecidable theorems. But by its very nature, paradox threatens such neat closure. To his dismay, Russell had to confront the issue head on when he formulated the paradox that is now known as "Russell's antinomy." It can be described as follows:

Classes seem to be of two kinds: those which do not contain themselves as members, and those which do. A class will be called "normal" if, and only if, it does not contain itself as a member; otherwise it will be called "non-normal." An example of a normal class is the class of mathematicians, for patently the class itself is not a mathematician and is therefore not a member of itself. An example of a non-normal class is the class of all thinkable things; for the class of all thinkable things is itself thinkable and is therefore a member of itself. Let "N" by definition stand for the class of *all* normal classes. We ask whether N itself is a normal class. If N is normal, it is a member of itself (for by definition N contains all normal classes); but, in that case, N is non-normal, because by definition a class that contains itself as a member is non-normal. On the other hand, if N is non-normal, it is a member of itself (by definition of non-normal); but, in that case, N is normal, because by definition the members of N are normal classes. In short, N is normal if, and only if, N is non-normal. It follows that the statement "N is normal" is both true and false. (Nagel and Newman 1958, 24)

The antinomy can be translated into seemingly harmless and entertaining puzzles. For instance, does the barber who shaves all and only those who do not shave themselves shave himself? Do all rules have exceptions? *All* rules?[7] But there are more disturbing examples, ones that go to the root of logic itself. What happens when we examine the indispensable logical (and metaphysical) law of the excluded middle, which is designed to preclude contradiction? The law of the excluded middle can be phrased as follows: "All propositions are either true or false." The law itself is a proposition; thus if the law were applied to itself, it would be exposed to the possibility of refutation. For the law to operate as a law, however, it must exempt itself from its own operation. A law determines what is and what is not legitimate, but it cannot justify its own legitimacy without implicitly resorting to a higher legitimacy, a higher law—a move that introduces, once again, the danger of infinite regress. To serve as the ground upon which logic builds, the law of the excluded middle must effectively *be* the excluded middle; it must simply be, rather than be either true or false.

To avoid the problem brought about by such reflexive applications of rules, propositions, and classes, Russell prohibited "impredicative definitions" (Henri Poincaré's term) by declaring that statements about totalities could not be part of the totality they describe (Kline 1980, 207). With his theory of types, introduced in 1908, Russell hoped to save the logicist program of mathematics by legislating a whole class of paradoxes out of existence. To block self-reference, he arranged propositions (or classes, etc.) into discrete hierarchies. Simple statements about individual objects are first-order propositions. Statements concerning those first-order propositions are one level higher, and are called second-order propositions. And the series could be indefinitely continued. Thus the proposition that states that all propositions are either true or false does not fall victim to self-reference because it is of a type higher than the propositions it subsumes. Similarly, set N, the set of all normal sets, is neither a normal nor a non-normal set but rather a second-order one—a "hyper-normal" set, one might say—that cannot be included within itself. Russell thereby avoids self-referential paradoxes—but at a price. Ironically, the theory of types, devised to avoid paradox, seems to mirror the cause of paradox, the infinite progression of Cantor's transfinite numbers that Russell originally set out to disprove. To refer to Wittgenstein's example again, the "fact" of the "totality of facts" would not be a fact within that totality, according to Russell's theory, but a fact of a higher order. As a result, however, the world that is the "totality of facts" would not be *the* world, but *a* world, one that can be observed by another "higher-level" world, the world within which the higher-level fact exists. Totality becomes totality deferred, referred higher and higher in the hierarchy of levels, such that any description of totality will inevitably be incomplete—at best, "totality minus one," so to speak. Once self-reference is excluded, there is no more possibility of proving the existence of a set of all sets than there is of finding the "greatest of all infinite numbers." Thus, though Russell's device avoids paradox, it does so by precluding completeness.[8]

It was the work of Kurt Gödel, however, that secured a permanent place in contemporary thought for self-reference, paradox, and incompleteness. Gödel showed, as is well known, that the logicist and formalist attempt at a complete and consistent axiomatization of mathematics was logically impossible. Recall that completeness of a mathematical system demands that every true statement within that system be deducible from its axioms; and consistency prohibits the system's axioms from demonstrating both a statement and its negation. Gödel devised a numbering system by which he could "'map' or 'mirror' meta-mathematical statements about a sufficiently comprehensive formal system in the system itself" (Nagel and Newman

1958, 63). He folded or collapsed metalevel statements into the basal level that those statements were about—in this case, logical rules of inference into arithmetical formulas susceptible to basic arithmetical operations (e.g., addition, multiplication, etc.). In this way, he could "construct an arithmetical formula G that represents the meta-mathematical statement: 'The formula G is not demonstrable.' This formula G thus ostensibly says of *itself* that it is not demonstrable" (85). In other words, he formulated a number within a given arithmetical calculus (based on the prime numbers) that "contained" within it or "represented" a self-referential statement. He could then show that this formula G is demonstrable "if, and only if, its formal negation -G is demonstrable" (85). If both the formula and its negation are demonstrable, the system in question cannot be considered consistent. If, on the other hand, one assumes the system to be consistent, then the formula G must be considered "formally undecidable." If the system is consistent, that is, then neither G nor -G can be uniquely demonstrated by the axioms of the system. Gödel then demonstrated that G, though not formally deducible from the axioms of the calculus, was nevertheless a true arithmetical formula. It was, in other words, a true but formally undecidable statement within the system formed by the axioms of arithmetic. Therefore, by definition, the axioms of arithmetic are demonstrated to be incomplete. "Moreover, Gödel established that arithmetic is *essentially* incomplete: even if additional axioms were assumed so that the true formula G could be formally derived from the augmented set, another true but formally undecidable formula could be constructed" (85–86). (Recall Spencer Brown's image: "In this sense, in respect of its own information, the universe *must* expand to escape the telescopes through which we, who are it, are trying to capture it, which is us.") In a similar way, Gödel mapped the meta-mathematical statement "Arithmetic is consistent" onto the calculus and demonstrated arithmetically that "if arithmetic is consistent its consistency cannot be established by any meta-mathematical reasoning that can be represented within the formalism of arithmetic" (96).

What Gödel did *not* prove is that math is inherently illogical, inconsistent, or incoherent. Despite (or perhaps because of) the collapse of the formalist and logicist ambitions, mathematics was enriched, not impoverished.[9] What Gödel *did* prove, however, is that there is no strictly immanent way of demonstrating the consistency and the completeness of any formally rigorous system; that there can be no expression of total or complete knowledge of a system made from within the system itself. Using modern, symbolic logic, Gödel demonstrated a tightly structured, microcosmic version of what Kant had already demonstrated with his antinomies of pure reason, namely that "there is no way for us to imagine in a consistent way the universe as a Whole; that is, as soon as we do it, we obtain two antinomical, mutually exclusive versions of the universe as a Whole" (Žižek 1993, 83). Thus, in the words of the logician and philosopher Patrick Grim, the inescapability of self-reference and the paradoxes that it can engender do *not* show that "our logic leaves out a totality of truths or a notion of 'all truths,'" but rather show that "given fundamental logical principles, there cannot *be* any such totality, there can be no consistent notion of 'all truths.' Given fundamental logical principles, the notion of total knowledge must prove similarly impossible; it is not simply omitted, not transcendentally ineffable, but logically incoherent" (Grim 1991, 128). Examining various versions of and attempted solutions to persistent logical paradoxes such as the Liar Paradox and the astonishing Paradox of the Knower,[10] as well as ramifications of Gödel's incompleteness theorem and Cantor's notion of power sets, Grim asserts that the *universe* is incomplete, not our knowledge of it. Indeed, it is our knowledge, not our ignorance—as classical, metaphysical rationalism claimed—that produces incompleteness. Modeling an ideal knower on the basis of the type of immanent formal system described by Gödel, Grim states:

No matter how much basic knowledge we imagine building into an ideal knower of this basic form—no matter what else is included among the recursively enumerable axioms of G—such a knower could never approach omniscience. If such a knower knows enough to handle basic number theory, in fact—no matter what *else* he knows—he already knows too *much* to know everything. At that point he already knows too much, in fact, to know the truth regarding all statements he can *express*—all statements in the language of G and thus, on our analogy, all statements in the general domain of his body of knowledge. (74)

And, using Cantor's notion of a power set, Grim shows that even a system as formally "thin" as language itself must be "expressively incomplete" and thus inadequate for the "expression of all truths" (82). Finally, even the existence of an omniscient mind proves categorically impossible:

Any omniscient mind would surely be self-reflective in at least the following sense: among its objects of knowledge, among those things it knows something about, would be its own conceptions of properties. . . . Any such mind will have at least as many objects of knowledge as conceptions of properties, since each of the latter will also be an object of knowledge. But by Cantor's power set theorem, there will be more actual properties of its objects of knowledge than objects themselves. Actual properties will outnumber its conceptions of properties. Thus some genuine property of its objects of knowledge, and therefore some truth, will fall outside even its range of *conception.* (83)

Grim's conclusion: An omniscient mind, to be omniscient, would have to be minimally self-reflective, but since it can be demonstrated that no such self-reflective mind can be truly omniscient, there simply can be no omniscient mind. Even for God, the universe is "incomplete." God may know everything, but God cannot know everything God knows.

Observation

What holds for God holds for all self-referential systems. They cannot construct themselves so as to be able to see themselves fully. Opacities remain, no matter how large the telescopes.

One such system, Luhmann asserts, is communication. Or, since communication is the basic, irreducible element of society: One such system is society with all its internally differentiated subsystems. "Only communication can communicate," he tells us (this volume, chapters 7 and 8), thereby neatly excising the act from any actor or agent. With his identification of society and communication, he effects, in fact, a dual cut. The individual (the person, the subject, the psychic system) not only disappears as the agent of communication and therefore no longer provides intention or conveys information but also, quite surprisingly, disappears from society altogether. Society is the aggregate not of individuals, according to Luhmann, but of communications. The psychic system, as Luhmann puts it, exists as the environment of the social system, just as the social system exists as the environment of the psychic system. And though the psychic system serves as a precondition for communication, it does not directly enter into it. Certainly we *attribute* communication to individuals (including ourselves), institutions, and so on, and therefore we address our communications to individuals (as "persons"), institutions, and so on, but what occurs in society is nothing less and nothing more than communication. It is communication—not minds, not persons—that reacts to and provokes further communication, for communication can no more know what goes on "inside" the "mind" than it can know what goes on "inside" the "atom."

Can we therefore say that the social world is the totality of communications? Yes. But we must also add that our social observation of this totality takes place *as* communication, and that any observation of this totality that cannot be communicated is not social. Accordingly, this communicated observation of communication must be included in the set that it describes. Our social observation—a communication—of the social world—consisting of communications—must therefore be incomplete. The observation of society, which, as communication, must be self-observation, presents us with the same set of problems as the self-observation of any other system. "Every operational act," Luhmann writes,

every structured process, every partial system participates in the society, and is society, but in none of these instances is it possible to discern the existence of the whole society. Even the criticisms of society must be carried out within society. Even the description of society must be carried out within society. And all this occurs as the criticism of a society which criticizes itself, as the planning of a society which plans itself and always reacts to what happens, and as the description of a society which describes itself. (Luhmann 1990b, 16–17)

To see society *sub specie aeterni* would indeed be the mystical feeling par excellence, for it would truly leave one speechless.

It is Wittgenstein, actually, who will help us understand this "impersonal" model of society. Although his assertion regarding the world as the "totality of facts" has been one of the foils of our argument, his recognition of the limits of language serves as a starting point for developing an adequate model of observation that incorporates its essential partiality. For the Wittgenstein of the *Tractatus*, the world is coextensive with language and logic. What is outside of the world is also outside of language and can therefore not be articulated; the same holds for logic. Wittgenstein expresses this in two ways: by saying, for instance, "Logic pervades the world" (Wittgenstein 1974, 5.61), but more commonly by speaking of limits. "*The limits of my language* mean the limits of my world," as we saw above, and "the limits of the world are also [logic's] limits" (5.6, 5.61). Does this notion of the world defined by the limits of language leave room for a subject who *uses* language? Apparently not. "There is no such thing as the subject that thinks or entertains ideas," he writes.

If I wrote a book called *The World as I found it*, I should have to include a report on my body, and should have to say which parts were subordinate to my will, and which were not, etc., this being a method of isolating the subject or rather of showing that in an important sense there is no subject; for it alone could *not* be mentioned in that book. (5.631)

Thinking with Russell, we might then be tempted to assume that the subject was a "class" located a level higher than the class of "facts" or propositions found in the hypothetical book. But Wittgenstein rejects Russell's theory of types, though he does affirm the prohibition against impredicative statements (3.331–3.333). Thus the subject does not hover over the world—neither transcendently nor transcendentally—but exists at or *as* its limit. It is of the same order as the world, but not in the world. "You will say," he reports, "that this is exactly like the case of the eye. But really you do *not* see the eye. And nothing *in the visual field* allows you to infer that it is seen by an eye" (5.633). Just as the eye remains the blind spot that defines, but is not contained within, the field of vision, so the "psychological self," the psychic system, remains external to the social system and becomes part of the system's environment. "The philosophical self"—and this holds for the social self as well—"is not the human being, not the human body, or the human soul, with which psychology deals, but rather the metaphysical subject, the limit of the world—not a part of it" (5.641).

What is this "metaphysical subject" who serves as the invisible but constitutive limit of the world? "Metaphysical," of course, is a loaded term. It sounds dangerously close to "transcendental," in the sense that the metaphysical subject should serve as ground and guarantor of the unity of experience or unity of the world. That, however, is not what Wittgenstein has in mind. To the extent that the Wittgensteinian subject is a condition of possibility, it is a formal device, a device that brings a world into being, much as the hypothesized eye creates the visual field. Luhmann, following Spencer Brown, keeps with the ocular metaphor and identifies this formal operation as observation. True, the ocular model brings with it some traditional baggage—the self-reflective baggage, in fact, that we have been unpacking up until now—but Spencer Brown *meta*physically (and certainly metapsychologically) converts the metaphor into a formal calculus—into the *Laws of Form* (the title of Spencer Brown 1979). Observation is a formal, binary operation that draws distinctions. A distinction, Spencer Brown notes, is "perfect continence," by which he means "a boundary with separate sides so that a point on one side cannot reach the other side without crossing the boundary" (Spencer Brown 1979, 1). A circle drawn in a plane represents such perfect continence. Using an ingeniously simple notational system of his own devising (consisting of two symbols: a right angle that can embed itself within itself multiple times and in multiple ways, and a blank space), Spencer Brown develops a highly abstract calculus, which, as he sets out to demonstrate, can be interpreted for mathematics (a primary arithmetic in his chapter 4 and a primary algebra in chapter 6) and logic (in appendix 2). Beyond these traditional uses of a formal calculus, Spencer Brown also believes that the "laws" he sets in motion with his first injunction ("Draw a distinction" [3]) have universal applicability:

The theme of this book is that a universe comes into being when a space is severed or taken apart. The skin of a living organism cuts off an outside from an inside. So does the circumference of a circle in a plane. By tracing the way we represent such a severance, we can begin to reconstruct, with an accuracy and coverage that appear almost uncanny, the basic forms underlying linguistic, mathematical, physical, and biological science, and begin to see how the familiar laws of our own experience follow inexorably from the original act of severance. (xxix)

Spencer Brown's *Laws of Form*, then, is an instruction manual on how to construct a world. First step: draw a distinction. Then, mark one side of the distinction (e.g., the inside of the circle) and leave the other side the unmarked state. From the marked state, one starts one's further operations, piling distinctions upon distinctions, until the form of the world takes shape. One may cross the line and enter the former unmarked state, but then one marks it, pushing the unmarked state beyond a further boundary, the boundary created by the distinction that was used to cross the original boundary. The world thus created can be formal (described by logic or mathematics) or physical (described, for instance, by biology). Its ultimate form, however, is contingent upon its starting point.

Luhmann's starting point is the distinction between system and environment, and the world he creates with his observations is social. Society, characterized by communication, is a system distinct from its environment (which includes other systems—physical, living, conscious). Within society—within, as it were, the marked state inside the circumference of the circle—subsystems proliferate (e.g., economics, politics, art, religion, etc.), each distinct from its particular environment (which includes other subsystems). Systems are operationally closed to their environment in the sense that they receive no informational or instructional inputs from the outside that determine their operations. Rather, they reproduce themselves autopoietically, in "perfect continence," though they are in constant contact with, and thus in a constantly irritated and perturbed state because of, their environments. Contact is maintained through communication—communication not *with* the environment but *about* system and environment—based on a binary code. The political system creates a world in which communication about anything is communication about having and not having power; the economic system a world in which it is about profitability; the legal system a world in which it is about legality and illegality; and so on. An event can be coded politically by sending troops to fulfill a particular mission in a delimited region of the world. Economically, that "same" event can be coded in terms of oil prices and adjustments in one's stock portfolio. Legally, it can be determined that the losers of the military confrontation were "war criminals" and thus were vanquished "justly." The "event" in question, however, does not exist for society outside of these coded representations. Even the mere physical description of what occurred is just that, a physical *description*, communicated (morally, journalistically, ecologically) according to well-established, if flexible, codes. Each description increases the complexity of the event and thereby the complexity of the social world that these communications reproduce.

Traditionally, one might speak of event and description in representationalist terms. We start with an experience and then encode it so that we might communicate it. The experience, though inaccessible, is thought of as the starting point that necessitates an exact and corrigible description. One would then speak of an event as if it preceded narrative. In the above paragraph, however, we spoke of distinctions that precede, or take precedence over, the distinction between event and description—distinctions such as having / not having power, making / not making a profit, and so on. These codes, which direct social function-systems, seem to "anticipate" events, such that the event emerges as an event—as a political, economic, legal, or natural-scientific event—only after it has been communicated. Perhaps it would be better to say that a system's code converts environmental perturbations—"noise" that comes as if from the "outside"—into events. Within a functionally differentiated society, therefore, events are communicatively formed; they serve as the means by which the modern, functionally differentiated social order reproduces itself. The economy, say, is "triggered" by political or scientific communications to narrate an economic "event" or "crisis" to which it must then respond. Such a communicatively secured "event" is neither a duplicitous charade nor a "reflection" of some "event-*an-sich*." It is reality itself—economic reality. It is, in fact, the discursively elaborated *decision* to devise the narrative in this way rather than that way.

Perhaps Wittgenstein knew this as well when he claimed that no part of our experience enjoys a priori status: "Whatever we see could be other than it is. Whatever we can describe at all could be other than it is. There is no a priori order of things" (Wittgenstein 1974, 5.634). The order of things is determined by a decision, a distinction, that itself is not ordered. To reconstruct the order of things, then, is to chronicle the formal consequences of the initial decision. Spencer Brown often talks as if the calculus he develops were a form of "direct recollection." We find ourselves in the midst of form, in the midst of a world, and try to understand it by "remembering what we originally did to bring it about" (Spencer Brown 1979, 104). We can trace our steps to the point of the "original" distinction, but must admit that it is, in fact, not original. To make a distinction, we must already be distinguished. The original distinction, the one that produces the world of observation, must be the distinction between what sees and what is seen. But even *that* distinction, as Fichte showed, presupposes the distinction between the absolute self and the self that is constructed so as to see itself as the distinction between the observer and the observed—and this original distinction simply cannot be seen. Though recollection is the process of making latencies manifest, there is no way to wipe the slate clean and start from the beginning. Embedded in this world, we can observe it only by severing it, by making another distinction and adding to its form. All distinctions are made *in medias res*; no distinction allows us to see the state of nondistinction.

Spencer Brown's genial stroke is to allow the Wittgensteinian observer to reenter the world. His world is not a totality of facts but a multiplicity of observers. Whereas Wittgenstein's subject defined the distinction between the world and transcendence, Spencer Brown replicates that distinction within the world itself. By repeating the basic inside/outside differentiation, each distinction opens up a new space within the world, enriching its texture, so to speak. The "inside" of the "original" distinction, the marked space, increases in complexity. The "outside" remains unmarked. Each distinction marks a different space, and no distinction can escape the consequences of its own operation. No distinction can reveal the world as a harmonious whole, as a totality of facts, or even as a totality of observations, because each distinction creates an unmarked outside that remains unseen. In this way, Wittgenstein's "metaphysical subject" becomes physical—not an observer in the psychological or physiological sense, not a real eye, but a measuring device, constructed in such a way as to "reveal" aspects of the universe that emerge only when they are seen. Observation does not map the world as if it were a spy satellite. It is an operation within the world and thus part of the territory that is the world. Spencer Brown's observer, then, does not act as an agent "manipulating" a distinction and "marking" it; rather, "the first distinction, the mark, and the observer are not only interchangeable, but, in the form, identical" (Spencer Brown 1979, 76). As Luhmann says, the observer, as the distinction, is the excluded middle or blind spot of observation. As the eye that remains outside the field of vision, the observer excludes itself from its own operations; yet, as one of many observers (distinctions) operating in the world, it is made visible by other distinctions, other observations. Thus, the social world is made up of observations (communications of distinctions) that open up a space, and observations of the latencies of other observations, each enabled by a further latency exposed to observational scrutiny. In Hegelian terms, we are faced with a bad infinity, a network of observations that never fully closes the circle, a structure of latency that never achieves complete transparency. In Nietzschean terms, we are immersed in a radically incommensurable perspectivism with no hope of an overarching coordination of viewpoints. In quantum terms, the talk is of a "complementarity" of observations, in which "every observation introduces a new uncontrollable element," such that "an independent reality in the ordinary physical sense can neither be ascribed to the phenomena nor to the agencies of observation" (Bohr 1961, 68, 54). The claim is not that the (physical or social) world is the figment of some demon's imagination but that its structure is fundamentally "unknowable," not because of the limits of human knowledge but because of the "interactively" alterable limits of the world itself. No matter what we choose to call it, however, this bad infinity of complementary observational perspectives is the social world we call home.

Reentering the World Within the World

If Russell finds paradoxes destructive and seeks to solve them, Luhmann finds them productive and watches them unfold over time. Luhmann's unacknowledged model here is Max Weber. Weber famously chronicled the rise of Western rationality as the result of its "loss of meaning." The peculiarity—and peculiar effectiveness—of modern rationalism, he maintained, results from the reduction of substantive (metaphysical) reason—which linked the human intellect to the inherent and comprehensible structure of the world—to a mere utilitarian, instrumental, means/end relationship. We can rationally judge no longer the legitimacy of ends but only the best means of achieving these ends. The choice of ultimate values, therefore, is a pre- or non-rational enterprise, as can best be seen in the functioning of modern institutions. Institutions or social systems can manipulate rationalities and technologies to actualize the values they prize, but they have no way of rationally justifying those values by means of these same rationalities and technologies. Medicine, to give one of Weber's examples, can determine the best way of saving a physically damaged life, but cannot determine whether, in individual cases, the value of preserving life at all costs is higher than a dignified death. Similarly, art can determine what is beautiful and what is ugly by the criteria of its choosing, but cannot determine whether the search for beauty is itself a "beautiful" or worthwhile enterprise. And most tellingly of all—especially since he was a keen analyst of modern, formal, legal positivism—Weber states that law can determine what in its field can be judged legal and what illegal, but it cannot place itself within that field in order to decide whether legality itself is legal. "Juridical thought holds when certain legal rules and certain methods of interpretations are recognized as binding." However, "whether there should be law and whether one should establish just these rules—such questions jurisprudence does not answer. It can only state: If one wishes this result, according to the norms of our legal thought, this legal rule is the appropriate means of attaining it" (Weber 1946, 144–45). The distinction between legality and illegality (or any other distinction) presents itself as the first or foundational distinction of a system, but it cannot affirm foundationally its right to do so; it can justify its right to decide the legality of issues only by means of its effective performance over time. Its justification is after the fact, accomplished through the construction of social forms in the shape of habits and conventions, including the convention of rational justification and de facto norms.

In this way, Weber anticipates Gödel. Not just the formally rigorous system of mathematics but all social systems fail to justify themselves strictly on their own terms; and reference to norms from some external source (from some other social system such as religion) is reference to a system that must suffer the same fate. Ultimately, a pragmatic approach must be assumed. Only as the legal (or any other) system unfolds, only as it "performs" within the structures it builds up, does what it determines to be legal become justified, become, in fact, the norm. The distinction legal / illegal, by which it observes the world, can in turn be observed, but no such meta-observation can serve as a normative foundation for the legal system. Indeed, any observation of the observations of the legal system only relativizes that system—that is, observes it from sets of distinctions other than its own. But such "relativization" is not (or not necessarily) destabilizing, for such external observations are observations made by a system that thereby reproduces itself through its own peculiar set of ungrounded distinctions that also become justified over time. And as these systems interact and continuously observe each other, patterns develop, patterns that we call rational. Thus, the "unfolding" of social systems over time is not "reasonable" in the sense that they are the concretization of natural law or the result of rational planning. There is no normative control over the development of modern institutions that can check "pathologies" against discursively and rationally achieved standards.

Perhaps, then, we can say not that modern rationality is the product either of reason or of the "loss" of reason but rather that reason, as we know it, is the product of modern rationality—or rather, the product of modern, "rationalized" institutions, the paradoxical and accidental development of which it was also Weber's achievement to describe. The paradigmatic case, of course, is his account of the capitalist money economy (Weber 1958). This most worldly of institutions owes its "spirit" and its inexorable spread to the most resolute denial of creaturely worldliness—Calvinist Protestantism. And this early modern example is just a special case of a more general tendency. Ascetic denial of the world produces more of the world it denies, as Weber clearly saw. "The paradox of all rational asceticism, which in an identical manner has made monks in all ages stumble, is that rational asceticism itself has created the very wealth it rejected. Temples and monasteries have everywhere become the very *loci* of rational economies" (Weber 1946, 332). Luhmann can explain the productivity of this paradox by way of Spencer Brown's notion of reentry. One makes a distinction and then operates on one side of the distinction that is made. One issues diatribes against irrationality, for instance, from within the realm of rationality. In like manner, one consciously discusses the unconscious. Or again, one communicates about the incommunicable. Such possibilities are enhanced when the distinction—communicable/incommunicable, say—reenters the space from which communication proceeds. One calls the incommunicable silence, or the sublime, and thus turns silence into a form of communication.

Within Catholic theology, one distinguishes between the immanent, worldly world and transcendence. One longs to occupy transcendence but can do so only if one reenters the distinction within the world. The absolute difference between the immanent and the transcendent becomes the immanent difference between the profane and the sacred. Consequently, within the world, monasteries are built, vows of poverty taken, celibacy imposed, silence embraced—and thereby new, immanent, and quite worldly institutions are formed that serve as educational, agricultural, economic, scientific, and even political centers. Within early modern Protestantism, on the other hand, profane activity, piously executed, is made the sign of the sacred, and asceticism becomes "inner-worldly." One works diligently and energetically at one's worldly vocation to demonstrate one's worthiness, one's eligibility for extraworldly salvation. In so doing, one creates wealth. Because asceticism prohibits the squandering of wealth, wealth itself is put to work. As a result, capital accumulates, and a whole new "worldly" ethic, an economic "system-rationality," takes hold.

In both instances—medieval Catholicism and modern Protestantism—the denial of the world complexifies the world. Systems and rationalities proliferate, subdivide, and reenter themselves; and any attempt to evade complexity or think the unity of distinctions only fuels the process. Good works become hard work—a self-justifying system. Indeed, that the strict, Protestant worship of an absent God, provoked by an intense concern for the otherworldly salvation of one's soul, should lead to the obsessive need to save and invest money, such that daily news of interest rates and stock market averages read like the weather reports of heaven—that this overwhelming desire to overcome the body should become embodied in money, the very emblem of worldly materiality—is just one of the ironies that reveals how paradox, far from paralyzing activity, does the essential work of the world.

In the essays in this volume, Niklas Luhmann formulates some of the pre-conditions for an adequate theory of modern society. Though the essays do not fall neatly into separate categories, I have arranged them under some of the key terms in Luhmann's vocabulary.

Under the heading "Husserl, Science, Modernity," I have included two essays dealing with the modern European philosophical and scientific tradition, in particular the phenomenology of Edmund Husserl. Readers of *Social Systems* (Luhmann 1995b) will quickly recognize the enduring in-fluence of Husserl on Luhmann's work, especially with regard to the concept of meaning and Luhmann's definition of communication in terms of a hori-zon of selections. In Chapter 1, a lecture delivered in Vienna to commem-orate the 60th anniversary of Husserl's 1935 lecture series "Philosophy and the Crisis of European Humanity" (Husserl 1970b), Luhmann pays tribute to Husserl and phenomenology, not by endorsing the philosopher's em-phatic belief in the universal mission of Greek philosophy and European humanity, but by "redescribing" phenomenology in systems-theoretical terms. Luhmann thereby not only defamiliarizes phenomenology and res-cues it from its more famous sociological appropriators but also gives the philosophically informed reader a handy guide to Luhmann's own thought. Chapter 2 picks up a Husserlian theme, the contours of modern science.

Under "Paradox and Observation" I have grouped four essays whose explicit task is to introduce the crucial notion of observation, as Luhmann, following Spencer Brown, defines it. Noting once again the present era's fascination with paradox, Chapter 3 examines the history of paradox as a logical problem and as a historically conditioned feature of rhetoric. In Chapter 4, Luhmann provides the reader with another "redescription" of twentieth-century philosophy, this time the deconstruction of Jacques Der-rida. Again, readers of Derrida may find in this essay a useful introduction to the ideas of Luhmann. They may also gain new insights into Derrida's own language-centered allegiances by seeing them translated into an ocu-lar vocabulary. Chapter 5 offers a comprehensive discussion of what Luh-mann finds useful in Spencer Brown's *Laws of Form*.[11] Finally, Chapter 6 builds on the previous chapters' discussion of observation and paradox to offer an account of their consequences for epistemology. This essay presents the most complete, if at times teasingly elliptical, exposé of Luhmann's cognitive constructivism in English.

The last major heading is "Communication," a topic conveniently glossed in catechistic fashion in Chapter 7. Here, the basic elements of Luhmann's theory of communication (and therefore of society) are laid out clearly and unambiguously. Somewhat more difficult is the important articulation of the difference between thought and communication in Chapter 8, a difference that underlies one of Luhmann's most radical and controversial theses—namely that the individual not only does not form the basic element of society but is excluded from society altogether, being situated instead in the environment of the social system.

Finally, as a coda that repeats in abbreviated form several crucial themes, I include a polemical talk that Luhmann delivered at a conference dedicated to investigating the continuing relevance of the critical thought of the Frankfurt School. For most of Luhmann's academic career, from the late 1960s to the late 1990s, the Frankfurt School (especially as represented by Jürgen Habermas) was the dominant, internationally known representative of postwar German social thought. It was Luhmann's firm (if exaggerated) belief that Critical Theory was a nostalgic, morally motivated rhetorical stance, an ethos, rather than a well-thought-out theory adequate to the task of understanding modern society. When asked to say where the answers to modernity's most perplexing questions were to be found, his answer was an emphatic: "Not in Frankfurt."

PART I

HUSSERL, SCIENCE, MODERNITY

1

The Modern Sciences
and Phenomenology

I

Sixty years have passed since Husserl's Vienna lectures, which are to be commemorated today—a long time, even for philosophical reflections.[1] Social conditions and above all the way they are observed and described have been transformed in significant respects. Sociologically viewed, this temporal distance carries such great weight that not much can be accomplished with a textual exegesis following hermeneutic directives. Instead, the text should first be placed back into the communicative situation of its time so that one can recognize what it was directed against *without this being said in the text itself*.[2] At the time of Husserl's Vienna lectures, dictatorial regimes that one retrospectively terms "fascist" seemed to be marching forward unstoppably. Bourgeois intellectuals kept an anxious eye on the few still-functioning democracies that, squeezed between communist and fascist dictatorships, seemed to keep alive a remnant of freedom. But with what prospects—above all in the face of war that was possible at any time? In this situation, attention was turned to politics; this occurred on the basis of a specifically European horizon of expectation. One of the most attentive sociological observers of National Socialist Germany, the American Talcott Parsons, had held until the end of the Second World War a very skeptical view of the effects of typical structures of modernity, above all its tendencies toward rationalization and differentiation. The diagnosis ran: destabilization, economic crises, political polarizations, antidemocratic regimes.[3] After the Second World War, the USA replaced Germany as the leading model, and the colors became brighter and friendlier. Ultimately, Parsons's optimistic variables read: adaptive upgrading, differentiation, inclusion, value generalization.[4]

Intellectuals who survived fascism and the Second World War tended at first toward a positive assessment of the situation. At the same time, the problems shifted to the confrontation of the "Cold War" and thereby to powers that were no longer perceived as European, even if their ideologies could not deny their European origin. After the collapse of this confrontation, a new international disorder arose, pointing with its conflicts toward global-societal problems, for instance toward the question whether the state—a European invention—really constitutes an appropriate model of order for territories marked by ethnic, tribal, or religious conflicts that cannot be represented by different, though electable, political parties.

In addition, economic and ecological problems are increasingly assuming the center of political attention. They appear before our eyes with a dynamic of their own and with their own temporal fatality, one that obviously poses too great a challenge to states and hence to politics. Perhaps among the most obvious changes can be counted the vanishing of the peasant-artisanal family economy everywhere in Europe, even in the South at a tremendous pace, without there being an adequate successor institution in sight on a structural level.[5] Similar transformations can be observed worldwide—and with much more catastrophic consequences in less affluent countries that lack a functioning "welfare state." Life may still take place in "families" or similar communities, but it is dependent down to its last detail upon the market and upon organizations of professional work, of production and service, and hence upon transformations felt by the individual to be external and intractable. The integration of individual and society is becoming a matter of market forces [*Konjunkturen*] and careers [*Karrieren*]—K.u.K., if you will.[6]

Transformations that are just as spectacular can be named on the macro level. The tremendously rapid development of international financial markets, the appearance of ever newer financial instruments, and the concomitant volatility of all monetary investments have literally swept from the market more or less profound attempts at a socialist politics motivated by social ethics, reducing them in politics itself to residues of rhetorical controversies. One does not see how the enormous amounts of money that are obviously available for investment can be motivated toward investments, nor can one manage to control politically the divergence that has arisen between maintaining businesses and maintaining wealth. The relocation of work to cheap-labor countries, on the one hand, and massive demographic movements, on the other, have become the topic of political perplexity, and will remain so despite a multitude of attempts at intervention. The fact alone that "regulation" and "intervention" have become prominent political concepts betrays a new kind of awareness of the problem.

In all this, the effects of science and politics upon the economy have not yet been mentioned. Consider the consequences that unleashing atomic energy has for the conduct of war and for energy production. Consider the unmistakable consequences of interfering in the genetic structures that have determined life on earth until now. Consider the challenges posed to science in the field of medicine as well as in other ecological questions, a science that today stands already largely in competition with self-induced transformations. If one takes all this into account, the problems that Husserl confronted in his critique of the modern sciences undergo a shift. The complaint about the absence of a humane-ethical orientation has not died down, but compounding this is the perhaps graver problem that the sciences, with each gain in knowledge, produce even more ignorance. This happens above all in the practically urgent questions of controlling the causality of transformations, for instance in the area of preventive medicine, with every kind of therapy, or in forecasting the ecological consequences of a technology that is already being practiced as compared with an altered one.

Finally, a word with regard to the status of technology. While Husserl mainly refers to an ancient European concept of reason, technology for him is a specifically modern phenomenon. It is no longer a matter of logos and cunning,[7] no longer a matter of weaving mechanical causes cunningly together into a complex causal constellation encompassing forms, matters, and final states. His reception of the tradition of rationality is thus highly abbreviated. His judgment with regard to modernity is equally one-sided. Certainly it is good to remind oneself of the astonishing—*admirabile*— manner in which Newton dealt with sun, moon, and stars. But that can hardly lead one to judge this negatively from the perspective of the counter-concept of the "lifeworld." For Husserl there exists a close connection between technology and modern science as an aberrant development of reasonable rationality. According to this view, technology is applied science, and the Fall of a rationalism gone astray lies in anticipating possibilities of

science's technical realization.[8] Today, we see that differently. Historical research into technology has shown that, as a rule, its development could not
depend on a preexistent scientific knowledge for solving its own problems;
that holds, for instance, in the case of the development of regulatable steam
engines. It holds for the invention of computers, and for the minimization
of their operative components, where the problem had lain almost exclusively in production technology. Current problems in technically combat-
ing consequences of technology (security technologies, exhaust purification,
trash deposits, etc.) convincingly show that one must resort to experimenting with model trials and cannot read up in books about how it is to
be done. This is not to dispute the fact that foundational scientific discoveries, such as those of quantum physics or biogenetics, had far-reaching
technological consequences in the course of time; but as theory, they were
not patentable.

Even the natural sciences have also been fundamentally transformed,
to be sure, in precisely the respect in which the humanities [*die Geisteswis-
senschaften*] could distinguish themselves from them. The natural sciences,
from physics to biology, have become self-reflexive. They are concerned
with objects that observe themselves. Cognition presupposes a memory
that functions in a quantum-physical manner. Microphysics transforms
through its observation the object it observes. Biology owes itself to living
biologists. The fiction of a reality that exists cognition-free already had to be
given up with Heisenberg; and if such a reality does exist, it does not display
any qualities to which an observation could latch on. I will return to this
point. For the time being, let us merely note that for such cognitions, contrary to what Husserl maintained, *Geist* is not necessary. Rather, they arise
out of the universalization of projects of cognition in the natural sciences,
and hence out of a program that compels autologies, self-application — or
that remains incomplete in its world-intention.

Not least of all, intellectuals, too, react more skeptically today. In the
so-called "postmodern" discourse, fundamental assumptions of modernity
are deemed to be refuted by facts: the rationality of the real by Auschwitz;
socialist hopes by Stalin; the principles of the market economy by enormous
financial speculations; and the expectations related to democracy by the
1968 movement and its consequences.[9] The motto of today, the "métarécit"
of today, runs: there are no longer any *métarécits* capable of consensus.

Many of the things that Husserl took for granted in his own lifeworld appear today as outdated, especially the presuppositions that had allowed him to put the modern project of a scientifically oriented technology in its place. This is no doubt especially true for the positive side of this critique, for the faith in the healing powers of the occidental telos of reason. As Joachim Ritter has impressively shown, philosophies can be inspired by the social problems of their time, without this being expressed in an unmediated way in their theoretical figures and arguments.[10] What can be proven in the case of Aristotle and of Hegel may also be valid for Husserl. A reencounter with Husserl's transcendental phenomenology and with the forms it takes in his late work will have to account for this. This should be understood neither as criticism nor, as is widely held among philosophers, as an autopsy or as objective textual management. Rather, it is a question of searching for a form in which the unconditional theoretical interest accepted under the name of philosophy can be continued in the face of changed conditions.

Philosophy itself has ultimately not taken any notice of Husserl's directional signs and probably was unable to do so. It set off on different paths simultaneously. Some philosophers are merely interested in the textual history of the discipline; others are interested in fashionable themes such as postmodernism or ethics; still others present the embarrassments of a comprehensive view literarily or in the manner of a *feuilleton*; and perhaps worst of all, the effort at more precision, which borders on pedantry. For the external observer, in any case, what Husserl pointed toward is not evident, namely an entelechy of self-critical reason. Critique—that only means, anymore, observing observations, describing descriptions from a standpoint that is itself observable.

II

The first task will therefore be to work out some peculiarities of Husserl's text with regard to which it is doubtful whether and how continuity is possible. In doing so, I shall refer for the most part to the Vienna lectures, but occasionally also to the text in its revised book form, *The Crisis of European Sciences and Transcendental Phenomenology* (Husserl 1954b; Husserl 1970a).

Most conspicuous, perhaps, is its Eurocentrism, such as one hardly finds it elsewhere in the twentieth century. European humanity finds itself in a crisis; European humanity must be saved—and indeed *by itself.* That surely has nothing to do with imperialism, colonialism, and exploitation, but rather, with a spiritual sense of superiority that not only excludes "the Gypsies who constantly wander about Europe" (Husserl 1970b, 273) but also envisions a Europeanization of all other human groups, "whereas we, if we understand ourselves properly, would never Indianize ourselves" (275).[11] No consideration of the political and economic relations around the globe, no thought of the possibility that the European tradition could slowly be dissolved into other, differently structured relations in a world society. The emphasis on crisis and salvation, autonomously achieved, is owing to these blind spots, which at that time were already non-credible and which would become obviously even less so after the Second World War.

A further problem lies in the evocation of culture. It is understandable that a universally oriented philosophy deals with culture among other things. In a manner of expression that became common at the end of the eighteenth century, one speaks of the philosophy of art, the philosophy of law, the philosophy of history, even the philosophy of religion, and so on. Why not the philosophy of culture as well? That philosophy takes itself to be culture should, on the contrary, be surprising. Philosophy is a result of a specifically European cultural development? There is thus a culture of eating, a culture of manners, a culture of habitation—and then also a culture of philosophizing. What might that mean?

Now, we should recall that the concept of culture as it is used today was an invention, a European invention of the late eighteenth century. At that time, it was apparently a matter of bringing under conceptual control the immense horizon of comparison of modern society, which was expanding from a regional and historical point of view. That things, texts, practices have and maintain their immediate use-meaning was by no means contested; but all human artifacts and finally even the way in which "nature" was seen or felt were duplicated and made into testimonials to culture as well. Only now was everything that was already present and everything that existed in other parts of the globe declared to be culture and explained as culture. Only now was there culture at all, because only now could one think in these conceptual terms and speak about it and write about it.

Cybernetically stated, a level of second-order observation is thereby created, and an observing of observers is laid over things. That the "naive"—as Schiller would say—or "natural"—as Husserl says—or "lifeworld" perspective is not thereby removed has never been contested. But what is added to this? Or what new limits result from the fact that naively practiced religion must now reckon with its being observed, compared, evaluated as a cultural phenomenon? And should one not also address this question to philosophy? Must philosophy now organize resistance against culture in the name of authenticity, genuineness, originality? But, if so, this, too, remains a mere reaction that has no concept for the unity of the difference between comparable and incomparable. This attitude is a familiar one since Rousseau: "Si je ne vaux pas mieux, au moins je suis autre" ("If I am not more worthy, at least I am different"), he says at the beginning of the *Confessions* (Rousseau 1959a, 5). But when this account is printed, cited, and copied, its fascination quickly fades. Culture absorbs even that.

Husserl escapes this question through the supposition of a historically unique process of, as he says, the "switch" from a natural to a theoretical perspective. Even if one concedes this point, one cannot avoid the question of which conditions philosophy must satisfy if it wants to be or has to be culture. If all of its assumptions are held to comparable under this rubric, and if, in the infinite horizons of comparability, the question of the location from which comparisons are made keeps popping up, must philosophy not then give up the search for a conclusive formula, whether it be called "spirit" or "transcendental subject," and find forms that can reconcile philosophy to its own contingency?

Husserl—and this is my third remark—solves or at least suppresses this problem with the help of a certain technique of making distinctions. It is a case of distinctions with built-in asymmetry, such that one side of the distinction dominates the distinction itself. In this way, moralists hold the distinction between good and evil itself to be good, and jurists do not doubt that courts are entitled to distinguish between justice and injustice as long as this occurs lawfully. With some perspicacity, one can recognize a hierarchical technique of domination in this form of drawing distinctions, with which the person who has the positive side of the distinction at his or her disposal makes him- or herself master of both sides. Louis Dumont has designated this form of hierarchy as *l'englobement du contraire* ("the encompassing of contraries") (Dumont 1966, 107–8). With Husserl, this hierarchy is no longer recognizable, unlike the form of making distinctions that, if one is not careful, reproduces hierarchical pretensions. In this way, with the distinction between the natural and the theoretical perspective, the latter is called upon itself to formulate the distinction (just as, with Schiller's distinction between naive and sentimental poetry, only sentimental poetry realizes that naive poetry is naive). And, in this very way, the humanities dominate the distinction between humanities and natural sciences, for only the humanities (according to Husserl) can ask in what spirit the natural sciences conduct research.

Logically, this technique of drawing distinctions honors the rule of the excluded middle and pays for it with the ambivalent positioning of the positive value. But it offers no substitute logic, no structurally richer logic such as, for example, Gotthard Günther had at least envisioned with the concept of transjunctional (neither conjunctional nor disjunctional) operations.[12] The observer who makes the distinction and for that very reason cannot appear within it secures himself a place on the side he prefers. Today, one can see through this maneuver. This places philosophy before the question of what it obscures when it produces and accepts this ambivalence without naming it. Does this give us a key to answering the question of how the peculiar, paradigmatic figure of European modernity is set in place by Husserl and of how it can then convincingly seem as if the solution to the problem of the crisis can be found only on the path of European self-help?

A fourth and final point of view concerns Husserl's relationship to tradition. Here, too, one discovers an ambivalence placed in a theoretically strategic manner, if not a paradox. The centerpiece of the European rationality of reason is the "peculiar universality of the critical stance, the resolve not to accept unquestioningly any pregiven opinion or tradition so that one can inquire, in respect to the whole traditionally pre-given universe, after what is true in itself, an ideality" (Husserl 1970b, 286; trans. modified). But exactly this theoretical perspective is itself introduced as tradition and legitimated through tradition. How else would one come simply to assert this on the seventh and tenth of May, 1935, in Vienna? Moreover, such a tradition of antitraditionalism can be seen for modern sciences as a whole.[13] But one would expect from philosophy that it reflect this as well. It appears to a later, external observer—that is, to us—that Husserl proceeds from a peculiar presence of tradition and also from the entelechy of European philosophy, from a presence of the origin as a still-possible motivation, indeed, one to be demanded, and from a presence of the idea of a goal that lies at infinity. Origin and goal are therefore, as presence, the same. Those are, as analyses of historical semantics could show, temporal structures of an aristocratic society, which derived its demands upon the virtue of those now living from the origin of a state or of a noble family and could therefore treat neither the past as vanished nor the future as open. It was a matter of perfection and corruption, of normative ideality and deviance. But the discovery of culture, which had established historical time as now only a horizon of comparison and the *Zeitgeist* as the precarious position of an observer, had introduced a break between experience and expectation (Koselleck), and that had made distinctions such as those between naive and sentimental poetry (Schiller) or Christianity and Europe (Novalis) possible. Husserl attributes to philosophy the capacity to bring about once more that unity of past and future, that entelechy grounded in tradition, in order to save Europe—but this in a society that, for many reasons, can no longer accommodate itself to this temporal formation, that can no longer recognize itself. How should that be? With the help of the desperate thesis "Ideas are stronger than all empirical powers" (Husserl 1970b, 289)?

If one does not only pursue a psychological suspicion of motives or a sociological suspicion of ideology but also poses the question of what remains unilluminated or excluded when one proclaims self-critical reason as the historical heritage and obligation of "European humanity," one ends with the question of whether (and how) this, too, may be recovered once more in self-critical reflection. That could indeed be. But if so, then it would demand entirely different theoretical figures than those that are held in readiness in the concept of the transcendental subject, Husserl's paradigmatic figure. At first, however, ignoring this question of the other side of the asserted form made a call to reason possible in a historical and political situation that sorely needed such a call. The alternative would have been to "deconstruct" even this and to give oneself over to the paradox of an uncritical self-critical reason.

III

The considerations that have been briefly indicated here could lead us to see Husserl's Vienna lectures as a historical event that is understandable in the context of its time but that for us and according to our conceptions of time lies in an ever-receding past, one that already today can interest only historians of philosophy. This would be accommodated by philosophy's tendency to make a museum of itself, or by the way critique is understood in Frankfurt as an emphatic rejection of the object of critique, or by the negligence with which sociologists even today speak of "phenomenological" sociology and thereby run into the trap of objectivism carefully avoided by Husserl. Moreover, this objectivism is bound to the non-concept of "intersubjectivity," as though there could be a compromise between objectivism and subjectivism, a partial, social constructivism that puts the sociologist in business.

Postwar sociology, for its part, did not espouse Husserl's critique of science and technology. On the contrary, it pursued a project of modernization built upon a collaboration of technical-industrial developments, the increase of wealth, the improvement of individual chances in life, and political processes of consensus building (key word: "democracy"). The functional differentiation of society was described as though all functional systems ultimately acted in concert to improve human beings' overall conditions of life. In this description, more wealth, more freedom, less coercion, more chances for individual self-realization were expected in part through an evolutionary development, in part through a scientifically informed politics. This double faith in evolution and politics could support the conviction that the idea of modernity contained an immanent rationality and that the modernization of society was to be expected as an achievement of society itself. In addition to the distinction evolution/politics, which left open the extent of the necessary interventions, the problem lay only in the political-ideological differences of opinion concerning a liberal-democratic or a socialist path.

In the last twenty years, this faith in the project of modernity has at first gradually and then as good as completely vanished. After the collapse of socialist state systems and even of socialist political ideas in the West, it would seem obvious to place all hopes on "freedom"—whether in the sense of a liberal market economy, or of freedom of opinion, or of electoral democracy, or of free research oriented solely according to its own prospects of success. And indeed, political rhetoric voices itself in this way—to its own detriment. For this concept of a largely successful path toward an ever more modern modernity is hardly credible any longer in view of consequences that are already evident. It would thus seem all the more appropriate to reflect upon Husserl's Vienna lectures and especially to dust off the fundamental thought concerning a self-critical reason and, as it is so nicely put, to "bring it into the conversation" once again.

If only difficulties with the texts that cannot be so easily skipped over hermeneutically or analytically did not exist! What one reads in this case, and especially the many misunderstandings that have adhered to the brand name of "phenomenology" like algae on a ship that has been at sea for a long time—all this makes it difficult to have an unbiased grasp of the fundamental idea of the theory. The second and third copies that have arisen since then, but also the forms of expression chosen by Husserl himself, do not in the least measure up to the rigorous consistency with which Husserl presents an interest in theory and defends it against every kind of doubt and despair, even in the sciences themselves. We do not have to concern ourselves with salvaging European humanity and perhaps not even with brand loyalty regarding the names "transcendental subject" and "transcendental phenomenology." One could even gladly forgo reason if one knew how the interest in theoretical reflexivity could be salvaged. For in this century there are but few examples of such a decisive interest in theory. In sociology, Talcott Parsons would be an additional case (though for understandable reasons he could not make anything of phenomenology as it was presented to him).[14] It should thus be worthwhile to look more closely and find out how theories at this level of sophistication were worked out—regardless of whether one thereby apprehends how one can continue this work, or instead sees oneself warned in view of the grave consequences of certain theoretical decisions.

For the present case, that means that we have to disentangle once again the peculiar fusion of historical and transcendental argumentation, of genesis and validity, that distinguishes Husserl's later work. This fusion is explicable only in light of its historical circumstances, and hence in light of Husserl's attempt to find an answer to the self-endangerment of modern Europe. This also means, though, that one will have to keep open the possibility of examining the theoretical foundations of transcendental subjectivism and perhaps submit them to a redescription.

IV

This much can be ascertained without doubt: Husserl's theoretical decision lies in concentrating on the transcendental subject. In contrast to all the digressions of "phenomenologists" of a first generation who took the summons to approach the things themselves in a literal and, so to speak, theory-free manner, Husserl insisted on a transcendental foundation of phenomenology. It is also clear what this decision was directed against, namely the psychologism of the end of the nineteenth century. Husserl formulated this, even in the Vienna lectures, as the rejection of an objectivistic conception of science that was, so to speak, void of spirit. However, it might well be—I have not double-checked this—that a certain insight also played a role, namely the insight that in empirical research the differences between individuals tend to be converted into the form of examinable variables, with the result that the peculiar operativity of consciousness, and indeed of every consciousness, is neglected. And Husserl's interest was directed toward precisely these fundamental structures of the operations of consciousness.

We can leave unresolved the question of whether Husserl was well-advised in his choice of the term "transcendental," which uncoupled him from the whole empirical realm. What is primarily interesting is how his analysis presents the operations of consciousness and, to repeat, of *every* consciousness. What does not fall under this description would accordingly not be a consciousness, at least not under the sign of transcendentality that represents the theory's claim to universality and hence the claim of validity for every consciousness.

Husserl (following Brentano) labels as *intention* the form in which consciousness carries out its operations. In today's conception, this formulation presupposes a causal attribution, an attribution of a purpose. If one wanted to take this into account as well, however, the unambiguousness of the concept would dissolve, for it would then depend on who does the attributing, which psychic and social systems (for example, courts of law) are attributing. For Husserl, however, who wishes to explain the life of consciousness from within consciousness itself and as a general form, this cannot be taken into account. One could think about taking exclusively self-attribution into account. But this, too, would not fit into Husserl's theoretical framework; for, as comprehensive psychological research shows, self- and hetero-attributions vary with other personal features and hence from person to person. We are therefore left with only the possibility, in the manner of a Husserlian epoché, of disregarding questions of attribution. But what, then, remains?

Perhaps one could say: intention is nothing more than the positing of a difference, the drawing of a distinction with which consciousness motivates itself to designate, to think, to want something determinate (and nothing else). That would accord with a mathematical theory that George Spencer Brown has worked out as a calculus of indications or as a theory of operatively produced forms.[15] The first and unavoidable commandment of consciousness would accordingly be to draw a distinction,[16] and to do so consciously—as an autonomous achievement of the self-reproduction of consciousness.

Husserl's concept of world would also harmonize with this. According to Husserl, "world" is an infinite horizon of ever greater possibilities, albeit one in which everything that is at all intended has to assume determinacy. "The indeterminateness [of the horizon—N.L.] necessarily signifies a *determinableness which has a rigorously prescribed style*," to quote from Husserl's *Ideas*.[17] In George Spencer Brown, the same statement would run along the lines that every distinction requires the crossing of a border (posited by the distinction itself) between unmarked space and marked space.

One could follow this by asking how this intentional filling of indeterminable horizons makes itself possible? Or more pointedly: How does it compensate for the risk that must lie in the fact that one treats indeterminacies as determinabilities and, in the serial fulfillment of intended determinations, one generates a history that one oneself then *is*?

The problem does not arise in Husserl because it is treated as always already solved—to be precise, solved through the double structure of noesis and noema. Distinction is introduced as a discovery of self-reflection, independent of all empirical evidence—as transcendental evidence, as it were. Everyone can find it in him- or herself—and no one has disputed this to date. For precisely this reason, causing phenomena to appear is an indispensable component of consciousness. The theory that describes this, relying on its own evidence, is hence called "transcendental phenomenology." It emancipates itself from cosmological precepts as well as from the ontological distinction between being and appearance. Phenomenology is now no longer a teaching of the world as it appears, no longer a temporary science that still faces the task of penetrating the appearance to reach a recognition of true being. Rather, phenomena are the things themselves, "realia" that are a part of the operation of consciousness, as is consciousness of consciousness, that is, the consciousness that consciousness operates consciously. There is accordingly no sense in demanding more or demanding knowledge in another form—at least there is no sense in placing such demands upon consciousness. This is explained in very detailed analyses—for example, in the analyses of perception with the help of the concept of "adumbration" [*Abschattung*] in §41 of *Ideas* (Husserl 1998).[18] Perspective variation is an accomplishment of consciousness that uses it to identify phenomena as things: "Each determination has *its* system of adumbrations" (Husserl 1998, 87). The continual multiplicity of appearance and perspective variation is necessary, according to Husserl, to constitute what remains identical within it. But experience itself does not turn itself off. "The adumbration, though called by the same name, of essential necessity is not of the same genus as the one to which the adumbrated belongs. The adumbrating is a mental process. But a mental process is possible only as a mental process, and not as something spatial" (88). Questioned how experience is possible as experience, then, Husserl would have presumably responded by pointing to the transcendental facticity and self-accessibility of experience. From here (and without posing a contradiction) it is but a short step to systems-theoretical reformulation. It would read: Experience is made possible by the fact that a recursive generation and reproduction of this inside/outside difference succeeds.

In other words, it is the *difference* between noesis and noema, between presenting [*Vorstellen*] and presented [*Vorgestelltem*], that ensures the describability of the world and that constitutes determinable "objects."[19] There is thus no sense—and here we come to Husserl's objection to the modern sciences—in using methodological provisions to neutralize the accomplishments of consciousness that subjectively create meaning. For with them, the world of objects would also vanish. According to Husserl, forgetting this was the aberration of the Galilean-Cartesian idea of science.

It is only a slight reformulation, though ultimately one with many consequences, to replace the distinction between noesis and noema with that between self-reference and hetero-reference. This is possible, it seems to me, without a loss of meaning and reveals more clearly that the two references condition each other. Consciousness cannot indicate itself if it cannot distinguish itself from something else; likewise, there would be no phenomena for consciousness if it were not in the position to distinguish hetero-referential indications from self-indication. The operational method of consciousness that steers by means of intentions is possible only on the basis of this distinction between self-reference and hetero-reference. This distinction keeps open for consciousness the possibility that, in its further operational course, problems may surface regarding the phenomena or consciousness itself. One could ask, "What can one make of this thing?" Or, "Have I made a mistake?" And expressed more formally, intentional operation is a permanent oscillation between hetero-reference and self-reference and in this way keeps consciousness from ever losing itself in the world or coming to rest in itself.

This already intimates the fact that time plays a role, not gratuitously, but rather for reasons that can be theoretically reconstructed and hence understood. Husserl himself presented comprehensive, introspectively gained analyses of the "inner temporal consciousness." [20] In this context, what is decisive is presupposed as a finding of introspection, namely that consciousness has access to its own temporality only in the moment of its actual operation (Husserl: in the moment of the life of consciousness)—neither before nor after. Consciousness exists as accessible to itself only in its own operations, and hence there can be time only in the form of momentarily present retention or protention. Everything else is a horizon-shaped reconstruction of a past that is no longer present and of a future that is not yet present, whereby a present arises that is inserted as an incision between past and future and that allows one to distinguish in turn differences and concordances (discontinuities and continuities) in an "objectively" appearing world. [21]

If temporality is found in this way in consciousness, one can still ask, why is that so? How does this peculiar temporality of consciousness cohere with the other characteristics of consciousness? And above all, why does consciousness cover up its own radically inner, "subjective" time with the assumption of an objective, chronological time in which it has to reconstruct itself as self-moving, as a stream of consciousness, so that a phenomenological technique of analysis is necessary to bring out the truth (if that is what it is)?

To inquire in this manner, to ask for an explanation in this way, is to go beyond the descriptive findings of a phenomenology that proceeds introspectively. But we are not returning to the premises of an ontological metaphysics that could ask only if time "is" at all rather than if it "is not." [22] We are wandering into a strangely precarious terrain where Heidegger himself could make out only confusing forest paths. [23]

If one asks the abstract questions "Who distinguishes time in the first place?" and "Who distinguishes time in time according to the schema before (retention) and after (protention)?" it is apparent that Husserl still remains beholden here to the metaphor of the river or of movement, and thus to a long European tradition. Since Aristotle, and again since the introduction of mechanical clocks in the fourteenth century, this tradition had treated the question of drawing a distinction as a question of numbers, of measurement, of chronology, and had presupposed movement as the substratum of chronology, as what was to be measured. For the time being, that sufficed to distance the observer from time, as an observer who reads, measures, and calculates time correctly or incorrectly. On this basis, however, because the measurement of time is itself already technical (for it must guarantee exact repeatability), the critique of technology that Husserl intended is not achievable with utmost radicality. If, on the contrary, one does not see the distinction of time in time as measurement or as number, what grounds would there be to hold on to an ontological or phenomenological substratum-concept of movement, of flowing, of streaming?

It is certainly difficult to renounce such a concept and at the same time to argue in an Augustinian way that we do not know what time *is*. Nevertheless, there are two important footholds. First, the operational manner of intending already implies time, at least in the sense of transcending the condition actualized in the current moment. Second, and above all, a constant oscillation between hetero-reference (phenomena) and self-reference (consciousness) can be established only if there is time available to redirect emphases and if one already knows, even while being fascinated by phenomena, that one will regret this and ask oneself: Why does that interest me at all? If one disregards time or if one relies on an ontologically oriented logic that cannot include time, one encounters paradoxes, as technicians of formal calculations know. One then must either "Gödelize"—that is, transcend the boundaries drawn by the premises of the calculus—or "temporalize," that is, endow the calculating system with time. It is then no longer a matter of true/false but rather of flip/flop.[24]

Husserl probably thought he could guarantee the unity of his transcendental phenomenology through the unity of its object, the "subject." We can already surmise that one can forgo it. The connection we have uncovered between operation, bistability (self-reference / hetero-reference), time, and oscillation supports itself—and is therefore probably demonstrable with regard to very different objects.[25] The unity sought could accordingly be *the oscillation itself,* namely the necessity, when occupying one side of a form (e.g., hetero-reference and not self-reference, object and not subject, what is observed and not what is observing, or vice versa), to release the other side for reoccupation. Among other things, that would presuppose that the system has a memory that grasps what has been released as capable of being reoccupied and *thereby generates the illusion of temporally enduring objects (or phenomena).* Memory objectivizes, it contracts, it reckons the relation of identity between the designations of observations that, as operations, can be carried out only one after the other.

This highly abstracted reformulation of Husserl's theoretical model can thus above all be used for theoretical comparisons. To name just one of these, there is a noticeable isomorphism with structures that have determined cybernetic theory since its beginnings. To be sure, cybernetics does not withhold judgment in the sense of Husserl's epoché. However, it, too, does not trust the world, and thus is interested in controls. That peculiar bilateral stability of self-referential and hetero-referential possibilities of linkage is also presupposed. In cybernetics, self-reference is represented by the well-known feedback loop (usually interpreted causally). One finds hetero-reference in the form of goal-oriented behavior. The manner of operation itself consists in the transmission of signals, and thus likewise consists in a sequence that requires time and has to be continued with constantly new information if the system is to keep operating—and operating means existing. In George Spencer Brown's calculus of forms, however, time first enters the picture in a very different sense. In the transition to equations of a second order, to recursive functions, to a reentry of forms into themselves, it becomes necessary to equip the operating system with two additional functions: memory and the ability to oscillate within the distinctions used. These functions, though, can be separated only if (without using a one-dimensional concept of time!) one divides them according to past (memory) and future (the possibility of oscillation). It appears as though distinguishing time in time is not a measurement, nor does it presuppose a processual substratum, but rather is necessary in order to endow systems with the possibility of operating in a sensible self-referential way. We cannot pursue this further here, but we note that, apparently, a multiple discovery of the same theoretical form has taken place in humanistic, technical, and mathematical areas of research.

V

If we translate the distinction consciousness/phenomenon into the distinction self-reference / hetero-reference, this seems possible without a loss of meaning. At the same time, though, it opens the way to more recent efforts toward an empirical epistemology, a cognitive science[26] oriented toward empirical systems.

If there are systems capable of cognition at all, one runs into the problem that these systems operate with a distinction between self-reference and hetero-reference and can calculate an idea of the environment only through hetero-reference (thus only "phenomenologically"). The environment remains operatively inaccessible, since the system cannot operate in its environment. On the other hand, one runs into the problem that systems themselves cannot distinguish between the environment as it really is and the environment as they designate it. "We can never be quite clear whether we are referring to the world as it is or the world as we see it."[27] This difficulty is covered up by an ambivalent use of the idea of "reality." Somehow, one thinks, not without cause, reality must be cognitively accessible, for otherwise the distinction between self-reference and hetero-reference itself would collapse. Hetero-reference (consciousness of phenomena) would be ultimately only self-reference, that is, consciousness. This consideration ought to have consequences for what one can understand as rationality and thus consequences for what Husserl had "projected" as self-critical Western reason.[28]

If one wishes to remove the illusion of reality, one ends up with the epistemology of radical constructivism. The environment is operatively inaccessible and therewith also simply inaccessible to knowledge; and on this very fact rests the capacity of cognition to observe it with the help of self-chosen distinctions (for which there is no correlate in the environment) and to make for itself an image of the environment. Since, however, radical constructivism as a self-marking theory resolves the distinction between hetero-reference and self-reference in self-reference, this in itself does not point toward an attainable system-rationality. Nevertheless, it might make sense to work with this limit-idea of paradoxicality and its correlate, an illusion of reality, and, indeed, especially when it is a case of the question of a concept of rationality adequate to contemporary circumstances.

In the tradition of logical-ontological metaphysics, which Husserl wishes to eliminate through an operation called epoché, the self-correction of knowledge had already been provided for. Logic had two values; it could thus mark true and untrue statements. All knowledge was thus subjected to testing for error (insofar as religion permitted). In the nineteenth century, this was expanded through a new kind of sophistry, a theory of latent, unconscious projection that projected outward the interests, repressed needs, or simply structural inconsistencies of the apparatus of knowledge. In the twentieth century, analyses of a language-dependent view of reality supplemented this. Marx, Freud, Whorf, Sapir would be the names that come to mind. In the period after the Second World War, the tendency to demand reflexivity, that is, the application of these theories to themselves, increased.[29] To an extent that is difficult to delimit, tools of self-correction were thereby complemented by tools of self-discipline, and not only with regard to the psychic structuring of cognition but also, especially, with regard to its social structuring. Thereby, the suspicion of projection was universalized, as, for instance, in the "strong programme" of the Edinburgh theorists of science, and made itself autonomous for the first time under the brand name "Radical Constructivism."[30] On the other hand, there is no consensus that reality as the world as it is thereby loses all significance, for that would mean the same fate for radical constructivism that had been predicted for classical skepticism: to fall into contradiction with itself and be able to appear anymore only as a paradox without consequences.

Both components of Husserl's projection, epoché and self-critical reason, now appear to make the transition to a new empirical problematic. One might ask, how can one save the illusion of reality if one indeed knows that everything figured to be cognition is produced internally and is therefore dependent on structures that secure the identification and distinctions of the system and their recursive use?

If one may trust the experiences of therapists, the function of the illusion of reality lies in its enabling the transition from one construction to another. As long as the therapeutic schema pathological/normal is still used, this means that "normality" can be defined not as a better adaptation to an external reality but, rather, as a less painful, more bearable construction. But even when therapy is not in question, the illusion of reality offers the possibility of making the transition from one construction to another. Modern society is a polycentric, polycontextural system. It applies completely different codes, completely different "frames," completely different principal distinctions according to whether it describes itself from the standpoint of a religion or the standpoint of science, from the standpoint of law or the standpoint of politics, from the standpoint of pedagogy or the standpoint of economics. There must be, in Gotthard Günther's terms, transjunctional operations that make it possible to change from one context (one positive/negative distinction) to another and in each case to mark what distinction one accepts or rejects for certain operations.[31] If, in doing so, one were to stick to a two-value logic and a methodology of testing for errors, one would ruin the distinction of a firmly cognizable reality. One would be able to establish, with Heisenberg, only that reality in itself, as an object completely isolated from knowledge, has no describable qualities. Suppositions of reality are needed, however, only in order to accept a multiplicity of incommensurable constructions and, when needed, to move from one of them to another.

Radical constructivism can accept exactly that. For reality is then nothing more than the correlate of the paradox of the self-referential unity of self-reference and hetero-reference (or of subject and object, or of consciousness and phenomenon). And this simultaneously implies that one cannot linger with reality in itself. Like a paradox, reality requires "unfolding." It is only an aid for reaching one construction from another. Consequently, the reality that is given as a paradox is the only knowledge that is unconditionally given, that cannot be conditioned in the system — and therefore remains unproductive.

One can now better understand which perspectives Husserl both opened up and obstructed. Reason is self-critical not because of its European heritage but only if and insofar as it can exchange its own belief in reality and thus insofar as it does not begin to believe in itself. The tests of its validity are found in therapy, which attempts to attain less painful solutions and itself maintains a disengagement in matters of reality. They are also found in claims to communication, in claims to a subtler language (to cite a book title)[32] that functions even under polycontextural conditions. Self-critical reason is ironic reason. It is the reason of the "Gypsies who constantly wander about Europe."

VI

Have we gone off course? Actually, we wanted to find out what of transcendental phenomenology and its turn to European history is dated and what can still interest us after sixty years. How can an extremely formal theoretical configuration help us in the face of the countless problems with which our society presents us and which we increasingly recognize as consequences of its own structures? One is reminded of Schiller:

> In the serene regions
> where the pure forms dwell,
> misery's gloomy storm blows no more.
> ("Life and the Ideal")

However, in order to gain some distance from the potentially dated terminology in Husserl's later philosophy, a terminology that reacts to historical situations and concerns, we had asked about form, which in his work takes on an emphatically theoretical interest. A variant of operative constructivism had thereby revealed itself, as it is represented today under different brand names: for instance, formal calculus; second-order cybernetics; the theory of closed, "autopoietic" systems; or radical constructivism.[33] Its disciplinary provenance is very heterogeneous, ranging from mathematics to biology and neurophysiology to the theory of automata and linguistics. Its manner of argumentation sounds rather naive to the ears of trained philosophers (above all in the cases of Maturana and von Glasersfeld). Obviously, at the creation of this conceptual world, no one bothered to ask philosophy, and it is all too understandable if philosophy now emerges as the angry fairy[34] in order to take her revenge. But the specialized sciences themselves are generally little inclined to take such radical considerations seriously and to orient their own research around them. Seen in the context of contemporary science (not to mention philosophy), it seems to be a matter of homeless constructs that, like Husserl's gypsies, are wandering about.

But how would it be if one could successfully show that Husserl already uses this theory, except that, with concepts such as "subject," "spirit," or "transcendental phenomenology," he places it within a tradition that already in his time had little chance of a future. In Husserl's time, Freud had already given up the idea of a quasi-substantial subjectivity of the subject and had replaced it with the supposition of a constant quantity of psychic energy that can take on different forms as it is burdened with demands for sublimation. We can replace this concept of energy, fashionable at that time, with the concept of autopoiesis that is fashionable today, for here too, freely interpreting Maturana, the principle applies that autopoiesis must be maintained as long as the system reproduces itself but can take on different forms according to which structural couplings the system reacts to. This leads to a conceptuality that is no longer bound to a certain type of operation—whether biochemical syntheses, neurophysiological changes in quanta of energy, processes of consciousness that direct concentration, or communications—but that can organize, on these different bases, the reproduction of a difference between system and environment and, independently thereof, can organize cognition.

But other prominent efforts toward a new theoretical orientation in the second half of this century are also marked by a turn away from the figure of the transcendental subject, whether in the efforts of Hans-Georg Gadamer toward an objective hermeneutics, in the "linguistic turn" of analytic philosophy, or in the invocation of insights gained from the philosophy of language in Jürgen Habermas's theory of communicative action. Also, the centering of theory around the human body begun by Husserl himself and developed by Merleau-Ponty should be mentioned. One has the impression that the currently urgent problems of philosophy are conditioned by the very refusal of achievements of unity that the transcendental subject had offered. On the other hand, these departures are mediated by distinctions that remain bound to this figure, whether the distinction is subject/object (or derivative/circular) or subjective (monologic) / intersubjective (dialogic). Within these distinctions, the understanding of history and reason shifts. But must one draw such distinctions? Or is a theoretical construction present in transcendental phenomenology that, if one may formulate it so paradoxically, can separate itself from itself, can become independent of itself?

The necessity of a transcendental (transempirical) foundation might have seemed appealing as long as no replacement was in sight[35] and, above all, as long as knowledge seemed to rely on an asymmetrical, noncircular grounding. But in philosophy itself, this is called into question by Heidegger, and in many formal sciences today, one openly discusses the necessity of a "break with symmetry" or of a "de-tautologization," of an "unfolding" of primordial paradoxes or, very generally, of the necessity of beginning with the operation of drawing distinctions. In this case, it is no longer merely a matter of unconditional prerequisites, but a matter of the demands of the structure of complexity (of calculations, of systems, etc.) which must be met in one way *or another* if one wants to attain any result whatsoever. And above all, it is no longer merely a matter of the peculiarities of consciousness, but a matter of the very emergence of order.

The rigor of this departure from the transcendental can be recognized if one considers the possibility of omitting consciousness as the medium of the formation of forms and, despite this, of maintaining the structure that was discovered by Husserl, namely the insight into the interrelation of the conditions of the capacity for operations, the separation and simultaneous processing of hetero-reference and self-reference as well as temporality from the standpoint of the respective operations. I believe that this is possible if one determines to presuppose meaning as the general medium for the formation of forms and then to distinguish whether systems are constructed on the basis of intentional acts of consciousness or on the basis of communication. For the case of acts of consciousness, one could repeat Husserl's analyses, but one would no longer need to characterize them as "transcendental." For the case of communication, one would have to find a parallel construction that demonstrates both what functions in the case of consciousness and also how it functions: as an operation present only in the moment, the drawing of a border, the simultaneous processing of hetero-reference and self-reference (thus "bilateral stability"), and further, recursive regressions and anticipations of currently non-actual but actually graspable temporal horizons of past and future, and, all in all, the inclusion of the excluded as the mode of processing meaning.

I think that such a theoretical program, which radically distinguishes between psychic and social systems, is practicable, but this is not the place to demonstrate this.[36] The question is only, How would the landscape of theory look if such a theoretical program were practicable?

We would have a new type of theory design, one built neither upon old-fashioned laws of nature, nor upon their statistical derivatives, nor upon the leitmotif of technically proven couplings. Husserl's criticism of the one-sidedness of Galilean-Cartesian idealizations and of the form of mathematics that is binding for them would be confirmed. Even so, we would not have a dialectical theory that progressed toward an attainable end (however positively or negatively one wishes to value that). It would of course not be a cross-indexing in the sense of Parsons' theory design, derived from the concept of action. It would not be a logic that seeks to guarantee consistency through the exclusion of paradox, but rather a theory that keeps the paradoxing and deparadoxing of its principal differences open in the event that the forms it can offer are no longer persuasive. It would be a theory of self-referential, nontrivial, therefore unreliable and unpredictable systems that must separate themselves from an environment in order to gain their own time and their own values, which limit their possibilities. It would be a theory that assigns to cybernetics the task of controlling the indeterminacies[37] that are generated in the system itself.

There is no question, then, that one can reconstruct the good old subject in this way. However, the decisive factor is that social systems, too—society, too—can be described with this concept.

VII

With the distinction of the operations constitutive of meaning according to whether they generate psychic or social systems in their recursive self-reproduction, we have come a good bit closer to our goal of introducing Husserl's intuition of theory into a completely different "lifeworld." One could imagine that a theory of society could be worked out on the basis of these sketched-out foundations, a theory in which communication would be understood as basic operation, information as hetero-reference, utterance as self-reference, and understanding as a prerequisite of the transferal of communicatively condensed meaning into further communications, with the option of looking for the focal point of the connecting communication either in hetero-reference or in self-reference, an option that perpetually reopens the theory and that is to be perpetually decided anew.[38] Communication can intervene operatively in its environment as little as consciousness can, for that would mean operating outside of the system in the system's environment. In one case as in the other, this fact can, however—with a permanent evolutionary remnant of risk—be compensated for in that the systems distinguish between hetero-reference and self-reference and can correspondingly observe in a way that is bilaterally stable and open to the future.

No one seems yet to have come upon the idea of transferring such a promising theory-type from the "subject" to the "social system of society." In view of the current perplexity in the judgment of the state of the world—for instance, the perplexity declared as "postmodernity"—the attempt would be rewarding. It could record the moods of the time, such as the fascination with self-referential circles and paradoxes,[39] the necessary incorporation of ignorance into knowledge,[40] and the interaction of construction and deconstruction on the basis of self-limiting system operations.[41] As far as ontological metaphysics is concerned, it would demand no longer only epoché, that is, renunciation of statements of being, but also the resolute prioritization of the distinction between "inside" and "outside" over the distinction between "being" and "not-being."[42] With this theoretical apparatus, one could replace the fascination with the problems of consensus, integration, and insightful civil society that is still common in the social theory of sociologists with the problem of the temporal dimension, memory, and the disposition toward a future that oscillates with regard to all distinctions.

At the moment, sociology is surely not prepared for such a reading. In hindsight, it is also apparent that Husserl—just as, by the way, Heidegger—did not take sociology into account. Apparently, the distinction between natural sciences and humanities had so strongly structured the realm of possibilities of knowledge that a third candidate had no chance. That is even more surprising since Alfred Schütz had attempted to draw attention to this limitation of vision and to enrich phenomenology (whatever that meant for Schütz) through Max Weber's theory of action.[43] It can be supposed that it was not a felicitous idea to enrich phenomenology on the basis of the concept of action whose rationality had already grown questionable in Weber and whose sociality could be determined only by recurring to subjectively intended meaning. This attempt could thus lead only as far as the problem of the subjectivity of intersubjectivity, a problem that Husserl had already failed to solve; or it would have to devolve into a scholarly objectivism that only bore the name "phenomenology" without continuing the awareness of problems connected with it.

It is surely idle to speculate about what could have gone otherwise under other circumstances or with the help of authors who might have come closer to Husserl's theoretical intuition. The development of science is not a straightforward process driven by flashes of genius. Like complex self-referential systems in general, science, too, must begin with a given historical and factual state of knowledge that defines and limits its susceptibility to stimulus. It is thus rather an evolutionary process that records certain chance impulses but cannot register others at all. Therein lies the flexibility in the *distinctions* that can be applied to a given way of formulating knowledge—thus, for instance, factually oriented objectivity versus the subject, or history versus reason, or acting versus knowing, or spirit versus matter. One who wishes to opt out of all of these distinctions has hardly a chance of being understood. On the other hand, it is entirely possible—and one can show this in the very case of Husserl—that one who opts within these "frames" is compelled to reformulate already-used-up thoughts, and thereby covers up the already visible theoretical intuition. One can experience this theoretical fate hardly more sharply than in Husserl's Vienna lectures. At the end of a lifelong process of reflection that is scarcely to be exceeded in seriousness and rigor, theory finds its conclusive formulation—and within this formulation, finds itself—in a proper name: Europe.

VIII

The analysis presented here of the Vienna lectures and of Husserl's transcendental phenomenology that originally motivated them was not intended as a "critique," hence not as a sorting out of what is tenable and untenable in this philosophy. Nor was it meant to be philosophy. For a sociologist, the windows in the philosophical lecture halls are too high.[44] If a sociologist operates on a theoretically comparable terrain, then he does so without the attitude.[45] However, we can also read Husserl's texts as communications that are formulated in a certain time and whose descriptions reacted to the society of their time. It is thus for us a matter of a new description of this description, a matter of a redescription in Mary Hesse's sense.[46] Such redescriptions of descriptions rank among the characteristic features of modern descriptions of the world. One need only consider Karl Marx's redescription of the political economy of his time, Sigmund Freud's redescription of the phenomenology of the contents of consciousness, the redescription of tonal music through atonal music,[47] or the redescription of the ambitions of the movement of 1968 by postmodernism. In view of the facility of this kind of textual production, one can redescribe it, too, and thereby surpass the self-understanding of its authors.

It is not a matter of striving for progress, of increasing or improving knowledge, or of hermeneutic exhumations of the real meaning, nor is it a matter, as already said, of critique. Rather, what occurs in this manner can be understood only as a continual transformation of necessity into contingency, of natural into artificial, conditional frameworks of knowledge and action. What was previously accepted as self-evident and, as it were, "life-worldly" is now made visible as a peculiarity of a certain way of observing. Insofar as the transition to other forms is successful—that is, insofar, for instance, as atonal music is really produced—what was previously valid becomes recognizable as a selection of a certain observer. The successful production of different forms of observation is an important and severely limiting precondition for this transformation. It is thus in no way a matter of "decisionism," as defenders of traditions always maintain, or of unleashing arbitrariness in the sense of "anything goes." The conditions for successful substitution are often difficult, and they are often recognizable only through further redescriptions. In any case, they are very strict conditions. The attempt to describe transcendental philosophy anew by the modern means of the theory of self-referential systems or by means of second-order cybernetics has to ask itself, therefore, if it can meet these demands.

The theoretical redescription of the redescription of descriptions is an autological concept. It is applicable to itself. It does not strive to supply a grounding, let alone a better grounding. It thus does not expose itself to infinite regress. It does what it does, and in this manner it represents itself. It itself operates autopoietically, without aiming for a palliative conclusive formula.

It could be that this style of thinking, in comparison with Husserl's, presupposes a radically different relation to time. Husserl had located the intentions of transcendental consciousness in time, a time that consciousness also observes, so to speak, out of the corner of its eye. And he had correspondingly located the crisis of the modern sciences in the historical time of the occidental history of reason. In all of this, time was conceived as a river, as movement, as process. The theory of redescription, by contrast, has to engage in a very different relation to time, for it envisions the described descriptions as its past and the prospect of further new descriptions of its own concepts as its future. It understands its present as the difference between its past and its future. It articulates its position no longer only in time, but rather *with the help* of time. No longer, then, can time be thought of in a late ontological manner, as it were, as a historical process, or as a copying of the measure of movement into the knowing system; rather, time is now a definite form of observation, a world-construction with the help of the difference between the infinite horizons of past and present. The grounds for the continual new description of redescriptions lie only in the fact that our society leaves no choice in this respect. Our future can never be like our past. As concerns action, we thus have to decide, and as concerns recognition, we have to describe.

How difficult it is to accept this can be seen in the emergence of fundamentalist countermovements, in the desperate demand for meaning and self-realization. Such concepts gain their energy from difference, and the same is apparently also true of the currently fashionable concept of civil society with which some intellectuals announce to the public that they, the intellectuals, exist. But this explanation of current phenomena is itself nothing other than a redescription of what has already been described. Apparently, the diagnostic of our time can no longer detach itself from this second-order level of description, although, and indeed because, a first-order observation is always co-produced. One will hardly be prepared to view this as a "crisis" in the continuation of self-critical occidental reason. But perhaps it is a theoretical description that does more justice to what we can actually observe at the end of this century.

Translated by Joseph O'Neil and Elliott Schreiber

2

The Modernity of Science

I

So far as one can see, science has never had any trouble representing itself as "modern," nor has it ever stood in need of doing so. The modern states—that has been a topic. The modernity of modern society is being discussed at length in sociology.[1] And today, one still asks what modern art is. Yet as regards the field of science, its modernity does not even seem worth questioning, let alone an argument.[2] Its modernity seems to go without saying.

As is well known, Max Weber attempted to determine the specificity of European modernity by way of a cultural comparison of immense dimensions. Since this attempt has never been superseded but, at best, only repeated with new data, sociology is today still under the spell of this thought experiment. Apart from all the weaknesses of the theoretical foundations of such a comparison, weaknesses that cannot be sufficiently clarified by the comparison itself but must be presupposed, it is the lasting merit of Weber's enterprise to have pointed out regional and historical contingencies. At the same time, however, the *regional* comparison does not do justice to what is *historically* new. For, as Max Weber indeed recognized, the novelty lies in the final analysis, not in the relation to Europe's own history. Otto Brunner's concept of "old European" structures and semantics does greater justice to this aspect. It, in turn, however, lacks any kind of theoretical analysis.

In the context of these data, one can at least begin to recognize that modern society produces its own newness (why does society have to be "new"?) by way of stigmatizing the old. The dismissal of the "world of one's fathers," its degradation to mere history, seems to be imperative for any self-description of modernity. This devaluation places increased burdens on the persuasive power of self-interpretations[3] and thus leads to irreconcilable controversies. Initially, science was able to distance itself successfully from these controversies, and today it feels the effects of the problematization of the semantics of the modern age as if from the outside—as an undeserved fate, as it were, an irrational attack, a lack of expertise. The modernity of science consisted in the progress of knowledge itself; science was more or less constant modernity. Caesuras came about through methodological and theoretical discoveries that opened up new fields of research, enhanced the power of dissolution [*Auflösevermögen*], or put the extensive and complex collections of knowledge in their final classical form: Euclid, Newton. Such a concept, however, makes it difficult to recognize a connection between modern science and modern society. The factual contents of knowledge resist a historical as well as (for the same reason) a sociostructural classification. And bivalent logic, together with the epistemology based on it, does not provide any alternatives to this situation. If knowledge is true, it is always true (which, of course, does not include the claim that the object of this knowledge must always have existed).

Up until Thomas Kuhn, all earlier descriptions of the world that did not correspond to the latest developments in research were regarded as more or less failed attempts at scientific knowledge—as double entries, as it were, in the bookkeeping of scientific progress under the directive of a unified truth in one and the same world. It is only with Kuhn's incommensurability thesis that precursor theories, insofar as they are based on different "paradigms," are released from the current world of truth and historicized. Together with this development, all stable foundations for the determination of the specific modernity of today's science went overboard. One could only say: we are dealing with a different paradigm whose claim to superiority can be formulated only by its own means. The constructivism of modern epistemology is grounded only in itself.

The analyses presented here[4] contradict this view. The basic idea is that of a connection between the functional differentiation of the social system and a constructivist self-understanding of science. Modern society's form of differentiation makes possible, or even enforces, the autonomy of separate functional areas; this is accomplished by the differentiation of certain operationally closed, autopoietic systems. Functional differentiation thus imposes on systems an obligation to reflect on their own singularity and irreplaceability, but an obligation that must also take into account that there are other functional systems of this kind in society. Knowledge—and indeed particularly demanding, advanced knowledge—is consequently only one form of social potency among others. Whether it is economically usable, whether it is to be supported politically, or whether it is suitable for educational purposes, these questions are decided elsewhere. It remains true that verbal communication already presupposes knowledge, and that society is unable to communicate—and therefore unable to exist—without any knowledge. Yet precisely for the expert knowledge of modern science this presupposition does not hold. Society is dependent on this knowledge only in a very specific sense, but not in the autopoiesis of its communication as such.

In a peculiar way, scientific knowledge must stand its ground and take itself back; it must continue to produce new achievements, and at the same time, it must refrain from defining the world for society. To be sure, no one seriously doubts the descriptions of the world furnished by science, insofar as science itself trusts them. Nonetheless, the effect is virtually nonbinding as far as other systems of communication are concerned.

The designations that usually register this state of affairs are relativism, conventionalism, and constructivism. One can summarize the meaning of these concepts in the thesis of a loss of reference. This thesis marks their negative content. Its negativity, however, arises only in a historical comparison with the premises of ontological metaphysics, with its religious safeguards, its cosmos of essences, and its normative concept of nature that prescribes a correct order, even if one accepts the irretrievable loss of these attitudes toward the world and feels compelled to align oneself with relativity and contingency, that is, with the hypothetical and merely provisional character of all knowledge. A kind of "discontent" with the modern culture of knowledge remains, and perhaps this discontent, too, explains why there is no effort to reflect upon the specific modernity of today's science. Such an effort would only confirm this discontent—or so it seems, given this as yet quite superficial reflection.

The formula "loss of reference" (some say "loss of experience" or, more drastically, "loss of meaning"—some even claim that others no longer believe in their own bodies) summarizes in a single focal point the distance to the old European tradition. The formula, however, is too compact and too negative to open up any future perspectives. What, after all, is "reference"—this is what philosophers are discussing—and what is the case when reference gets lost? What is the "other case" that must be cointended by the form of the formula "loss of reference"? In order to pursue these questions, we have to dissolve the problem with the help of further distinctions.

The tacit assumption that truth is not possible without reference to an external world (because this is precisely what is meant by "truth") has led to endless and unproductive discussions of the problem of realism.[5] If, however, the very operation of referring—we spoke of designating—must be understood as a real operation, one can no longer seriously think that only what it designates (refers to) is real. On the other hand, it is not sufficient simply to change over to the opposite position and maintain the reality of the referring operation. The operation is inaccessible to itself, and for an observer it could be referred to only as something that he designates. This way, one is left only with the existing controversy between realism and constructivism—as if these were incompatible positions.

For us, the impossibility of solving a problem posed in this way indicates that modern society needs to formulate its epistemological problem differently.

First of all, problems of reference and problems of truth must be clearly distinguished. A bivalent logic has tempted (forced?) people to conflate the two perspectives. Its only positive value, "truth," designated "being," and therefore articulated reference. The countervalue "untruth" only served to control the act of referring (designating, claiming, recognizing). Under these presuppositions, the loss of reference had to appear as a loss of truth resulting in the paradox of "nihilism," which states that consequently only the untrue could be the truth. Logic was structurally not rich enough to represent more complex relations, and this condition was sufficient for social relations that went along with a world described in a monocontextural fashion. The talk of the loss of reference (or its semantic equivalents), however, clearly indicates that these conditions have changed.

A first step toward the comprehension of modernity therefore consists in the distinction between problems of reference and problems of truth.

The following reflections arise from the difference-theoretical starting point of our investigations. In other words, they arise from the conception of reference and of truth as *form* in the sense of Spencer Brown—as a two-sided form, as difference, as the marking of a boundary whose crossing takes time.

For truth, the matter is clear. We have interpreted it as a code, that is, as an intrinsically self-referential difference between *truth and untruth*. In the case of reference, a distinction must be made between *self-reference (internal reference) and external reference*. Both sides of this distinction are given only together with their respective opposites. A retreat into pure self-reference in the face of the lamentable condition of the world would be a futile endeavor. Even the exquisite forms of *l'art pour l'art*, and precisely these, still remain forms.

If one accepts this distinction of reference into self-reference and external reference, then the problem of reference poses itself on two levels. Reference itself is nothing but the achievement of an observational designation. Each observation designates something (traditionally speaking: it has an object). The opposite concept here is simply operating.[6] In contrast to referring, operating is an objectless enactment. In the observation, the difference between observation and operation can be reformulated in an innovative way as the distinction between self-reference and external reference. Self-reference refers to what the operation "observation" enacts. External reference refers to what is thereby excluded.

After these theoretical revisions, the predicate "real" can no longer simply be attributed, or (in the case of an error) denied, to what is designated. The value of reality shifts from the *designation* (reference) to the *distinction* that is co-actualized in every designation. Real is what is practiced as a distinction, what is taken apart by it, what is made visible and invisible by it: the world. And this holds for every distinction—for the distinction between self-reference and external reference as well as for the distinction between true and untrue.

The distinction between the problem of truth and the problem of reference thus leads to a distinction of distinctions, namely, to the distinction between the distinction true/untrue and the distinction self-reference / external reference. The two distinctions are located at right angles to each other. They have no mutually unbalancing effects. That is, self-referential observations and descriptions, as well as those of external reference, can be both true and untrue. This takes away the Cartesian privilege of the subject. There is no truth preference for introspection. The insight remains

valid that if self-observations and self-descriptions are enacted, they are enacted with a certainty lacking any criteria. This move, however, has only
put the operation of observing (that is, its inability to see) beyond doubt.
What it refers to (designates, objectifies, recognizes) can nonetheless be
designated as both true and false—depending on the programs that serve
as criteria for a correct classification of these values. Things remain the
same: each system has a different access to itself than to its environment,
which environment it can construct only internally. Yet this advantage—
and after Freud even theoreticians of consciousness ought to agree with
this—cannot be interpreted in the sense that self-knowledge is easier to
achieve, produces better results, or has a higher probability of truth than
external knowledge.

For psychic systems, this state of affairs has been played through and
laid open above all in modern literature.[7] Our topic, however, is the social
system, and here the same facts are even more evident. The observing operation is always a communication that exposes itself in its very enactment,
and not only in its effects, to further observation. The question of whether
it thematizes the communicating system itself (society itself) or something
else is posed with the "form" of the system and is open to both options.
Only the distinction as such is being enforced—simply by virtue of the
fact that the system is operating. Self-reference as well as external reference
can be encoded in one and the same code—and this encoding takes place
in a different way, depending on which of its function systems society uses.
The same problem repeats itself at the level of function systems, which
themselves distinguish between self-reference and external reference in
their operations. The modern pattern of the social system is articulated
throughout the individual function systems. In this way, the function systems participate in the structural richness of modern society—a society
that only they in turn put into this form.

Consequently, modern society's form of differentiation, the differentiation through functions, accounts for the need of descriptions that are
rich in structure, and this need requires the distinction between problems
of reference and problems of encoding as the distinction of distinctions.
The semantic forms that take these requirements into account are specifically modern. They are historically conditioned both in their sociostructural
cause and in their semantic expression. Only to the old thinking must such
a "relativism" seem suspicious. The modern form of the self-description of

society and its function systems can integrate this factor. Indeed, it is unable to articulate itself differently; for in retrospect, premodernity has to appear to it as ontologically fixed and incapable of distinguishing between problems of reference and problems of encoding.

In constructivist epistemology, modern science has found the form in which it can reflect upon this state of affairs. One can describe this as an achievement of theory that, from Plato to Descartes, Locke, Hume, and Kant, has described cognition in an increasingly radical way as a self-produced distance. This description creates the impression of a progress in knowledge that gradually yields an increasingly improved knowledge of knowledge [*Erkennen*]. This portrayal is not wrong. It is incomplete, however, and it does not allow us to comprehend the break between transcendental idealism and radical constructivism. Continuity is an indispensable prerequisite for every evolution, and the emergence of any new forms presupposes prior achievements, *preadaptive advances*, materials in which they can establish themselves. Equally important, however, is the recognition of abrupt discontinuities. In a mere historiography of ideas, this side remains underexposed. A social-theoretical analysis explains discontinuities via the reorganization of the form of differentiation of society. The reason for the experience of modernity (in contrast to all older social formations) is therefore given with the functional differentiation of the currently realized social system. This form enforces a separation between problems of reference and problems of encoding. And this separation results in the semantic experiments associated with modernity.

The first implementation of this program via ideals of the future, transcendental-philosophical reflections, hopes of progress, and ideas of self-realization was insufficient, as the arts and literature had already registered with disappointment in the nineteenth century. On the level of such an insufficient structural richness, one can today only formulate a theory of postmodernity or act out one's aversions to the factually supporting structures of our social system.[8] Since, however, modern society is, and continues to be, factually without alternatives, there is little sense in semantically resorting to irrelevance in such a way. If, on the other hand, one defines modern society structurally in terms of functional differentiation and derives from this principle its semantic requirements through such concepts as polycontexturality, second-order observation, and the distinction of distinctions—especially the distinction between problems of encoding (for example, true/untrue) and problems of reference (self-reference and external reference)—then, in any case, an opportunity for observations and descriptions presents itself that is richer in structures..

That this, too, is only a communication, only a description, only a theory that exposes itself to observation, follows from the communication itself.

II

By an alternative route we also arrive at the insight that the specificity of modernity must be sought in the differences that are produced when an observer designates something and thereby makes a distinction. We infer this insight from the observation that important statements about modern science take the form of a critique that does not start from a perspective immanent to science with a view toward possible improvements but, in principle, complains about the fact that modern science, as science, leaves something essential out of consideration.

What is at stake in such a critique is the form of modern science—that is, the difference made by the fact that science exists. We are leaving aside the often-heard complaint that science serves capitalism (and should rather serve socialism) because it is insufficiently articulated from the perspective of social theory. There is, however, another description of science, equally critical of modernity, that targets its center. It takes aim at a one-sided tendency toward formalization, idealization, technicalization, accounting, and so on. In this sense, Edmund Husserl, as has already been discussed elsewhere,[9] spoke of a crisis of the modern sciences.[10] What is at stake here is not the dependency of technology on science but the dependency of science on technology—and not in the sense of a simple "finalizing debate" that takes only goals into account. At stake is the fact that science accepts technology as a form of its own. We are leaving open the question of whether anything is to be criticized, improved, or avoided. We are only asking: in what sense is technicalization (we continue to use this word) a form? And what is the other side of this form?

According to Husserl—and many have reiterated his view—technicalization forgets the "lifeworld," the always already employed, concrete foundation of meaning for subjective intentions, whether in the form of a naive "putting-into-it" [*Geradehineinstellung*] or of a reflexive attitude. Against this forgetting, Husserl reminds us of the special telos of European history: the complete self-realization of reason under the guidance of philosophy. Accordingly, the other side is the concrete actualization of meaningful human life under the guidance of reason. In a different version, which today is represented by Hans-Georg Gadamer,[11] the problem lies in our negligence toward language (dialogue) and textuality (hermeneutics) as the prerequisites of all understanding.

But technicizing abstraction is itself a means of achieving and securing consensus, in disregard of everything that might lead to different paths; what is especially disregarded here is the concrete endowment of the individual human being with attitudes, interests, motives, preferences—in short, the human being with a living memory. In the theory of the modern state, the confessional, legal, and moral judgments of individuals had to be regarded as arbitrary in order to make intelligible the necessity of concentrating such arbitrariness at the apex of the state.[12] Likewise, the concrete sense qualities and the entire sphere of "experience" [*Erfahrung*] and "opinion" in the realm of cognitive experience [*Erleben*] had to be understood as unreliable in order to set against them a mathematical calculus and its corresponding demonstrable measurement. This insight can still be garnered from the radicalism of Spencer Brown's *Laws of Form*: once one has made a distinction—and one cannot begin without one—and then continues in one's action, then an order of increased complexity arises, intelligible to everyone, which leaves only the options of either agreeing or refusing to join in.

Consensus can be achieved only by reduction; or, in order to formulate it paradoxically, by relinquishing consensus. The Romans had already discovered in their own way that, in the case of a dispute, one had to pose the *questio iuris*, define the legal problem, and, starting from there, search for similarities in the given law in order to separate the dispute from the network of kinship ties and political friendships. Nothing else is meant when we speak of differentiation in the terminology of systems theory. In exactly this sense, technicalization (or, to remind the reader, formalization, idealization, etc.) can be regarded as a specific element of modern science. A critique of this conception would be futile in a recognizable sense.

This in no way means that science has to confine itself to what is technically feasible, nor does it mean that science has to see its ultimate goal in technology, in the sense that freedom for thought experiments would be conceded only to preliminary reflections in accordance with the ultimate goal. Finally, it does not mean that now technologies, for their part, must conceive of themselves as applied sciences and, accordingly, wait until science is able to explain why something works. Such conceptions can be refuted with reference to real situations. Scientific theories and technologies, however, converge in their use of simplifications—that is, simplifications in the sense of disregarding other things whose reality remains undisputed.

The understanding of technology as a simplification that works allows us to include the technology of money and bookkeeping (concerning companies and nations in the most general sense). Accordingly, it becomes possible to balance the costs of labor and of materials. Indisputably, this process functions in the sense of calculating economically profitable or unprofitable modes of production in view of the question whether scientific discoveries are translatable into economic turnovers or not. It is equally indisputable that, in doing so, one abstracts from the evident fact that human beings work in a different sense than material. In other words, we are viewing as parallel the Marxian and the Husserlian critique of the disregard for what a human being is for himself. Obviously, modern society has made itself dependent on this abstraction, and for that very reason has left it to the individual to distance himself from this dependence and imagine his ownmost being [*sein Eigenstes*] as the center of the world—in a mode "free of technology," if one may say so.

Pitted against illusions that were perhaps indispensable at the beginning of the modern era, the understanding of technology as simplification indeed does not mean that the world even in its basic structures is simple and that this fact would have to be discovered. Science is not discovery but construction. Nor is it necessary to break through the surface of the phenomenal world and unmask it as mere appearance in order to discern the mathematical or categorical framework that carries the world. These are theories of the premodern world. On the contrary, science (just like, in its own way, technology) tries out simplifications, incorporates them into a given world, and seeks to determine whether the isolations necessary for such experiments are successful. Modern science can comprehend its own modernity only if it reflects upon this situation.

There are numerous ways in which this reflection can occur; in all cases, however, it requires double formulations. Systems theory speaks of differentiation by way of the operational closure of a system that is simultaneously *inclusive* and *exclusive*. In the language of Parsons's *pattern variables* one can say that *universalization* can be achieved only through *specification*. This amounts to an avoidance of particularities, of concrete loyalties, for example, and of diffuse generalizations toward an all-encompassing indeterminacy. Yet another formulation succeeds if one aims at complexity. Then we must say that the construction of complexity can be initiated only by a reduction *of complexity*.

The modernity of all function systems, including science, consists in the effects of these interrelated conditions. These effects block a description of the world as an object given to (or "standing opposed to") the observer. Correspondingly, the problem of the unity of the difference between cognition and its object loses the classical significance it used to have in guiding reflection. Science can no longer comprehend itself as a representation of the world as it is, and must therefore retract its claim of instructing others about the world. It achieves an exploration of possible constructions that can be inscribed in the world and, in so doing, function as forms, that is, produce a difference.

Once we understand the crisis of modern science as a becoming-visible of its simplifications, its technical character, its functioning without any knowledge of the world, then it is conceivable that this insight could be channeled back into science, to a greater extent than has hitherto been the case, and become the object of normal research. Neither the critique of political economy nor phenomenology "as a rigorous science" has been able to accomplish this. Likewise, the thematization of "technology and science as ideology" failed to link up to normal research.[13] Only recently, indications abound that the costs of these—after all, inevitable—simplifications are becoming objects of scientific research. This holds, for instance, for the evaluation of the consequences of technology and, above all, for risk research. To begin with, these disciplines seem to be greatly restricted in their scope and are initiated and carried along by topical interests. At the same time, however, models of "autological" research of science on science have been developed at the margins of available theories of reflection concerning the scientific system. If we succeed in regrounding these theories of reflection to a greater extent on a constructivist foundation and in scientifically rehabilitating them with the help of suggestions from the quite heterogeneous "cognitive sciences," then even those topics traditionally relegated to a rather external critique of science could become topics of research. Science would continue to observe itself in terms of the schema of its own code, that is, "true" and "false"; and it would still not think of thematizing the paradoxical nature of this code, that is, of asking whether the distinction of this code is itself a true or a false distinction. Yet it would be able to recognize to what extent it shares its peculiarities and its risks, along with all the characteristics we have discussed, with other function systems, and to what extent it ultimately owes these peculiarities to the structures of modern society.

III

A social theory that intends to take such considerations into account encounters a particular paradox, and this paradox arises to an equal extent for a description of society and for a description of the world. On the one hand, it is hard to dispute the fact that a comprehensive global social system [*Weltgesellschaftssystem*] has developed as the result of a long evolution. In addition, our concept of the world is not suited to perpetuating the old doctrine of the plurality of worlds; this doctrine has become inconceivable. Everything that is communicated is communicated in society. Everything that happens occurs in the world. This, too, holds for observations and descriptions, no matter with what kind of authorship (subject, science, etc.) they wish to equip themselves. For this very reason, the unity of society (of the world) cannot be reintroduced into society (the world). It cannot be observed or described as a unity, especially not on the basis of a representation without competition or on the grounds of some didactic authority. For each observation and description requires a distinction for its own operation. The observation of the One within the One, however, would have to include what it excludes (that against which it distinguishes its designation). It would have to be enacted in the system (in the world), just as the distinction between self-reference and external reference is enacted in the system (in the world). Such an enactment is possible, and it gives its paradox the form of a "reentry," but the solution requires an imaginary space (as one speaks of imaginary numbers), and this imaginary space replaces the classical a priori of transcendental philosophy.[14]

The result can be explained further if one considers that each paradox can be unfolded in a nonlogical (creative) fashion if one replaces it with
a distinction. In our case, this would be the distinction between operation
and observation (the distinction must take into consideration that all operations, if they are communications, are self-observing operations, and
that all observations must be enacted as operations; otherwise, they do not
take place at all). We can then say: the unity of the system is produced and
reproduced *operatively*. The operation, at the same time, observes itself—
yet it does not observe the unity that includes it, that comes into being, and
is being changed, in this enactment. The *observation* of unity, in contrast,
is a special operation in the system (in the world), which must use a special
distinction (for example, the distinction between system and environment
or the distinction between world and being-in-the-world) and which itself
can also be observed in the process of its distinguishing and designating.
The observation and description of unity from within unity is therefore
possible, but only as an enactment of precisely this operation, only on the
basis of the choice of a distinction whose own unity remains imaginary,
and only in such a way that the operation "observation" is itself exposed to
observation.

We have thus reached the point where the significance of second-
order observation becomes evident. In the architecture of theory, but also in
the self-understanding of modernity, it takes the place formerly occupied by
natural or transcendental premises. Instead of appealing to final units, one
observes observations, one describes descriptions. At the second-order level,
we arrive again at recursive interrelations and begin to search for "eigenvalues," which remain unchanged in the course of the system's operations.
Perhaps these eigenvalues are only "places" occupied temporarily by values,
with the consequence that after each change, these places must be refilled
because they cannot remain empty, a task for which there is only a very limited (or no) choice of other possibilities available. Put differently, they are
perhaps only functions to be fulfilled while a very limited choice of functional equivalents is available. Thus one can say that research and therefore
science fulfills a function and thereby reproduces a stable eigenvalue of
modern society. One cannot simply refrain from research without trigger-
ing catastrophic consequences—catastrophe understood here as the re-
orientation toward other eigenvalues. It is therefore obvious that if one

does not wish to flee into the imaginary space of an "other society," then the critique of research can be carried out only as research.

The observation of observations can pay particular attention to what kinds of distinctions the observed observer uses. It can ask itself what the observer is able to see with his distinctions and what he is not able to see. The observation of observations can be interested in the blind spot of its own use of distinctions or in the unity of its distinction as the condition of possibility of its observation. Here, the traditional interests of the critique of ideology and of therapy can be sustained, but only as secondary variants that are themselves exposed to observation by the question of why the second-order observer cultivates precisely this view instead of making use of other possibilities in the observation of latent conditions. At the level of second-order observation, society is able to operate in a very general sense with the distinction manifest/latent, and indeed in such a way as to include, autologically, the second-order observer also. No one can see everything, and one gathers possibilities of observation only by engaging in distinctions that are functioning blindly at the moment of observation because they take the place of, and must hide, the unobservable unity of the world. Distinctions serve as two-sided forms that direct the operations of designating, referring, and connecting. They serve as the unity of the representability of conditions of their own possibility, which themselves must remain invisible. And this circumstance helps us realize that the eigenvalues achieved thereby must assume the form of places or functions that "are" nothing but limitations for possible substitutions.

In the modern world, distinctions are therefore not, as it were, penultimate instruments that can be transcended with a view toward unity, whether of the world or only of absolute spirit. On the contrary, any attempt to designate a unity requires new distinctions and, in turn, renders the ultimate goal invisible. Knowledge serves—as does, in a different way, art [15]—to render the world invisible as the "unmarked state," a state that forms can only violate but not represent. Any other attempt must be content with paradoxical or tautological descriptions (which is meaningful as well).

A reflection upon this situation does not have to result in "nihilism," for such a conclusion would make sense only within an ontological frame of reference that presupposes the distinction between being and nonbeing. Nor are we dealing with a variation of the religious tradition that seeks support in the invisible in order to lament in turn the loss of this possibility today using the semantics of the invisible. Carrying along ultimate symbols [*Letztsymbol*] such as indescribability, invisibility, and latency only reflects the contingency of the employment of all distinctions. The soundness of this reflection, however, arises—and this can still be ascertained by this reflection—from a form of social differentiation that no longer allows for any binding, authoritative representation of the world in the world or of society within society.

Translated by Kerstin Behnke

PART II

PARADOX AND OBSERVATION

3

The Paradox of Observing Systems

I

In spite of several attempts, it is still difficult to submit formal sciences such as logic or mathematics to a sociological analysis. Such an analysis would entail discovering empirical correlations between specific social conditions and specific formal structures. Both the conditions and the structures would then have to be treated as variables whose "values" would appear as contingent, despite their claims to be "natural" (as society) or necessary (as the principles, axioms, and rules of logic). One would have to assert that the natural is artificial because it is produced by society and that the necessary is contingent because under different conditions it may have to accept different forms. These are paradoxical statements, but we need them when we have to distinguish different observers from each other or when we have to distinguish self-observations from external observation, because for the self-observer things may appear as natural and necessary, whereas when seen from the outside they may appear artificial and contingent.[1] The world thus variously observed remains, nevertheless, the same world, and therefore we have a paradox. An observer, then, is supposed to decide whether something is natural or artificial, necessary or contingent. But who can observe the observer (as necessary for this decision) and the decision (as contingent for the observer)? The observer may refuse to make this decision, but can the observer observe without making this decision or would the observer have to withdraw, when refusing this decision, to the position of a nonobserving observer?

All this does not affect the self-claimed validity of logic or mathematics; and we may find comfort with Dr. Johnson: "When speculation has done its worst, two and two still make four" (Johnson 1963, 114). We may, however, pursue a less trivial, a less commonsensical interest and continue to ask: Who says it? Who is the observer?

II

Paradox was invented—that is, discovered—more than two thousand years ago, at the beginning of serious experiments with second-order observing.[2] Since that time we find two different, even contradictory uses, the one logical, the other rhetorical. The logical tradition tries to suppress paradox. It exploits the ontological distinction between being and nonbeing to say that only being exists according to its own distinctions, above all: *hypokeímenon/symbebekos*. The observer can make true and false statements and can correct him- or herself (or be corrected by others) because being is what it is (not *as* it is, as we probably would say). Being is framed by such secondary distinctions (or categories) *and not by its distinction from nonbeing*. Being does not need to be distinguished from, or to exclude, nonbeing to be itself. It simply is, by itself (nature) or by way of creation. Disregarding this structure of ontological metaphysics, it has been claimed, would lead cognition the wrong way. It would end with paradoxes and destroy the telos of thinking. The appearance of unacceptable self-contradictions at the other side of the ontological scheme is then said to prove ontology as metaphysics. Thinking has to stay on the right path and avoid paradoxes.

The rhetorical tradition that invented the term[3] introduced paradoxical statements to enlarge the frames of received opinions—therefore "para-doxa"—to prepare the ground for innovation and/or for the acceptance of suggested decisions. At first sight, this seems to be a completely different notion, and the collection of examples of rhetorical paradoxes hardly ever demonstrates logical contradictions.[4] After the introduction of the printing press, such collections were in fact recommended and sold as amusing jokes. "They are only but exercise of wit," Anthony Munday excuses himself, sending his book on paradoxes to the king,[5] and Ortensio Lando adds to his book on paradoxes a second publication trying to extinguish the fire (Lando n.d.). But why do we communicate paradoxes in the first place if we are not supposed to take them seriously?

The conventional answer seems to be—exercise of wit.[6] This may be a good advertisement for selling books, but it is not the whole truth. When we go back to the traditional definition of paradoxes as going beyond the limits of common sense,[7] the immediate intention seems to be to deframe and reframe the frame of normal thinking, the frame of common sense. The communication of paradoxes fixes attention on the frames of common sense, frames that normally go unattended. If this is the function, then it will not surprise us that deframing again needs its own frames. Therefore, we find comments on paradoxes in prefaces, in letters of dedication, in other books, or at the end of the text (as in Erasmus's *Praise of Folly*), and it seems to require other texts to frame the deframing, to look at it from the outside and to lead back to common sense—it is only an exercise of wit.

But cancellation can hardly be the whole meaning of the operation, for it could not explain Shakespeare's theater with its elaborate use of paradoxes and frames within frames, or Plato's cave as a stage for the shadows of ideas to appear on, that is, as a frame for these shadows. And the cave is also itself framed by Plato's theory of ideas and of the ways we are able to remember them, which explains that in daily life we only use the cave-frame and need not, indeed cannot, reflect the double closure of the frames.

The interest in paradoxes emerging in the sixteenth century directs attention to the frames of common sense. It seems, when we are allowed to appeal to a further frame, to indicate the appearance, the coming on the stage, of a new historical interest, the interest in frames as frames or in limits as parts of a form that are neither inside nor outside but in a certain sense nowhere or "nothing" (da Vinci 1954, 73). If paradoxes are teleological operations aiming at a perfect state, then this state could be described as enriched common sense. However, it may be more rewarding to ask whether the assumption of a natural end is adequate or whether we are not observing a discovery that, like Kant's final cause without finality, is inherently paradoxical.[8] The rhetorical paradox, then, may be an autological operation, infecting itself with whatever is a paradox.

During the eighteenth century, rhetoric lost its traditional reputation, partly because of the spread of literacy, partly because the hierarchical structure of the estates of society was replaced by a class structure. The rhetorical figure of the paradox that was still in use was definitely seen as frivolous play and as insolence.[9] And finally, during the nineteenth and twentieth centuries, with the increasing development of formalism in mathematics and logic, and with the increasing interrelation of logic and mathematics (e.g., Cantor, Frege, Russell), paradox was treated as something to be avoided by all means, be it by simple interdiction or by constructing "hierarchies" of types or levels and presenting them as logical or linguistic necessity. However, if we maintain an interest in frames, we may well describe such hierarchical distinctions as frames, this time not of commonsensical opinions but of logical operations, and revive the curiosity of the sixteenth century to see what would happen if we deframe these frames. In such a revival of sixteenth-century curiosity, we will receive the support of systems therapists who say that everyday communication cannot but confuse these levels and reproduce paradoxical communication,[10] and we will receive the support of Gödel, who would say that one cannot cleanly separate (and I would like to add: in communication) the statement about numbers from the statement about statements about numbers.

If at the end of this history, observing frames is a serious consideration, does it then make any sense to maintain the traditional distinction between the logical interdiction and the rhetorical recommendation of paradoxes? Or is this double tradition but another sign for the inherent paradoxicality of the paradox?

III

We began our investigation by asking how a sociology of knowledge can include among its objects formal sciences such as logic and mathematics. We now have to answer the question: How is it possible to observe frames? Whatever difficulties may emerge during this investigation, we will certainly need a medium that is the same on both sides of the frame, on its inside and on its outside. I propose to call this medium *meaning*, and thereby exclude two other possibilities—the world and truth. The world, as an unqualifiable entity, an entity without information, seems to be too large. Truth, on the other hand, is too narrow because it itself serves as a frame, as the inner side of a form whose outside would be everything that is not true. But what, then, is meaning?

If we want to observe paradoxical communications as deframing and reframing, deconstructing and reconstructing operations,[11] we need a concept of meaning that does not prevent or restrict the range of such operations. "Meaning" cannot be understood as the result of obedience to the methodological instructions of the Viennese school of "logical empiricism," which would exclude metaphysics and much more as "meaningless,"[12] nor can it be understood in relation to the subjective aspiration of individuals and what seems meaningful to them and for them.[13] Such definitions of meaning exclude unmarked possibilities and are valid only within their methodological or subjective frames. They are, that is, deframable (deconstructible) meanings and do not fulfill the requirements of a medium that gives access to *both* sides of *any* frame.

To avoid such limitations, we need a concept of meaning that is (for systems that can use meaning as a medium) coextensive with the world. Meaning in this sense will have no outside, no antonym, no negative form. It knows, of course, negative meanings, even artificially constructed nonsense meanings (nonsense poems for example), but every possible use of this medium called "meaning" will itself reproduce meaning, and even an attempt to cross the boundary of meaning into an unmarked space will be a meaningful operation. (The unmarked space has, for this purpose, the name "unmarked space.")

With reference to Husserl's transcendental phenomenology, we can conceive of meaning as the simultaneous presentation (in Husserl's terms, intention) of actuality and possibility (1995b, 59ff.). The actual is given within a "horizon" of further possibilities. Since operationally closed systems consist of operations only and have to renew them from moment to moment, they can maintain their self-reproduction only by continuously actualizing new meaning. This requires selection from many possibilities and, therefore, will appear as information. The internal dynamics of communication (in the case of social systems) and living experience ("Erleben" in the case of psychic systems) is possible only because, strangely enough, actual operations are also possible operations. The distinction actual/possible is a form that "reenters" itself.[14] On one side of the distinction, the actual, the distinction actual/possible reappears; it is copied into itself so that the system may have the sense of being able to continue actual operations in spite of an increasing change of themes, impressions, intentions.

If we observe such a reentry, we see a paradox. The reentering distinction is the same, and it is not the same. But the paradox does not prevent the operations of the system. On the contrary, it is the condition of their possibility because their autopoiesis requires *continuing* actuality with *different* operations, *actualizing different possibilities*.

That psychic and social systems are *based* on a reentry has dramatic consequences. From a purely mathematical point of view (following Spencer Brown), it means (1) creating an imaginary space that includes unmarked states and makes it possible to introduce expressions of ignorance, and (2) producing a system with unresolvable indeterminacy—the system becomes incalculable and therefore nontransparent to itself. Furthermore, (3) the system nevertheless has to start every operation from a historical state that is its own product (the input of its own output) and needs a memory function to distinguish forgetting from remembering, and (4) it has to face its future as a succession of marked and unmarked states or self-referential and hetero-referential indications. It needs, in other words, to be prepared for oscillating between the two sides of its distinctions. An oscillating system can preserve the undecidability of whether something is inside or outside a form. It can preserve and reproduce itself as a form, that is, as an entity with a boundary, with an inside and an outside, and it can prevent the two sides from collapsing into each other. A self-referential system that continually regenerates its reentry will be, in Heinz von Foerster's terms, a nontrivial machine, structurally determined by its own output and therefore *unreliable* (von Foerster 1984, 8ff.).

A system that is bound to use meaning as a medium constitutes an endless but complete world in which everything has meaning, in which everything gives many cues for subsequent operations and thereby sustains autopoiesis, the self-reproduction of the system out of its own products. To see (and we will say: to observe) possibilities and to use meaning as a medium, the system will use the distinction between medium and form.[15] "Medium" within this distinction means a loose coupling of possibilities without regard to actual happenings, and "form" means tight couplings that construct the form, for example a thing, with an outside. Again, the medium is inside and outside, but the attention of the system has limitations and observes only forms. Forms are actualized in time just for a moment, but since the system has memory it can reactualize well-tried forms and direct its operations from form to form, thereby reproducing the medium. The distinction medium/form serves as a frame without outside, as an internal frame that includes, via reentry, its own outside.

IV

Now we are sufficiently prepared to observe the observer, to enter the circle of "observing systems" (in the double sense of von Foerster's *Observing Systems*). As with so many other terms, the expression "observing/observer" has to be adapted to this theoretical context. It does not mean only attentive sensual perception, though it does not exclude this particular definition. In more recent literature, initiated by George Spencer Brown, Humberto Maturana, and Heinz von Foerster, the term corresponds to the autopoietic self-reproduction of systems, to the operation of reentry, and to the oscillation between marked and unmarked states, to the inside and the outside of forms and self-referential and hetero-referential indications.[16] Observing means making a distinction and indicating one side (and not the other side) of the distinction.

The other side can be left completely unmarked—say, Bloomington and nothing else. But normally our indications will frame our observations with the effect that the other side implicitly will receive a corresponding specification—say, Bloomington and no other city, the university in Bloomington and no other university. In this case the indication implies a double boundary, the inner boundary of the frame "cities," "universities," and the boundary of this frame that excludes animals, numbers, fine wines, and everything else, that is, the unmarked space. Our next operation may cross the boundary that separates Bloomington from its unmarked state and may select another frame. For example, we may ask whether it would be possible to find fine wines in Bloomington, and this would lead us to look for a further frame—say, restaurants or shops. One will thereby be led to places where one can find fine wines. Proceeding in this way from frame to frame or from form to form will, by necessity, reproduce the unmarked space.[17] It will maintain the world as severed by distinctions, frames, and forms, *and maintained by its severance*. "We may take it," to quote Spencer Brown, "that the world undoubtedly is itself (i.e., is indistinct from itself), but, in any attempt to see itself as an object, it must, equally undoubtedly, act so as to make itself distinct from, and therefore false to, itself. In this condition it will always partially elude itself" (1979, 105). This partiality precludes any possibility of representation or mimesis and any "holistic" theory. It is not sufficient to say that a part is able to express or to symbolize the whole. The miracle of symbolization, the marvelous, that which has been most admired by our tradition, has to be replaced by a difference that, when observed, always regenerates the unobservable.

The operation of observing, therefore, includes the exclusion of the unobservable, including, moreover, the unobservable par excellence, observation itself, the observer-in-operation. The place of the observer is the unmarked state out of which it crosses a boundary to draw a distinction and in which it finds itself indistinguishable from anything else. As such, the observer as a system can be indicated, but only by way of a further distinction, another form, a frame, for example, that makes it possible to distinguish one observer from others or psychic observing systems from social observing systems. We arrive, then, at the autological conclusion that the observing of observers and even the operation of self-observation is itself simply observation in the usual sense—that is, making a distinction to indicate one side and not the others.[18] And this again can only happen in the world and by severing the unmarked space, crossing the boundary that thereby comes into existence as a boundary separating a marked from what now can be marked as "unmarked" space. We resist the temptation to call this creation.

V

It is by no means necessary to conceptualize this situation of meaning-producing operations. To clarify the world or to indicate the unmarked space as unmarked is a requirement neither of daily life nor of autopoietic reproduction. To elaborate on its self-description remains one of the possibilities an observer sees and can, if required, actualize. But even then, it will just change its frame, cross the boundary between self-reference and hetero-reference; it will mark itself as a thing among others or as an observer among others. Switching frames, proceeding from form to form, is the normal way of observing operations, and the "self" of the system can appear and disappear as suggested by circumstances. Language may make the speaker more visible if it is required to say "I love" and not simply "amo."

For social systems, the emergence of organizations that can communicate in their own name makes all the difference. No other social system can do that, no society, no societal subsystem, no interaction. If the "estates" of the old European society wanted to have a voice, they formed a corporation ("Standschaft" in Germany), and if the economy wants to have a voice in political affairs, it sends representatives of its organizations. Nations have names, but to be able to participate in communication they form "states." Names, addresses, persons (in the traditional sense) [19] are taken for granted. Their use has to adapt to the speed of perception, thinking, or communication, to the speed required by the necessity of replacing vanishing events by other events. There is simply no time to include the world or the complete reality of the observing systems (as "subjects" and as "objects") in the operation.

But if an observer—again, a psychic or a social system—wants to observe and describe the continuous deframing and reframing of frames, the autopoietic operation of observing systems (including itself), it will end up with paradoxical formulations. It would have to say that the different is the same; that the distinction between marked and unmarked is *one* distinction among others; that any distinction is a unity, a frame that separates two sides and can be used to connect operations only at one side (at the positive side, at the inner side of the form) and not at the other side. The other side remains included, but as excluded. The excluded third, or the "interpretant" in the sense of Peirce, or the operation of observing in our theory, or the "parasite" in the sense of Michel Serres, or the "supplement" or "parergon" in Derrida's sense, is the active factor indeed, without which the world could not observe itself. Observation has to operate unobserved to be able to cut up the world.

When observers (we, at the moment) continue to look for an ultimate reality, a concluding formula, a final identity, they will find the paradox. Such a paradox is not simply a logical contradiction (A is non-A) but a foundational statement: The world is observable *because* it is unobservable. Nothing can be observed (not even the "nothing") without drawing a distinction, but this operation remains indistinguishable. It can be distinguished, but only by another operation. It crosses the boundary between the unmarked and the marked space, a boundary that does not exist before and comes into being (if "being" is the right word) only by crossing it. Or to say it in Derrida's style, the condition of its possibility is its impossibility.

Obviously, this makes no sense. It makes meaning. It makes no common sense; it uses the meaning of "para-doxon" to transgress the boundaries of common sense to reflect what it means to use meaning as a medium. However, even paradox cannot be observed without a distinction, but one that is involved in two different ways. On the one hand, paradox is always the unity of a distinction (for example, in the case of the Liar's Paradox, the unity of the distinction true/false); and on the other hand, one may find ways to deparadoxify or to "unfold" (Löfgren 1978) paradox (again, in the above case, by making a rule to separate types or levels and to forbid "strange loops" [Hofstadter 1979]). It seems, then, that any distinction can be paradoxified and deparadoxified, depending on conditions of plausibility. The distinction used to make the paradox visible and invisible has to be presupposed to apply a second distinction, the distinction between the paradox and its unfolding, its visibility and its invisibility. Only the paradox itself provides for unconditioned knowledge; the distinction used for unfolding the paradox depends on conditions of acceptability. Paradox, then, is, as unconditioned knowledge, a transcendental necessity, the successor of what was supposed to be a performance of the transcendental subject. But all usable, connectable knowledge will be contingent.

The paradox, then, would be the *parergon*, a supplement to the work that remains to be done and that has already been done.[20] It has a double identity, a logical identity by oscillating in itself between positive and negative versions of the same, and an empirical identity due to the recursive network of operations of a system that paradoxifies and deparadoxifies its distinctions.

VI

And now, we are on our way back to a sociology of knowledge within the framework of a theory of society. Neither ontology nor cosmology, neither nature (with its substances, its essential and accidental forms) nor knowledge of God (theology) will help. We will have to distinguish observers, and the most important of them will be society, that is, the encompassing social system.

Society produces culture—memory—and its culture will decide whether distinctions and indications may be communicated as natural (not artificial), as normal (not pathological), and as necessary or impossible (not contingent). In periods of semantic uncertainty and structural transition, paradoxes will become fashionable, as in the sixteenth century after the introduction of the printing press and after the Protestant Reformation and during its civil wars.[21] We may find society, now world society, at the end of the twentieth century in a similar situation of uncertainty, for very different reasons, of course. And again, paradox has become fashionable, if not *the* predicament of the century.[22]

There are at least two interconnected reasons for this renewed interest in paradox. One is the establishment of a world society with a plurality of cultural traditions. The invention of "culture" at the end of the eighteenth century was still a European affair, opening European perspectives for historical and regional comparisons (Luhmann 1995a; Williams 1958). With the two world wars of this century and with the dissolution of the colonial empires, Europe lost its centrality in both structural and semantical terms. We may now imagine shifting centers of modernity (Tiryakian 1985), but no one center can presume to be the center of society as a whole.

Secondly, that we have to live with a society without top and without center is due to the fact that the structure of modern society is determined by functional differentiation and no longer by a coherent hierarchical stratification or by a one-center / periphery differentiation. Functional differentiation requires polycontextural, hypercomplex complexity-descriptions without unifying perspective.[23] Society remains the same but appears as different depending upon the functional subsystem (politics, economy, science, mass media, education, religion, art, and so on) that describes it. The same is different. The integration of the system can be thought of no longer as a process of applying principles but rather as a reciprocal reduction of the degrees of freedom of its subsystems. Reason and consensus are replaced by evolutionary tests, that is, by uncertainty, and motivating orientations shift from symbols of identity, principles, and norms to boundaries and differences, to ecological problems, to individuals as distinct from society, or to more or less fundamentalistic oppositions. This very condition implies that there is no need to adapt to it, but theories of society that refuse adaptation will increasingly be described as counterfactual, as purely normative, as having a conservative bias toward ideas, even as being ideological.

VII

A final consideration returns us to forms in which our Greek, Roman, and European tradition treated, nourished, and killed paradox.[24] We examine here two distinctions that were probably the most important ones, the distinction between being and nonbeing, elaborated as ontology, and the distinction between good and bad, elaborated as ethics.

Ontological metaphysics presents itself, hiding its paradox, as the science of substances and essences, of individual beings (substances) and generic entities (essences) that may exist and be visible (for angels only) as ideas. There is no nonbeing in this world, this *universitas rerum*, but there are perfect and corrupt natural forms and, in cognition, true and false opinions. Cognition, too, is a natural process of being impressed by substances and essences. On this view, cognition exists, either with true or with false results. Its distinguishing capacity (*dihaíresis*) is its very essence, but it relates only, via mimesis, to the substances and generic forms of being. Reflection (including the reflection of reflection) is nothing but a particular way to be, a special capacity among others of the human psyche, and the category of the "infinite" serves as the asylum for all questions that cannot be solved with this approach (Günther 1979b, 8). "Something is or it is not; that is all there is to it in ontology" (Günther 1979a, 286).

But why are we supposed to observe the world with this primary distinction between being and nonbeing, and why are we to treat the distinction finite/infinite as a supplement to this primary distinction? Why don't we, operating as observers, that is, as systems, start from the distinction between inside and outside (Herbst 1976, 88)? Apparently, being is the strong side, the powerful side of this distinction. It is the "inner side" of the ontological form. You can operate on the side of beings but not on the side of nonbeings. Only beings have connecting value. The exclusion of nonbeings from beings is a natural and (logically) necessary aspect of their being. But what would happen if we set out to observe the natural as artificial and the necessary as contingent? That is, what would happen if we permitted the question of what kind of society lends plausibility to these ontological assumptions?

The same series of questions emerges when we look at "ethics" in its classical, premodern form. Here, the guiding distinction is good and bad or, taking the human origin of action into account, virtue and vice. Perfect action is good, corrupt action is bad; human perfection is virtue, human corruption is vice. In human society, only good actions have connecting capacities, whereas bad action or vice is seen as an isolated event or an isolating habit. This leads to the conclusion that being is good (*ens et verum et bonum convertuntur*) and that the world and society can be accepted. The good is the form that is taught in ethics, and the form itself is good, which means that it is good to distinguish the good from the bad and that ethics itself is morally good. The good represents both the positive side of the distinction *and the distinction itself.* In our logical and linguistic frames, its unity is due to a confusion of levels. In social communication this presupposes authority—for example, of the old over the young, of men over women, of noblemen over commoners, of clerics over laymen. In structural terms, this form of unfolding the paradox presupposes a society with hierarchical and/or center/periphery differentiation.

What we label "modern" society, then, reacts to the dissolution of these premises. The printing press and technological advances may mean that the young have access to better knowledge than the old (Thomas 1988) and that the reading public may have the better judgment compared to the local magnates or the clerics bound by orthodoxy (M. James 1974). First the aristocracy and its political apparatus and then finally everybody needs money, so money becomes the medium, at least for this transitional period, organizing the differentiation of social status (Stone 1965). As a result, recruitment patterns of organizations (state bureaucracies, enterprises, universities) become more and more independent of family origin, that is, nobility. Having to digest these social changes, the social and political semantics has to change its conceptual frames.[25] But it also—and this is our point—has to provide new patterns for the unfolding of the paradoxes inherent in all distinctions that are used for framing observations and descriptions.

During the second half of the eighteenth century, new problems were invented, not to describe this social change but to cope with increasing uncertainty. The traditional ontology became superseded by the Kantian quest for the condition of possibility of experience, and in order to provide a solution, the *hypokeimenon/subiectum* became the subject, the observer himself. Moreover, good behavior now needed no longer good manners but good reasons, and ethics became an academic discipline branching out in transcendental and utilitarian theories. So, in the subject it is now easy to recognize the observer, and in good reasons for good behavior it is easy to recognize the ambivalent duplication of the good, that is, the veiling of the paradox. The social—treated in the tradition as either naturally domestic (economic) or naturally political (civil) society—became thereby pulverized as the culture (*Bildung*), language, economy, or state of individuals. The social, then, could be reconstructed only by an inherently paradoxical term—intersubjectivity.

The old-European tradition resolved its paradox by fetishism and disavowal, to use (or misuse) these Freudian terms. It used a reentry of the distinction between being and nonbeing into being and a reentry of the distinction between good and bad into the good. The substantial being and the reasonable good take the place of the paradox. This solution could efface the original differences and reconstruct them in terms of internal distinctions so successfully that medieval theology accepted it as cosmology and saw no need to reflect on paradoxes or even to retain the word. Only with Nicholas of Cusa and the early modern mystics did the problem come back and paradoxical formulations reemerge as a form to communicate ineffable experiences rationally.[26] But the so-called "modern" solution could never achieve a similar stability. Its "present time" became "pregnant with future," that is, with the unknown and with the prospect of oscillating within the framework of its distinctions—now described as "ideologies." There were many competing distinctions, such as society and state, society and community, individual and collectivity, freedom and institution, progressive and conservative politics, and, above all, capitalism and socialism, but in none of these cases did the unity of these distinctions, the sameness of the opposites, become a problem (Luhmann 1990a, 123–43). The paradox now becomes resolved as oscillation, that is, as the still-undetermined future. Supported by a universally accepted "open future," these distinctions (and others as well) stand in for the paradox of any frame used by an observer.

If "modernity" relies on its future for its deparadoxification, it is, and will always remain, an "incomplete project" (Habermas 1981). The future never becomes present; it never begins but always moves away when we seem to approach it. But how long are we supposed to live with or wait for this future if we run into troubles with our present society? The more pressing need might well be to describe the present condition, but then we might have to acknowledge that there are many possible descriptions, so that we will have to move from first-order to second-order descriptions.[27] This will require a transclassic logic in Gotthard Günther's sense and will certainly go beyond the suggestions we find in Spencer Brown's *Laws of Form*.[28] I have no idea how this can be worked out in sociological terms, but if we could develop theoretical frames of sufficient logical and structural complexity to dissolve our paradoxes, we may find that there still is one paradox left— the paradox of observing systems.

This theory of paradox is in no way a theory that founds itself explicitly or implicitly on systems theory, that is, on the distinction between system and environment or inside and outside. All distinctions—this one too—can be paradoxified. We need only ask the question "What is the unity of this distinction?" to see the paradox. And what prevents us from doing precisely that?

We would have to use the distinction between paradoxification and deparadoxification of distinctions. We would have to admit that all distinctions, including this one, can be reduced to a paradox. In this sense, paradox is an invariant possibility, and all distinctions are of only temporary and contingent validity. We can always ask: Who is the observer? And then, Why do we distinguish him or her? If there are sufficient plausible reasons in present-day disciplinary and interdisciplinary research, systems theory may offer itself as a way out of the paradox—for the time being.

4

Deconstruction as
Second-Order Observing

During my work on this paper I had the opportunity to see a television report on the admission of homosexuals into the army. What I saw (and I may well have seen things that were not shown) may serve as an introduction to the rather difficult and, if I may say so, postconceptual topic of deconstruction and second-order observing.

The report showed discussions in the United States Senate and individual interviews with privates and officers of the army. A lot of distinctions came into the foreground. The main questions were as simple as they were difficult, namely whether or not the admission of homosexuals would weaken the strength of the army and how strong would objections and resistance be on the side of the army. The issue was introduced for political reasons in the electoral campaign of Mr. Clinton, but it seemed to get out of hand. There were legal distinctions showing up from time to time, for instance whether or not the present practice was in conformity with the constitution (constitutional/unconstitutional) and whether or not the law would be able to control illegal behavior such as sexual harassment or violence against homosexuals in the army (effectiveness/ineffectiveness of the law), but behind all of this was the undisputed distinction between heterosexuals and homosexuals.

Such a situation gives an occasion to open the deconstruction kit and see what would happen if we applied the instrument. We would have to deconstruct the distinction heterosexual/homosexual. This, of course, would destroy the presupposition of a "hierarchical opposition" in the sense of an inherent or "natural" primacy of heterosexuality. At least we would *see*, if not effectively destroy, what Louis Dumont would call *l'englobement du contraire*[1]—that is, the inclusion of oppositions in a hierarchical structure of preferred lifestyles.

But this can be said in the terminology of "prejudices" and without using the ambitious and transconceptual operation of deconstruction. And Derrida himself explicitly warns against such a strategic and political use of deconstruction.[2] His aims are more far-reaching—and less specific. Deconstruction draws attention to the fact that differences are only distinctions and change their use value when we use them at different times and in different contexts. The difference between heterosexuals and homosexuals is not always the same; it is subject to *différance*.

No objection. But what if we asked the question: Who (that is, which system) is using the distinction as a frame (or scheme) of observations; or, Who is the observer? What does he invest in making this distinction, and what will he lose in maintaining it?

Then immediately a variety of observing systems appear: the political system, the interaction of a session of the United States Senate, the army, individual privates and officers, rejected homosexuals, females and males, and we at our television sets. The illusion to be deconstructed is the assumption that all these systems designate the same object when they use the distinction heterosexuals/homosexuals. The stereotypicality of the distinction leads to the assumption that all these systems observe the same thing, whereas observing these observers shows that this is not the case. Each of them operates within its own network; each of them has a different past and a different future. While the distinction suggests a tight coupling of observations and reality, and implies that there is only one observer observing "the same thing" and making true or false statements, a second-order observer observing these observers would see only loose coupling and lack of complete integration.

But this is not the end of the story. We forgot the most important observer—most important at least for this case—the body. It also makes its own distinctions and decides whether or not to be sexually attracted. Observing this observer leads us to ask whether or not it dutifully follows cultural imperatives,[3] or whether there is an unavoidable *akrasia* (lack of self-control),[4] as the Greeks would have said, a lack of *potestas in se ipsum* (self-control) in humans and in social systems.

If this *akrasia* is taken for granted, can a soldier know how his body would observe the situation if it included homosexuals without the protection of privacy—under the shower or in sleeping quarters or in a lot of similar situations? Even if society and the military prefer heterosexuality, and even if the mind of an individual accepts this definition for himself and for his body, could he or she be sure that his or her body plays the same game?

The television interviews report that the soldiers, these strong and healthy, well-nourished young men with oversized arms, legs, and bodies, confessed to being afraid of having homosexuals around them. But this would be (assuming that the law effectively prevents sexual harassment) completely harmless. Could it then be that the soldiers are worried about the possibility of their bodies reacting as observers on their own and that others would see that? It may be a very small chance of surprise, but a possibility amplified by uncertainty.

If this is true—and it is indirectly confirmed by the fact that female soldiers are much less concerned about the possibility of having lesbian comrades because their bodily reaction would be less distinct and more easy to conceal[5]—the whole definition of the problem changes. When the Greeks spoke about *akrasia* and the Middle Ages about *potestas in se ipsum*, the frame for observations was defined by the distinction between reason and passions, and reason was the position of an observer who was supposed to be created by God to observe His creation in one and only one way. Deconstruction destroys this "one observer—one nature—one world" assumption. Identities, then, have to be constructed. But by whom?

The problem of admitting homosexuals into the military is the problem of how to protect the fragile and eventually self-deceiving constructions of individuals; it is the risk (not untypical for soldiers anyway) of wearing badly fitting garments. It is not a problem, as many would like to see it, of protecting hypocrisy. It is not a problem of the freedom of the individual, either. The United States Senate would probably never call on experts in deconstruction or second-order observing, and these experts would not offer a political solution. However, could the political system, blinded by its own rhetoric, ignore that a more complex definition of the problem is available?

I

The American discussion about deconstruction has reached its stage of exhaustion. By now deconstruction looks like an old-fashioned fashion. There was a time when one thought to use deconstruction as a method to analyze literary or legal texts, replacing older, more formal methods of revealing the immanent meaning of a text. At the same time, hermeneutics lost its stronghold in subjectivity and became a method of creating circularity and of putting meaning into a text in order to be able to find it there; it taught how to construct something new by reading old texts. However, hermeneutics retained the idea that interpretation had to penetrate the surface of an object (that is, a text) or a subject (in other words, a mind) to reach its internal depths where truth was to be found.[6] It therefore retained the traditional idea of a boundary between the external and the internal that only Derrida dared to deconstruct.[7] There were also available the Hegelian version of dialectical method and Peirce's semiotics, both of which aimed at transcending distinctions in the direction of a third position. Deconstruction, however, was designed, if it was designed at all, to be none of these. Deconstruction seems to recommend the reading of forms as differences, to look at distinctions without the hope of regaining unity at a higher (or later) level, or without even assuming the position of an "interpretant" in the sense of Peirce. Deconstruction seems to be adequate for an intellectual climate heading toward cultural diversity. But are there any firm rules and any hope for results in the deconstruction business—that is, are there any framings that are not themselves deconstructible? Or would applying deconstruction lead only to reflexivity, recursivity, and self-reference resulting in stable meanings, objects, or what mathematicians call *eigenvalues*? It seems that there is only *différance*.

Derrida himself reacted to this discussion with well-studied amazement. In his "Letter to a Japanese Friend," he explains, "What deconstruction is not? Everything of course! What is deconstruction? Nothing of course!" commenting thereby on the presupposition of traditional ontological metaphysics and its logic according to which everything must either be or not be.[8] Deconstruction, then, is deconstruction of the "is" and the "is not." Deconstruction deconstructs the assumption of presence, of any stable relation between presence and absence, or even of the very distinction between presence and absence. It is an unstable concept subject to an ongoing *différance* of any difference it makes. It changes places and dances together with other unstable indicators such as *différance, trace, écriture, supplément, blanc,* and *marge* around a center that can no longer be characterized as either present or absent. It is like dancing around the golden calf while knowing that an unqualifiable god has already been invented. Or, in systems terms, is deconstruction the self-organization of this dance, complaining about a lost tradition and becoming, by this very complaint, dependent upon this tradition, so that it cannot decide and need not decide whether such a center is or is not present? It may be sufficient for maintaining the dance to be aware of the "trace de l'effacement de la trace" ("trace of the erasure of the trace").[9]

Looking at this discussion of deconstructionists and their critics, the most remarkable fact may well be the narrowness of its span of attention. It is almost a one-word discussion, or a text/context discussion, where deconstruction is the text and the history and the usages of the word the context. It seems as if hermeneutics takes its revenge by interpreting deconstruction. But if the concept really catches some elements of the "spirit of our times," of the intellectual climate at the end of this century, there will be other similar attempts in other corners. And there are of course other "postmetaphysical" theories that start and end with differences and focus on paradoxes and their unfoldings. These theories use time as the main formal medium of shifting connections. They rely on self-reference and recursivity to fix entities (as fictions) in systems of operations, mathematical or empirical, that maintain themselves in dynamic stability.

Given the narrowness of academic citation circles, there are many possibilities of cross-fertilization that remain unused. We may leave them to future "historians of simultaneity."[10] But to some extent we could explore these possibilities ourselves.

An alternative concept of knowledge, starting and ending with *difference,* emerged in the late 1960s from very different sources. Gregory Bateson, to begin with him, defines information as a difference that makes a difference.[11] On this basis, information processing has to be conceived of as transforming differences into differences. A system has to be irritated by a difference to be able to bring itself into a different state. But the two differences can match only if they are constructed by the same system. Other systems, other information.

George Spencer Brown assumes that any mathematical calculus has to begin by drawing a distinction to indicate one and not the other side of it.[12] Such drawing has to establish (and thereby to cross) the boundary between the unmarked and the marked state.[13] Then the distinction can be observed as form. It can be marked, and the processing of the mark may lead to forms of higher complexity—not only arithmetic but also algebraic forms, for example. The mark (indicating one and not the other side of the form) can be observed as the observer who makes the distinction. In other words, any kind of observing system, whatever its material reality (be it biological or neurophysiological or psychological or sociological), can be described as determined by the distinction it uses.[14] In the case of autopoietic (that is, self-reproducing) systems, this would mean that an observer has to focus on the self-determined and self-determining distinctions a system uses to frame its own observations.

This has led Heinz von Foerster to explore the possibilities of second-order cybernetics or second-order observations.[15] On this level one has to observe not simple objects but observing systems—that is, to distinguish them in the first place. One has to know which distinctions guide the observations of the observed observer and to find out whether any stable objects emerge when these observations are recursively applied to their own results. Objects are therefore nothing but the *eigenbehaviors* of observing systems that result from using and reusing their previous distinctions.

One should also mention Gotthard Günther's concept of transjunctional operations.[16] These are neither conjunctions nor disjunctions but positive/negative distinctions at a higher level.[17] If you find such distinctions being applied by a system (say, a moral code of good and evil, specified by a set of criteria or programs), you can, at the level of transjunctional operations, either accept or reject this frame. Then you may reject this very choice and may look for another form, such as legally right and legally wrong. Transjunctional operations become unavoidable as soon as a system shifts from first-order to second-order observations or, in Günther's terminology, to polycontextural observations. This comes very close to Derrida's attempt to transcend the limitations of a metaphysical frame that allows for only two states: being and nonbeing. It comes close to a rejection of logocentrism. But it does not imply a rejection of logics or of formalisms. Günther is not satisfied with the fuzziness of verbal acoustics and paradoxical formulations and tries, whether successfully or not, to find logical structures of higher complexity, capable of fixing new levels for the integration of ontology (for more than one subject) and logics (with more than two values).

II

There are some important lessons that could be drawn from this research on second-order observing systems for reformulating the intent of deconstruction. It is not our task, however, to try to clarify what Derrida possibly means. Derrida himself distinguishes *le sens de sens* ("the meaning of meaning") and *signalisation*, which could mean "making and deferring distinctions" on the one hand and "indications" on the other.[18] His writings are *écriture* in his own sense (that is, "inscriptions").[19] It remains open what they indicate. They have to be self-deconstructive to show how it works. And this is a form that exactly fits its philosophical intentions. But this does not mean that there can be no further steps. Derrida does his best to keep out of sight the presuppositions of using distinctions. But also one can pursue the contrary objective of making the architecture of theories as clear as possible so that an observer may decide whether to follow their suggestions or choose at certain points an alternative path.

One interesting convergence is already visible. A famous dictum of Humberto Maturana (within the context of his biological theory of cognition) says: Everything that is said (including this proposition) is said by an observer. The Derridean interpretation of Joseph Margolis leads to a very similar result: "Everything we say . . . is and cannot but be deconstructive and deconstructible."[20] For language use itself is the choice of a system that leaves something unsaid. Or, as Spencer Brown would say, drawing a distinction severs an unmarked space to construct a form with a marked and unmarked side. It may go too far to say that language use *as such* is deconstructive. But observing an observer who uses language certainly is. For on this level one can use transjunctional operations and reject (or accept) the distinctions that frame the observations of the observed observer. At the level of second-order observing, everything becomes contingent, including the second-order observing itself.

But what do we gain by this transition from deconstruction to second-order observing? What do we gain by avoiding the deconstruction of deconstruction and taking into account some of the results of more recent research on observing systems? There are several points to be mentioned:

1. Observations are asymmetric (or symmetry-breaking) operations. They use distinctions as forms and take forms as boundaries, separating an inner side (the *Gestalt*) and an outer side. The inner side is the indicated side, the marked side. From here one has to start the next operation. The inner side has connective value. For example, it is the immanent (and not the transcendent), the being (and not the nonbeing), or the having property (and not the not-having). The inner side is where the problem is—the problem of finding a suitable next operation. In the formal language of Günther, it has a positive (designative) but not a negative (reflective) value. Nevertheless, all observations have to presuppose *both* sides of the form they use as distinction or "frame."[21] They cannot but operate (live, perceive, think, act, communicate) *within the world*. This means that something always has to be left unsaid, thereby providing a position from which to deconstruct what has been said.

2. If one tries to observe both sides of the distinction one uses at the same time, one sees a paradox—that is to say, an entity without connective value. The different is the same, the same is different. So what?

First of all, this means that all knowledge and all action have to be founded on paradoxes and not on principles; on the self-referential unity of the positive and the negative—that is, on an ontologically unqualifiable world. And if one splits the world into two marked and unmarked parts to be able to observe something, its unity becomes unobservable.[22] The paradox is the visible indicator of invisibility. And since it represents the unity of the distinction required for the operation called observation, the operation itself remains invisible—for itself and for the time being.

This leads to the conclusion that parts of the world (or for that matter of any unity) have higher reflective potential than the unity itself (which may have none). This is definitely not a "holistic" approach. It is not a dialectical theory in the Hegelian sense, which ends with the "absolute spirit" that itself is nothing but a paradox, namely an entity excluding only exclusion. But it is in a sense a reconstruction of deconstruction.

It is the wisdom of Greek and Roman rhetorics, flourishing again in the sixteenth century, that grants paradoxes the function of stimulating further thought. The normal "doxa" is questioned by a para-doxa, and then you have to make a decision. Whereas the medieval techniques of *quaestiones disputatae* (points of disputation) relied on authority to decide between opposed opinions, with Ockham, and then with the printing press, authority itself became questionable. The opposed opinions were reformulated as paradoxes,[23] and the issue was left open. Finally, religion was divided at its institutional level, and the wars about truth began.

Today logicians say that tautologies and paradoxes need *unfolding*—that is, they have to be replaced with stable identities. In one way or another one has to find distinctions that protect from the error of identifying what cannot be identified. But distinctions again become visible as paradoxes as soon as one tries to observe their unity. Unfoldments, then, are the result of unasking this question. This means that one has to observe the observer to see when and why he takes the risk of an unfoldment—of a deconstructible unfoldment.

3. This may suggest, and correctly so, that the distinction between a paradox and its unfoldment is itself a paradox. (We keep in mind that deconstruction itself can be deconstructed.) Given this dead end, only time can help. Time can teach us that there is no end; everything goes on, and systems continue to operate as long as they are not destroyed. Spencer Brown's calculus of forms is strictly temporal, is a time-consuming program of building up complexity. In his terms, one can cross the boundary of any form (= distinction) and reach the other side. But this requires a next operation. If the other side is the unmarked space, you can do nothing but return. But thereby you obey the *law of cancellation*. If you come back, it is as if nothing has happened. But if, crossing the boundary, you try to find something specific, the other side will again be a distinction severing the unmarked space, reproducing the world as an unobservable entity. You defer the problem, and that seems to be what Derrida means by *différance*. If we start with the form of *nature* and cross its boundary with a specific intent, what do we find? Perhaps *grace*, which presupposes new distinctions, such as grace/work, grace/justice, grace / creation of order. The other side may be *civilization*; it may be *technology*; and we will feel the need for further distinctions such as civilization/culture, or tight coupling (technology) and loose coupling. The other side can be specified in several distinct ways. One can choose, at certain times, a religious or a secular context. Such possibilities of *antonym substitution* may be used to adapt the semantical structures of a society to changes in social structures.[24]

4. Within the theory of empirical systems, we can observe a similar trend to "temporalize" problems of identity and stability, and to replace theories of structural stability with theories of dynamic stability. Structuralism presupposed that systems need structures to limit the range of possible changes. Structures, then, seem to differentiate between fast changes (short waves), slow changes (long waves), and destructive changes (catastrophes). But contrary to a hidden assumption of structuralism, the only component of a system that can change is its structure. So if we focus on the form (= distinction), what is the other side of this form?

On the other side we find events or the operations of the system. Events (and this includes operations) cannot change because they have no time for change: they disappear as soon as they appear, they vanish in the very process of emerging.[25] So again, one of these cheerful paradoxes: the only unchangeable components of systems are inherently unstable.

Systems, therefore, have to use their operations to be able to continue to use their operations to be able, et cetera. This is, roughly, what has been called, following Humberto Maturana, autopoiesis.[26] Autopoietic systems are the products of their own operations. They have properties such as dynamic stability and operational closure. They are not goal-oriented systems. They maintain their autopoietic organization of self-reproduction as long as it is possible to do so. Their problem is to find operations that can be connected to the present state of the system. In this sense they are what Heinz von Foerster would call nontrivial machines or historical machines. They use self-referential operations to refer to their present state to decide what to do next.[27] They are unreliable machines, to be distinguished from trivial machines that use fixed programs to transform inputs into outputs. Autopoietic systems rely not on tight coupling but on loose coupling to move from one state to the next, and this makes it possible for them to evolve into different structural types according to random links between the system and its environment. They do not use cognition as a technique for adaptation and survival. Their environment is much too complex and nontransparent. But they develop, by evolution and learning, cognitive capacities for temporary adaptation to temporary states of the environment. And this makes it possible for them to have memory, which is the capacity to delay the repetitive use of forms.

5. A system that can observe may have the capacity to observe itself. To observe itself it has to distinguish itself from everything else, that is,

from its environment. The recursively interconnected operations of the system draw a boundary and thereby differentiate system and environment. The operation of self-observation requires a *reentry* (in Spencer Brown's sense) of this difference into itself, namely the operation of distinguishing system and environment *within the system*. (This is another way of saying that a part of an entity may have higher reflective capacities than the entity itself.) In this sense, all conscious systems and all social systems use the distinction between self-reference and external reference as an invariable structure of their own observations. This is a well-known assumption of the classical theory of the (conscious) subject that knows that it does the knowing in all its operations. But the same holds true for all communicating systems and in particular for the societal system. Communication requires the concomitant distinction between information and utterance, between constative and performative aspects of its operation. And understanding means nothing but observing the unity of this distinction.

But a reentry is a paradoxical operation. The distinction between "before" and "after" the reentry is the same and not the same. This shows that time (that is, the temporal distinction of an observer) is used to dissolve the paradox. And it shows also that a theory of the mind (the conscious subject) and a theory of society ultimately have to be founded on an unfolded paradox.

III

Who, then, is the observer, the constructing and therefore deconstructible observer? Nobody, of course, might be the answer in Derrida's style. Or everybody. The problem lies in the copula "is," used to formulate the question. But we can easily avoid its ontological implication (that there is an observer) by using the second-level observation. The question then becomes: Who is to be observed and by whom and for what reasons? This means: an observer has to declare (or even justify) his preferences for choosing and indicating a specific observer to be observed—that one and not another one. At the level of transjunctional operations any observer can accept or reject this choice. He can share the observer's preferences in focusing on this one (and not another) observer, or he can refuse to follow and, using third-level observation, describe the second-level observer as a specific system with specific preferences for selecting specific observers to be observed — say, as a family therapist with an interest in the intricacies of reciprocal observations of observations in families that so easily take a pathological path; or as a philosopher with an interest in deconstructing the distinguishing forms of distinction used in ontological metaphysics.

There is, in other words, no logical, ontological, or even natural primacy involved in using the distinction being/nonbeing. An observer may continue to use this distinction and thereby become visible as somebody who continues the distinct observational mode of our metaphysical tradition. Or he may reject this focus and become visible as entangled in all the difficulties of observing without using the distinction being/nonbeing — blurring, for example, its boundary without trying to replace it with other observational instruments.

A sociologist can find a relatively comfortable place in this game of *observing systems*. He may, for good reasons, focus on the societal system as the most important observer to be observed. Conscious systems (minds, individuals, subjects) are uninteresting for the simple reason that there are too many of them and it would be difficult to justify choosing one out of five billion or more.[28] And other social systems — science, for instance — are only subsystems of the societal system with a very specific (albeit universal) mode of observing.[29] The preference for observing the observer society remains a selection, remains contingent on specific observational interests. But it would be difficult to deny that in our present historical circumstances we are very concerned about not simply what modern society is but how it observes and describes itself and its environment.

Taking the society as an observer and even as the most important observer needs, of course, theoretical preparations. Some of these have been explained in section II. We have to define the concept of observation abstractly so that it can be applied to psychic and to social operations, to perception and thinking and to communication as well. Observation is nothing but making a distinction to indicate one side and not the other, regardless of the material basis of the operation that does the job, and regardless of the boundaries that close a system (brain, mind, social system) so that it becomes an autopoietic system, reproduced by the network of its own operations, and eventually irritated but never determined by its environment.

Accordingly, we have to redefine the concept of society. Conceived as an observing system, society cannot be described as a collection of different, somehow interrelated items such as human beings, or actions, structures and processes, elements and relations—or whatever our traditional frames suggest. In this way, the unity of such "collections" becomes incomprehensible, and as we already know, this ambiguity protects the underlying paradox that cannot be permitted to appear. However, recent developments in systems theory suggest frames and more promising unfoldings of the underlying paradox. We can think of society as the all-encompassing system of communication with clear, self-drawn boundaries that includes all connectable communication *and excludes everything else.* Hence, the society is a self-reproducing system, based on one, and only one, highly specific type of operation, namely communication. It excludes other types of operationally closed systems—cells, neurons, brains, minds. All this, and much more, is of course presupposed in the very process of communication. It is presupposed in the sense of a necessary environment (and we remember: the *form* of a system is the *difference* of system and environment). Living systems and conscious systems can produce only their own reproduction, replacing states of awareness by and with other states of awareness. They can never, by their own mode of operation, communicate. For communication requires the production of an emergent unity that has the capacity to integrate and disintegrate the internal states of more than one operationally closed system.

Operational closure seems to be the necessary *empirical* condition of observations.[30] Without closure, the system would continually mix up its own operations with those of its environment, conscious states with external states or words with things. It could not make the (reentering) distinction between self-reference and external reference. It could not even match external and internal states. It could not separate the observer from the observed. It could not produce cognition. What we know from brain research is also true for communication. *The lack of an operational access to the environment is a necessary condition for cognition.* And therefore, all constructions remain deconstructible by other observers. They can do it—if they can.

How, then, does society observe and describe the world by using itself as a system-reference, by developing the higher reflection capacities of a system, and by using the distinction between system and environment (between words and things) to dissolve the paradox of the world as a frameless, undistinguishable totality that cannot be observed?

IV

Conceived as an operationally closed system, modern society is world society.[31] Its function systems could never agree on regional, national, or cultural boundaries. The system of science, the economic system, the system of mass media operate and observe clearly on a worldwide level. But the political system nowadays, too, is a world system, segmented into "states" to achieve a better fit between political power and changing conditions of public consensus. States, in their phase of dissolution into ethnic groups or economic congregations, remain the prime address of political communication—national and above all international. But this does not mean that the society ends and begins at political boundaries—say, between the United States and Mexico, or between Germany and Austria. Tourists enjoy (to some extent) legal protection and the staged authenticity of customs and traditions all over the world. We can intermarry, whatever our national origins. Conversion from one religion to another is possible, if religions care at all for an exclusive identity and membership. But in spite of all this, the global system or modern society seems not to be able to produce one and only one self-description.

This leads to the question of how the world society can observe and describe itself and its environmental conditions given the enormous variety of living conditions, of cultural traditions, of political regimes, of religious orientations, of the impact (or lack of impact) of law as a constraint in daily life, of class structures, of career structures, of corruption, and of the degree of exclusion of large parts of the population from any participation in function systems in a very unequal distribution over the regions of the world?

The answer is surprisingly simple. This observing and describing is done by the mass media. What we know about the world we know from books, from newspapers, from movies, from television—be it German reunification or the living conditions of the pandas, the size of the universe or the increase of violence in Rio de Janeiro or in Los Angeles. To a large extent, mass media create the illusion that we are first-order observers, whereas in fact this is already second-order observing. All three main sectors of mass-media operations—that is, news and reports, advertisements, and entertainment—cooperate in producing a rather coherent image of the world we are living in. We know that this is preselected information, but we do not and cannot in everyday life reflect upon and control the selectivity of this selection. To see the contingency of the result, we need a more reflective second-order observing to see not *what* but *how* mass media select.

This selective presentation is not, as most people would be inclined to think, a *distortion* of reality. It is a *construction* of reality. For from the point of view of a postontological theory of observing systems, there is no distinct reality out there (who, then, would make these distinctions?), but instead all distinctions (indications, identities, classifications, and so forth) are made by an observer. And there is, at least in our society, no privileged observer—be it the highest class, the citizen (distinguished from countrymen), the clergy, the literati. The last semantic construction claiming to be in this position has been the "transcendental subject." But there is no transcendental subject. We have to rely on the system of mass media that construct our reality—transforming the artificial into the natural, the contingencies of their constructions into a mix of necessities, impossibilities, and freedom (or rather freedoms).

If there is no choice in accepting these observations, because there is no equally powerful alternative available, we have at least the possibility of deconstructing the presentations of the mass media, their presentations of the present. At this point, it again becomes important to replace *deconstruction* with *second-order observing*. We can very well observe their observing. There is already a lot of empirical research with well-known results. Mass media prefer discontinuity over continuity because they have to produce information. They prefer conflict over peace, dissensus over consensus, drama over normal and dull life. They prefer stories of local interest. The mass media like quantities that need no further explanation because they are distinctions themselves. They prefer bad news over good news, but good advertisement over bad advertisement. In their entertainment section, they draw clear moral distinctions, although the good guy sometimes has to cut corners to bring the story to a good end. They prefer morality and action. This means that we may overestimate the importance of decisions and of the influence of decisions (and individuals) on decisions, and that we will translate the uncertainty of the future into a risk of decision making. We will insist on responsibility and will evaluate decision makers accordingly, knowing very well that the future remains unknown and that values and criteria are and remain an object of controversy. Decisions do not come about without situational influences; quantities do not translate easily into developments; and discontinuities disconnect what we know from the past from what we may expect from the future.

This overall tendency to emphasize discontinuity, surprise, conflict, agency, decision, and moral evaluation seems not to lead to a unified world-view, replacing the old cosmology of substances and essences (*hypokeime-non, subiectum, ousia, essentia*) with a new one. What has become visible after some centuries of impact of the printing press and after a hundred and more years of mass media is a much more complicated, some say *hyper-complex*, description of complexity—hypercomplex in the sense that within the complex system of society there are many competing descriptions of this complexity. The unity of the complexity becomes unobservable. Intellectuals occupy themselves and others with describing description, philosophers become experts on philosophical texts—and literary criticism takes over, nicknaming "theory" something that we suppose has been done elsewhere.[32]

In comparison with what has become by now our old European tradition, this state of affairs appears very unsatisfactory. But do we have to compare? It could well be that our society is the outcome of a structural and semantical *catastrophe* in the sense meant by René Thom—that is, the result of a fundamental change in the form of stability that gives meaning to states and events. If this is so, the deconstruction of our metaphysical tradition is indeed something that *we* can do *now*. But if so, it would be worthwhile to choose the instruments of deconstruction with sufficient care so that by using them we could gain some information about our post-metaphysical, postontological, postconventional, postmodern—that is, *postcatastrophical* condition.

V

Ever since history became a narrative, and certainly since the invention of the novel and of historicism reflecting upon itself—that is, since the eighteenth century—describing history has been a semantical device presenting the unity of the past as a guarantee of the unity of the present. One could almost say the unity of the past had to compensate for the lost unity of the present. The unity of the past had to be presented as a coherent sequence of events, as a unity of diversity, a unity of some agency, such as the hero of the novel or the world spirit who is using history as a movement with the preordained end of self-realization. The German *Historische Schule* (historical school) did compensate for the lost *Reich* and for the not-yet-achieved national unity. Ever since, national and regional education programs have been focusing on the past to create unity within a present, glossing over different historical roots and cultural diversity.

But how did historical societies observe their world and themselves within their world? Raising this question dissolves the unquestioned value of history in forming identities. To return to history, then, means to return to diversity. The common heritage, the canonical texts, the "classics" all require a new reading. The deconstruction of our metaphysical tradition pursued by Nietzsche, Heidegger, and Derrida can be seen as a part of a much larger movement that loosens the binding force of tradition and replaces unity with diversity. The deconstruction of the ontological presuppositions of metaphysics uproots our historical semantics in a most radical way. This seems to correspond to what I have called the *catastrophe* of modernity, the transition from one form of stability to another.

Sociologists, then, have to look for the structural conditions and limitations that frame the frames within which observations and descriptions can operate. In other words, a sociological theory would have to formulate correlations between social structures and semantics. It is well known that Marx used the concept of *class structures* for this purpose and constructed a typology of changing modes of production that generated historical ideologies. We could enlarge this framework by substituting *forms of differentiation* for *class*. This opens the classical sociology of knowledge for more structural complexity and gives us the possibility of using the sophisticated framework of systems theory to elaborate on *forms of differentiation*. Differentiation becomes system differentiation; system differentiation becomes a reentry of system-building within systems, new boundaries within already bounded systems, forms within forms, observers within observers.

Developed societies of the past were differentiated according to social strata (nobility/commoners) or center/periphery (city/country) distinctions. Families (and therefore individuals) had to live on the one or the other side of this internal boundary. They found themselves placed by the social structure. This had the advantage that society provided privileged positions for observing and describing itself and the surrounding world. The highest strata or the center, the polis, had undisputed authority for observing and describing, for producing *ontology*. Critique could focus on bad moral behavior. Ethics and virtue were prominent devices to cope with the negative, in China, in the Greek city, in Rome, and in the Middle Ages. The moral worked as a protest-absorbing mechanism. There was no lack of authority for stating the truth. The world—be it the *universitas rerum* (world of things) or *hic mundus* (this world) in its religious, rather negative sense—*contained* the society of heroes and sinners, of exemplary modes of living. It framed and supported its structures. Words such as *environment, environnement,* and *Umwelt* are neologisms of the nineteenth century.

This is "the world we have lost," the world of ontological metaphysics, the world of "being or not being," the world of the two-value logic that presupposed one (and only one) observer who could make up his mind simply by looking at what is the case. Cognition, but also passion such as love, was a passive reaction to a reality out there, a "being impressed," and errors in cognition or passion could be corrected by reason.

The breakdown of what we may call (following Otto Brunner) *old-European semantics* became inevitable when society changed its primary form of differentiation, when it shifted from the very elaborate order of hierarchical stratification, conceived of as "the order," to the primacy of functional differentiation. With this move, function systems became independent of stratification, organizing their own boundaries, their own modes of inclusion and exclusion of persons, their own ways to transform equality into inequality and freedom into restraint. Society could proclaim equality and freedom for everybody since its function systems generated the contrary state—a quite new form of unfolding the paradox. Morality could no longer absorb protests but became a device for an enduring self-irritation of the society; it became individualistic and in need of reasoned elaboration—the new Bentham/Kant sense of ethics.

As lately as the last decades of the eighteenth century, European society became aware that the old order was gone. This has nothing to do with the so-called Industrial Revolution or the French Revolution, which became important only because society was prepared to see and to interpret a new order. Around 1800, a new semantics of modernity (the modern world, the modern states, and so forth) tried to catch up with the changes. The future was projected as open for improvements (more freedom, more equality, the constitutional question, more education, and, above all, emancipation). The problem of God became the problem of religion. During the nineteenth century, a series of new distinctions emerged, such as state and society, individual and collectivity, community and society, but the "and" of these dualities was left uninterpreted; that is, the unity of the distinction (= the paradox) remained invisible. Obviously the modern society was yet unable to observe itself, to identify the observer. Special problems such as "the social question" and national imperialism became controversial issues, but framing them in terms of problems and problem solutions could not contribute much to a self-description of the society. Only the mass media succeeded in serving this function.

Are we, at the end of this century, in a different position? Do we have other choices that could be made?

It can and has been said that the semantics of modernity has been a transitional semantics. But the concept of *postmodernity* does not provide us with further information; it simply repeats this insight. Reflexivity may be the predicament of the philosophy of this century.[33] But what does this mean, projected into a societal context? *Entzweiung*, difference, lack of unity, destruction of all canonical certainties—these were already the complaint of the nineteenth century, and we are only intellectually better prepared to accept them as inevitable. Finally, *deconstruction* seems to be the key word, suggesting that we could *do this*. This may appeal to the pragmatic sense of Americans. But the question remains: Should we do it? and why? or why not?

From a historical point of view deconstruction seems to be the end of history, history consuming itself. At the same time it can go on, it can never be completed, it never can reach the plenitude of nonbeing. It is and remains writing, constructing, and deferring differences. Given these unlimited prospects, understanding deconstruction as observing observers reduces its complexity. The only possible object of deconstruction would be observing systems. But observing means using a distinction for indicating one side and not the other. We then can distinguish (being observable in doing so) different observers. So by reducing complexity we gain complexity and therefore the structured complexity of self-observing systems. We do not lose the individual, the mind, the body as an observable observer. But we can also focus on society as a self-observing, self-describing system. Seen in this way, deconstruction will survive its deconstruction as the most pertinent description of the self-description of modern society.

5

Identity—What or How?

I

"What or how"—that is easy to say. The switch from "what" questions to "how" questions conveys the appearance of intellectual refinement—at least since Kant commended to any future metaphysics as its point of departure the form of questioning, "How is something possible?" But what is meant by this? Or: How is what is meant by this meant?

For Kant, metaphysics had become a problem. The way in which it had described the world was now to be described for its part and, where necessary, revised. What the world is and is not, along with the reason why it is what it is, could now no longer be taken without further ado from the world itself. One had first to observe how the world was observed, perhaps in order to correct the manner of observation. One should recall that, at the same time, historiography came to reflect its own historicity. It should also be recalled that, at this time, the modern novel began to give readers the ability to observe what the heroes and heroines of the novel could not themselves observe, above all, in a pre-Freudian way, their sexual interests.

As a sociologist, one sees no mere coincidence in these congruencies. They take place at a time in which modern society begins to understand as irreversible its break with all of its predecessors. This demands a distance from immediately fact-related observations and descriptions, demands a second level, on which one can observe and describe observations and descriptions themselves. Following Heinz von Foerster—although there are many, approximately contemporary parallel inventions—one speaks today of second-order cybernetics,[1] cybernetics understood here in the sense of a circular network of knowledge operations. The distinction between "what" questions and "how" questions is directed at this distinction between two levels of observation. Or, in any case, this interpretation gives it a usable meaning.

However, one should not thereby make it so easy for oneself. It is not a case of a logical or linguistic architecture of levels, not a case of a hierarchy of types invented in order to solve the problem of paradoxicality. Rather, this distinction is meant empirically, and, among philosophers, it may be appropriate to emphasize this explicitly.[2]

Every observation designates something and distinguishes it therewith from other things. What it designates can be another observer. When an observation observes another observer, it uses a more complex, two-tracked process of distinction. It must first of all distinguish the observer from what he observes, and at the same time, it must be able to distinguish the operation of observing from other operations, for instance from the mere generation of a difference. How can an observation do that? Note that we ask, "How?"

First, one readily observes that the second-order observation can do so only as a first-order observation. It must indeed designate *something* (namely, an observer). It can do so only as a simply executed operation. Thus, there is nothing esoteric or transcendental about this. The observation does what it does, like every operation, and when it does not do so (which, however, only another observer can establish), it does not. Everything that an observation can observe of a first-order observer is valid for that observation itself. It can claim no extraworldly, privileged standpoint. It is not to be understood as the activity of a subject, therefore not as the activity of a carrier that is founded upon itself. Its particularity lies only in the *autological* components of its observing,[3] that is, in its drawing conclusions about itself on the basis of the activity of its object. To this extent, it itself is that from which it distinguishes itself. The observation is itself what it is not. It itself, as a second-order observation, is a first-order observation. And "autology" then means nothing more than the dissolution of this paradox through the recursive calculation upon itself of its own establishment.

But second-order observation is indeed not only first-order observation. It is both more and less. It is less because it observes *only* observers and nothing else. It is more because it not only sees (= distinguishes) its object but also sees what the object sees and sees how it sees what it sees, and perhaps even sees what it does not see and sees that it does not see that it does not see what it does not see. On the level of second-order observation, one can thus see everything: what the observed observer sees, and what the observed observer does not see. Second-order observation conveys a universal access to the world. The world thus becomes the imaginary metaworld of all worlds that form themselves when systems distinguish system from environment. The reduction of complexity that lies in observing only one observer and having only to designate and distinguish this one is the condition of possibility for an increase in the complexity of possibilities of observation. Only one thing is necessarily excluded: the observation that is actualized in the very moment of observing, its functioning as a first-order observation. For the distinction necessary for every observation cannot distinguish itself in the very moment of its use (for then another distinction would be necessary). It makes a difference [*Unterschied*] that this distinction and no other is used. It produces a difference [*Differenz*], but it cannot observe it. That is perhaps what Michel Serres meant when, greatly exaggerating, he said, "The observer is the unobservable."[4] For every observer, the unity of the distinction he uses for the designation of the one (and not the other) side serves as a blind spot, for the first-order observer as well as for the second-order observer. For it is exactly the meaning of this drawing of distinctions that it is foundational as difference and not as unity.

Ontology must also submit itself to this necessity.

II

In the following, ontology is understood to be a certain form of observing and describing, to wit, that form that consists of the distinction between being and nonbeing.[5] This is not a metaphysical concept of ontology and certainly not one that cannot be transcended. (If we wanted to designate a historical peculiarity, we could speak of ontological metaphysics.) Rather, general—one could perhaps say meta-ontological—rules of the use of form apply to the ontological manner of observation.

Form is not to be understood here as the image of a thing [*Ding*] or, more generally, of a thing [*Sache*] in the sense of *res* that displays certain qualities owing to its form. Form is neither beautiful nor not-so-beautiful appearance. Form is also determined neither by opposition to matter nor by opposition to content (for that would only lead to the question of the form of this very object). Rather, form is the marking of a difference [*Differenz*] with the help of a distinction that compels one to designate one or the other side, in our case, either the being or the nonbeing of something.

There are different versions of this idea of form, which is two-sided in principle. With Gotthard Günther, one can assume the distinction between a positive and a negative value and subject this form to rejection or acceptance by means of a second-order observation. In another determination, which George Spencer Brown places at the base of his calculus of form,[6] no negation is presupposed at first. (This is appealing above all for the reconstruction of biological processes.) In its application to ontology, form, in Spencer Brown's notation, is at first called: $\overline{\text{being}}\,\rceil$. Form has an inside and an outside. That from which being distinguishes itself is the outside of the form, namely that which is left over from the "unmarked state" when the caesura of the form is posited. The inside of the form, that is, being or the positive value, designates the possibility of attaching further observation and description. The outside is the side from which the form is reflected, the contingency of the other side is perceived, and conditions of connectability can be established.

The different variants of the realization of a form in observation have in common that the concept of form designates a border that one must cross in order to pass from one side to the other. If one wants to cross, one must give a designation to the other side of the distinction. The "unmarked state" becomes "nonbeing." But, thereby, the distinction being/nonbeing becomes itself specifiable. Being becomes applicable as a concept. Out of $\overline{\text{being}}\,\rceil$. arises $\overline{\text{being}\,\lceil\text{nonbeing}}\,\rceil$. From ontics (which does not carry this designation) arises ontology. In any case, no operation of distinction can completely eliminate what is affected by the distinction as the remainder of the world, as an "unmarked state."

Crossing the border requires an operation. An operation requires time, for, even though both sides are simultaneously given, one cannot operate on both sides at the same time, for that would mean not using the distinction as a distinction. The form thus represents a paradoxical (and in exactly this sense realistic) temporal relation, namely the simultaneity of the before and after in a time that anticipates further befores and afters. A calculus of form thus applied leads therefore to a nonstationary logic that makes itself asymmetrical over time. Interpreted as an instrument of observation, this concept of form leads to a theory into which time (and by way of time, system formation) is built in foundationally and does not have to be added retroactively (as in our tradition through the form of motion in contrast to the unmoved).

We must explicitly maintain that the form is settled not merely on one side of the border, as in distinctions of the type form/matter, form/content, form/medium, but instead on *both sides*. In the case of ontology, it is not a form of being but the form being/nonbeing. Thus it does not vanish when one crosses the border (for one can always return). It would disappear only if one were to erase the marking of the border, but that would reproduce the "unmarked state" in which one can observe nothing.[7] The concept of form is therewith a concept of world, a concept for the self-observing world. It designates the wounding of the world through an incision, through "writing" in Derrida's sense, through the differentiation of systems in the sense of systems theory. It retains the wounded world as that which becomes unobservable through the installation of possibilities of observation (of whatever form). It does not cancel out the world; it only transforms it—as a latter-day descendant of the Fall—into a world in which time and work are needed in order to reach one side from the other, or, as already indicated, into a world in which time itself can be observed only paradoxically, namely as the form that exists as the simultaneity of the two sides *and* (on the one side of this temporal form) as the before/after of the positions that can be designated.

In principle, no objections can be made to ontologizing observation. We do it every day when we look for something and do not find it. Without holes, we can neither play billiards nor recognize Swiss cheese. The problem with ontological metaphysics lies in its reduction of all distinctions, including the observer himself and his claims to truth, to the ontological distinction between being and nonbeing. That leads to a theory that is extremely impoverished structurally and that has a corresponding need for completion. And one can suppose that it owes its success to religion, namely to the logically and ontologically inescapable filling of this need for completion. Not by coincidence, God appears under these cognitive conditions as the one observer who does not need to draw a distinction (not even Himself??) in order to be able to observe and, consequently, cannot be described ontologically. "Deum nequam concipi debere habere esse" ("It is senseless for God to be conceived as having being").[8]

III

Meanwhile, the impression may have arisen that this lecture is about philosophy or logic, or even theology. I must object to that. This is a sociological matter, namely the question of how modern society can observe and describe itself. And the answer can only be: in any case not in the form of an ontology, a special kind of thing, of living being, of human being.

Among the consequences of an ontological dissection of the world, one that differentiates being and nonbeing is this one: that the identity of what is [des Seienden] must be presupposed. On the basis of this cognitive requirement, there is no possibility of generating identity (although one can produce it, of course, by putting parts together into a whole). Nor does binary logic offer any other possibilities. It must insert a value for the designation of what is not, or, when applied to second-order observation, a value for the correction of errors. It therefore has only one value—a "designation value," as Gotthard Günther says[9]—available for designating what is. For this reason, the principle of identity belongs to the premises of this logic, as does, furthermore, the necessity of giving a reason why something is and why it is not the case that it is not. All statements are therefore attributed to something identical, which, from this point of view, can take on names such as substance or subject.

Modern society has to give up this requirement, and it is not sufficient, as one might hope at first, to convert from substance to subject (in the modern understanding of the concept), for this only implies a shift from the observed to the observer, while the operation of observing is still understood as monothematic (Günther again!).[10] Since the eighteenth century, it has become increasingly clear that the problem lies in the observation of observers and not only in the plurality of subjects that can somehow be aggregated into a unit. Without presenting deeper social-structural causes, we have already indicated some manifestations of second-order observation: the position of the reader vis-à-vis the hero of a novel, the manifest/latent schema of observation, the way historiography has become itself historical. One could add the romantic arsenal of critique, irony, "sensibility," and mystification as the play of self-observations of the observer, or the inexorable insight into the dependence of political and social valuations upon ideology. In this context, there arises the new kind of reflection that emphasizes the observation of oneself as an observer and the inquiry by those means into the conditions of possibility of knowledge and action. This form dominates historically recent epistemology (an expression that was created in the nineteenth century for just this purpose). However, when one observer observes what *another* observer establishes as identical, he can take the liberty of identifying otherwise; of using other distinctions; of interpreting based on other, contrary concepts; in other words, of treating the same as not the same.

Note that it is not a case of simple differences of comprehension—one person thinks something is a hare, the other thinks it is a rabbit. The problem is rather that one can observe an observer only when one allows what the other sees to be given to one by the other. Otherwise, two different first-order observers would simply be looking into the world side by side. Putting a finer point on it, it is not about psychic systems existing next to each other that generate and process information according to the standards of their own structures, with the effect that the results do not agree. Instead, it has to do with a problem of social communication in which communication in society is broken up through latent structures and must as a result factor in incommunicabilities. Society as a whole then operates as a system that can see that it cannot see what it cannot see. And in spite of this, the system is in a position to continue communication, even if it has difficulty describing how.[11]

IV

Renouncing claims to identity makes possible the question of how identity is produced and what presents itself as a consequence of this manner of production. This question aims at a genetic theory of the constitution of meaning. If it can be answered, one will gain access thereby to the phenomenal complexity of the world. Such access need neither describe in its manner of appearing what presents itself ("presents" in the sense of phenomenology) nor, since this would be too much, reduce it to kinds, genera, or types.[12] The genetic perspective is marked by the form in which the question is posed. We do not ask *what* something identical is, but *how* something *is generated* that, as identical, grounds observation. With this, the concept of identity shifts in the direction that is today designated as "constructivist." It no longer designates the form in which what is exists in accord with itself, but, first of all, designates "idealistically" the achievement of the synthesis of impressions that originate externally, which as such cannot for this very reason be identified. Finally, in the context of a theory of autopoietic systems, the concept of identity designates only the form that secures the continuing of the sequence of operations in a system; to be exact, it secures them through the distinction identical/nonidentical.[13]

Reduced to the most elementary level, all observation is a distinguishing designation, or, more precisely, the designation of the one (and not the other) side of a distinction. This does not yet require what is designated to be maintained as identical. One must only be able to distinguish it. An identification is first required when the operation is to be repeated, hence when a system is formed that reproduces itself in the linkage of operation to operation.

To be able to grasp how identification and, with it, system formation are possible, we use a distinction suggested by Spencer Brown.[14] If the system executes an operation of linkage, it can thereby *condense* the first and the second operation into one single operation. The referent is posited as identical. The person greeted did not notice the greeting; one greets him once more. The same content can also be read in another direction. One *confirms* the greeting, namely what it intends, in performing it again. Depending on the direction of the reading, one condenses two acts into one or expands and confirms one act through its first *and* second execution. In the one direction, one sees that identity is formed as the condensation of a plurality of operations. In the other direction, one sees that confirmation requires a second operation and thus another situation. The second greeting is, and is not, the first. It is not simply another, a further greeting. It is a second greeting as second to the first greeting, a first *and* second greeting. An identity is formed that is compatible with different situations and that therefore designates a certain playing field of possibilities.

In rudimentary form, this analysis explains to us the genesis of meaning, the result of which Husserl describes. In this way, a reactualizable core of meaning arises and, inextricably bound up with it, a horizon of reference to other possibilities. Or, more concisely formulated, the simultaneous processing of condensation and confirmation generates the difference between actuality and possibility, which we see as the constitutive difference of the medium that is meaning.[15] The genetic account of meaning explains its form, so that form is here, as always, defined as the unity of a distinction, as a border the crossing of which (in this case, from the actual to the non-actual) requires an operation.

The observation of the generation of meaning, the observation of repeating, condensing, and confirming, is always a second-order observation, even when it is for its part repetitively condensed and confirmed and concomitantly forms autological concepts adequate to its ends. In the immediate execution of meaning [*Sinnvollzug*], whether in thinking or in communicating, one does not need to think or communicate as well that this is a condensation or a confirmation. This would be just as superfluous and a violation of Grice's principle of the Quantity of Conversational Implicature, that is to say, of communicative economy,[16] as if one wanted to constantly maintain references to the autologies of the second-order level on the first-order operative level. The levels of observation thereby remain separated. And one can say—admittedly with an imperfect analogy—that a communication system is equipped with a network of second-order communication just as an organism is equipped with a nervous system, in order to be able observe its own condition and *only its own condition*.

If one grasps meaning in this manner as the unity of a distinction, whether it is the distinction between condensation and confirmation or the distinction between actuality and non-actuality (virtuality), it makes no sense to designate meaningfully in turn that from which these distinctions are distinguished. The reference for this goes missing. To that extent, meaning is a concept without difference. Nevertheless, one must always presuppose an "unmarked state" as the other side of the distinction (here, the distinction between distinctions), as what remains when meaning as form (border, caesura, cut) is introduced into the world. One would then have to write: $\overline{\text{condense}|\text{confirm}|}$ or $\overline{\text{actuality}|\text{virtuality}|}$. And to this extent, it makes sense to speak of meaning as if it could be observed from outside.

This genetic account of identity does not determine which distinctions the observer begins from. In everyday life, it would be a matter of referents that are distinguished from *everything else*. We shall call them *things* [*Dinge*]. In learning invariances at a higher level, it is specified *from what* the referent is distinguished—for example, a good grade from a bad one (and not from the teacher, the textbooks, etc.). We would like to name such referents *concepts*. Obviously there are countless distinctions that can function as the context of the formation of identity, among them the ontological distinction between being and nonbeing with which one can generate "somethings." However, ontological metaphysics had also additionally assumed that there is a central context of the genetics of identity, namely the distinction being/nonbeing, and that the world is therefore monocontexturally ordered. I would contest this terminologically and also as a matter of fact, with reference to Gotthard Günther.[17] Neither consciousness nor communication has ever been able to generate the world monocontexturally as the result of its operations. Only world-descriptions have supposed this. However, such descriptions have become hopelessly inadequate today, and the question for the sociologist is, "Why?"

V

Retrospectively we can now note that we prematurely gave the title nonbeing to the unmarked state that is left over when one distinguishes being. We can at least still uncover the ambivalence lying therein. With this distinction being/nonbeing, ontology arouses the impression that something distinguishable is given on the other side. However, this cannot be presupposed if one wounds the world with a first distinction. If one presupposes it, one presupposes the principle of the excluded middle and places oneself under the sway of classical logic. One is then incapable of distinguishing in turn the distinction of ontology, and one explicates, without seeing other possibilities, an ontological metaphysics.

Our distinction between things and concepts also makes it clear that ontology, which begins with the distinction being/nonbeing, must from this perspective be ambivalent. It distinguishes what is from everything else and in so doing grasps it as a thing. But it distinguishes being from nonbeing without distinguishing this second distinction from the first, and thereby conceives being to be a concept. This double status of what is positively designated as thing-and-concept or as comprehensible thing lends to ancient European philosophy its objectivity and hope. But we explode this indistinctness by demanding that there be a distinction between "unmarked state" and "nothing." But that also means that we have to devote more attention to this other side than was devoted to describing the genealogy of identity. How does one reach this other side? And how can one operate from there?

We attempt to explicate this problem with a further distinction. When one starts with being and crosses the border and returns, it is as though one had never done so. One stands once again at the starting point. Spencer Brown names this axiom "the law of crossing" and calls the corresponding form "cancellation."[18] In this manner, the other side is always treated as what it is to begin with, as a residue of the unmarked state. But what happens when one (temporarily!—everything is temporary) does not return but rather remains on the other side and wishes to operate from there? In this case the other side becomes "nonbeing," and from there one can observe the contingencies of being. The to and fro is considered in Spencer Brown's calculus as cancellation and compensation. There is no room on this elementary level of exposition for the act of remaining in the state that must be called "nonbeing," because it would require a further distinction and, in our sense, the formation of an ontological concept.

One can imagine that the simple forth (cancellation) and back (compensation) in the societal system is expressed as *religion*. Religion compensates in this sense for the experience that not even nothing, but rather only the unmarked state, is held available on the other side. It is, then, already a consequence of the reflection of this state that this is positively referred to as the unity of a difference.[19] In contrast, if one observes being from the other side, one could situate oneself for example in the *economy* and ask oneself if one wants to buy for the suggested price something that is. In all of this, the observer himself always remains factually in operation; he does not annul, compensate, reflect, and so on, himself. The scheme being/nonbeing offers him only the position of the excluded middle. Nevertheless, he can still work toward a structurally richer form of observation.

VI

The transition from an ontological construction of the world to a constructivist one, and from a strictly bivalent logic to a calculus of processing distinctions (forms), should not be justified as progress in the framework of a program of knowledge. We lack independent criteria for such a justification, and there may be good reasons for the tenacity with which the contemporary old Europeans cling to their viewpoint. It suffices just as little to collect the many indications that second-order observation is well under way and presents itself today in such a universal way that it reconstructs all possibilities of observation, itself included. That may be, and it may press the case for searching for structurally richer theories, but it does not yet answer the question why this is so.

Rather than announce and cash in on claims of superiority, we shall employ a social-theoretical argument. Douglas Hofstadter would probably describe that as "supertangling." In any event, we operate autologically and circularly insofar as we derive the demands for a theory that describes the world and within it society from the structures of this society itself. The system doing the describing and the system in the world-form system/environment are one and the same. We communicate.

A high measure of functional differentiation ranks among the structural characteristics of modern society that are relevant for us. Associated with this is the establishment of binary codes that allow all operations using such a code to be ascribed to the corresponding system — and this not at the discretion of an external observer (there cannot be one) but rather as a procedure of recognition [*Erkennungsverfahren*], as a condition of self-identification, as a condition of the autopoietic operation of the relevant systems themselves.[20] We mean such codes as true/false, loved / not loved, having property/ having none, passing tests / not passing, or good/bad grades, right/wrong, dominant /subject to power as defined through state offices, government/opposition, immanent/transcendent, winning/losing in sports, sick/healthy. It is obvious that these codes cannot be made congruent in the sense that one side is the positive one, that one side of a dichotomy always corresponds with one side of another, for instance the sick as sick are not loved, have no rights, are powerless, and so on. The differentiation of functional systems instead presupposes that these codes, independently of one another, fulfill functions that direct operations, and that it is also impossible to integrate them through a supercode, for instance through the code of morality. It is, rather, essential for the separation of the codes that one refrain from viewing the one side as morally good and the other as morally bad, for example bureaucratic power as good, being subject to such an office as bad, possession of property as good, lack thereof as bad. This has not been possible at least since the internalization of conditions of moral approval or disapproval;[21] and that also means that morality can function only as one code among many others.

With a terminology deriving from Parsons, one can also say that all these codes claim universal (not particular) and specific (not diffuse) relevance. They are valid for everything that becomes relevant within the horizon of information of the corresponding system (and thus for the world, seen from the corresponding perspective). Simultaneously, though, they constitute a specific distinction that is made operational with the help of programs assigned to them, and they make possible clear assignments (to the exclusion of others). And we also follow Parsons in treating the combination universal/specific as particular to modern society.[22]

If one wishes to describe a society that describes its world and itself according to these conditions, one must choose polycontextural forms. What that specifically means has not yet been clarified, despite the efforts of Gotthard Günther. In any case, one can quickly see that the individual values of the codes neither join together nor allow themselves to be expanded into multivalent codes. One is aware that all efforts toward a transitive, or otherwise ordered, architecture of values have failed. It is conceivable that, for the purposes of an analysis of the whole of society, one could assign transjunctive operations to every code, operations with which the code accepts itself and rejects all others. In this manner, system-relative functional primacies could be formulated. An observer using these descriptive means will, as a second-order observer, simultaneously be able to see what the coded systems (the observer himself as science included) *cannot* see. He will be able to see how they employ their codes as distinctions by the operative use of which they generate identities that owe their existence to the distinction and hence remain dependent on what must continue to be presupposed as a distinction. For the theory of science itself, that leads to a radical (but neither idealist nor subjectivist) constructivism.[23]

Society is an operationally closed, autonomous system of communication. Consequently everything it observes and describes (everything that is communicated about) is self-referentially observed and described. That holds for the description of the societal system itself, and it also holds with the same necessity for the description of the environment of the societal system. The self-descriptions and the hetero-descriptions are self-referential descriptions. Consequently, every description of the world made in the autonomous system designates self-reference as the point of convergence between self-reference and hetero-reference—and remains unsayable. It is as though the distinction between a map and a territory—a territory in which the map has to be made—itself has to be inscribed on the map.[24] This point of convergence can serve only as a reference to the unmarked state, which every distinction wounds and can then only symbolize as a distinction.

This problem was conceivable in a theological-ontological version just so long as it appeared only once—as a problem of the societal system. It could then be represented and covered up with a conclusive formula, the concept of god, or with a principle of "categories" as components of the concept of being. However, modern society reproduces this problem in many ways, namely for each of its operatively closed functional systems as well as for each individual, now understood as the subject of himself; indeed, if one may trust biologists, for every living cell, every immune system, every brain, and so on.[25] In this situation, the paradox of drawing a distinction takes the place of the conclusive thought that testifies to unity. One gains thereby not a "solution to the problem" but rather a more precise understanding of the fact that the solution of the paradox can employ various distinctions and thus diversify the problem.[26] Since its first attempts at self-description, that is, since the eighteenth century, modern society has developed a "critical" relationship to itself—whether by becoming aware of the high costs that progress incurred but at first seemed to justify (key words: new poverty, uprooting, alienation), or by recognizing each self-description as situationally conditioned ideology, even at the cost of devaluing the Enlightenment. Ultimately, as "critical theory," it could pride itself that it knew what it had to reprimand. This self-critique is further radicalized when it has to recognize that self-descriptions of society cannot escape what all descriptions (even those of a second order) are burdened with, namely having to draw a distinction. Nevertheless, that produces the freedom to choose distinctions. It includes operating with the distinction between being and nonbeing. But it excludes the metaphysical primacy of this distinction.

VII

A few closing comments should reinforce (confirm!) the suspicion that with our previous considerations we have engaged in an insoluble relativism. Everything, even ontology itself, depends upon what distinctions an observation is based on. In this context, distinguishing and designating are understood to be the operations of an observer. This observer operates with reference to his own other operations, and thus operates as a system. That is to say, he differentiates himself from an environment by observing; and he can observe himself only by distinguishing himself from his environment. The world always remains as the unmarked state that can be observed only by tolerating in itself differentiation, and hence the construction of form.

However, it is deleterious to combine this relativism with modern subjectivism. This combination, which recommends to us a "vitalist" [*"lebensphilosophische"*] hermeneutics stemming from Dilthey, would lead to the consequence that human beings, understood as self-grounding subjects, can *choose* the distinctions with which they dissect the world and designate what is to be observed. They could accordingly accept this or that theory, live in Euclidean or post-Euclidean spaces, select an Aristotelian or a Newtonian or an Einsteinian physics. This, though, is an untenable notion.[27] For all system operations, as undisputed research into the logic of self-organization has shown, are possible always only as conditioned operations.[28] And human beings are socialized through participation in social communication to such a degree that they can choose only from within the framework of possibilities that have been made accessible for this choice. If one looks at individuals, any notion of choosing at will disappears. The rule of second-order observation then runs: observe the conditionings by which they distinguish and designate. And if one is not satisfied with observing these individuals—which from among the five billion?—and instead wishes to observe modern society, this rule again holds: observe the conditionings by which it distinguishes and designates.

Only "subjects" require "spirit"—that is, disciplining of the form: in themselves and from above. If one abandons this figure of thought, one gains access to the complexity of a modern society that is no longer hierarchical and that can no longer be comprehended as the ordinance of motives, as well as to its nervous system of second-order observation. The renunciation of the metaphysical primacy of the distinction between being and nonbeing has its consequences. It is achievable not only hierarchically through a prefixed "post." What is new about this society does not come about through invalidating the old; it would have to be able to rely on a theory of society.

Translated by Joseph O'Neil and Elliott Schreiber

6

The Cognitive Program of
Constructivism and the Reality
That Remains Unknown

I

Interest in epistemological questions is not limited to philosophy to-day. Numerous empirical sciences have, in the normal course of their re-search, been forced to proceed from the immediate object of their research to questions involving cognition. Quantum physics is perhaps the best-known example, but it is no exception. In linguistics the question is raised today of what problems arise from the fact that research into language has to make use of language. Cognitive instruments have to be acquired via the object investigated by means of these very instruments and not, for ex-ample, through reflection of consciousness upon itself.[1] Brain research has shown that the brain is not able to maintain any contact with the outer world on the level of its own operations, but—from the perspective of in-formation—operates closed in upon itself. This is obviously also true for the brains of those engaged in brain research. How does one come, then, from one brain to another? Or to take a further example: the sociology of knowledge had demonstrated at least the influence of social factors on all knowledge, if not their role as sole determinants. This is also true, then, for this statement itself since no justification for an exception can be found, in the sense, say, of Mannheim's "free-floating intelligence." What conclusion is to be drawn from this? It was thought that one would have to found all knowledge on "convention"[2] or that knowledge was the result of a kind of "negotiation."[3] But these attempts only wound up designating an ancient problem—that of the unity of knowledge and reality—by means of a new concept. Not without reason have these attempts been criticized for epistemological naïveté,[4] since one either learns nothing about the relationship to reality or the connection is made only through theoretically unacceptable "both/and" concessions. There is little more to be gained by calling such "constructivism," as has recently been done, "radical"[5] since what is identified here as "constructivism" at first hardly seems unfamiliar. It might be that the theory of knowledge—at least in some of its traditional variants—will be confirmed rather than caught unaware. Science is apparently reacting here to its own power of resolution. This can already be found in Plato, who reduces everyday experience to mere opinion and raises the question of what reality lies behind it. As a result, these philosophic reflections were termed, at first, "idealism." As we come to modern times the emergence of modern science led more and more to the conclusion that this "underlying" reality was knowledge itself. This altered the meaning of the concept of the subject, although only in our century has the name "idealism" been replaced by "constructivism." There was a shift in emphasis in the conflict between realism and idealism, but it is not easy to discover in this a new theory. There is an external world—which results from the fact that cognition, as a self-operated operation, can be carried out at all—but we have no direct contact with it. Cognition could not reach the external world without cognition. In other words, cognition is a self-referential process. Knowledge can know only itself, although it can—as if out of the corner of its eye—determine that this is possible only if there is more than mere cognition. Cognition deals with an external world that remains unknown and, as a result, has to come to see that it cannot see what it cannot see.

So far there is nothing new here, unless it be in the definiteness and self-confidence with which all this is presented as knowledge. One has to look more closely at the theoretical distinctions with which this view of things is presented in order to discover something new. Insofar as constructivism maintains nothing more than the unapproachability of the external world "in itself" and the closure of knowing—without yielding, at any rate, to the old skeptical or "solipsistic" doubt that an external world exists at all—there is nothing new to be found in it. Nonetheless, the theoretical form in which this is expressed has innovative aspects—even such radical innovations that it is possible to gain the impression that the theory of a self-referring cognition closed in upon itself has only now acquired a viable form. One can express this more precisely: it has only now acquired a form in which it can represent itself as knowledge. A problem arises here, however. With the word "constructivism" (taken over from mathematics), premature victories have been proclaimed, and one has to accept that there will be those who step aside, with a shake of the head, denying the validity of these claims. It is important, therefore, to investigate the question of what is new and convincing here—and this will lead the discussion far afield.

II

For reasons that can be clarified only subsequently, we begin our investigation with the question: By means of what distinction is the problem articulated? That is, we do not begin with the Kantian question: "How is knowledge possible?" We have avoided this form of the question because it might lead us to the premature response: "In this way!" At first the difference is of no great consequence. The one form of the question can be translated into the other (if one is not afraid to face problems of logical hierarchies as well as their failure). One can answer the question "How is knowledge possible?" with "By the introduction of a distinction." In contrast with the tradition involving such concepts as "diapherein"[6] or "discernment,"[7] here the concept of distinction is radicalized. For in order to recognize knowing, it is necessary to distinguish it from what is not knowing. As a result, the question with regard to the foundation of knowledge is transformed into a question with regard to the distinction of distinguishing, that is, into an obviously self-implicative question.[8] The passage from the search for a founding—and therefore asymmetric—relationship with regard to some unity is transformed into a search for an operatively employed difference. It is, further, easy to recognize that circularity and paradoxes can no longer be rejected but will come to play a role.

So, once again, the question is: By means of what distinction is the problem of knowledge articulated? (And, for the sake of clarity, let it be said once again: We are aware that with this question we have taken upon ourselves the difficulty of the distinction of distinguishing.)

In any case one will not be able to approach constructivism if one proceeds from the old controversy of whether the knowing system is a subject or an object. The subjectivist problem was to state and to show how it is possible by means of *introspection*—that is by passage to the self-reference of one's own consciousness—to form judgments about *the world of others*. That "intersubjectivity" is only a word, which therefore does not solve the problem, should be obvious. Objectivism, on the other hand, came up with the idea of describing knowledge as a condition or process in a particular object that was often called "organism." [9]

The mistake here lies in the assumption that it is possible to describe an object completely (we won't go so far as to say "explain") without making any reference to its relation to its environment (whether this relation be one of indifference, of selective relevance and capacity for stimulation, of disconnection, or of closure). In order to avoid these problems, which arise from the point of departure taken, both subjectivist and objectivist theories of knowledge have to be replaced by the system/environment distinction, which then makes the distinction subject/object irrelevant.

With this we have the distinction central to constructivism: it replaces the distinction transcendental/empirical by the distinction system/ environment. The concept of environment (as well as the corresponding one of system) was not available during Kant's day. What we call "environment" today had to be conceived of as the state of being contained and carried (*periechon*), and what we call "system" had to be thought of as order according to a principle. Both of these were already objects of knowledge. In order to answer the question of how knowledge is possible without falling into a self-referring circle, the distinction transcendental/empirical was developed. Hardly anyone accepts this distinction today despite the labor that goes into the exegesis of historical texts. But if one drops this distinction, how does one then avoid the circle of the self-founding of knowledge? Why must one avoid this circle? Can't one simply say: Knowledge is what knowledge takes to be knowledge?

The distinction system/environment and a fully worked-out systems theory provide the means for answering these questions. Virtually automatically, all systems-theoretical research becomes potentially relevant for a theory of knowledge. In contrast to the procedure in transcendentalism, investigations bearing relevance for epistemological questions do not need to be carried out primarily with this end in mind. The relevance emerges as a side effect of other investigations (e.g., of investigations in neurophysiology or in the history of science), and one only has to take care that the transitions are smoothed over and now and then put in order, for example by adequate terminological recommendations. A good example of this is

Humberto Maturana's use of the word "cognition" ("conocimiento") for the extension of operations under the condition of interaction with the environment,[10] however annoying this terminology might be for professional epistemologists afraid of a biological invasion of their domain.

It has been known for quite some time already that the brain has absolutely no qualitative and only a very slight quantitative contact with the external world. All stimuli coming from without are coded purely quantitatively (principle of undifferentiated coding); furthermore, their quantity, as compared with purely internal processing events, plays but a marginal role.[11] Incoming stimuli are also erased in fractions of a second if they are not stored in internal storage areas with somewhat longer retention times (short-term memory)—an event that is more the exception than the rule. With this, even time is made to serve the internal economy of complex processes. Apparently it is fundamental for the functioning of the brain that selected information is enclosed and not that it is let through. As if it were already information (or data) before it motivates the brain to form a representation. Such knowledge as this was not used by theoretical epistemology, and it is only a formulation in terms of systems theory that leads to an insight that must seem surprising to epistemologists:[12] only closed systems can know. The sociology of science has arrived at similar conclusions (which are still, for the most part, rejected as being too shocking).[13] Whoever still maintains that knowledge is the construction of a relation to the environment that fits things as they are is welcome to his opinion, but he is forced to begin his theoretical reflections with a paradox: it is only nonknowing systems that can know; or, one can see only because one cannot see.

Philosophical epistemology has become scientifically marginal if not completely isolated, a situation that has often been lamented.[14] This was the case for the neo-Kantians and is the case for the neo-Wittgensteinians. Nonetheless, anyone familiar with both sides is aware of the numerous possibilities for contact. Systems theory or, more precisely, the distinction between system and environment could play the role of mediator here.

The effect of the intervention of systems theory can be described as a *de-ontologization of reality*. This does not mean that reality is denied, for then there would be nothing that operated—nothing that observed, and nothing on which one would gain a purchase by means of distinctions. It is only the epistemological relevance of an ontological representation of reality that is being called into question. If a knowing system has no entry to its external world, it can be denied that such an external world exists. But we can just as well—and more believably—claim that the external world is as it is. Neither claim can be proved; there is no way of deciding between them. This calls into question, however, not the external world but only the simple distinction being/nonbeing, which ontology had applied to it. As a consequence, the question arises: Why do we have to begin with precisely this distinction? Why do we wound the world first with this distinction and no other?

Systems theory suggests *instead* the distinction between system and environment.

III

If one accepts this suggestion, the answer to the question "How is knowledge possible?" is, to begin with, "As the operation of a system separated from its environment." If one, further, takes seriously that the system always has to be operationally closed, then to the initial idea of separation assumptions are added regarding self-reference and recursivity. Operations of this kind are possible only within the context of a network of operations of the same system toward which they point and on which they are founded. There is no single operation that can emerge without this recursive network. At the same time the network itself is not an operation. "Multiplicity does not act as a relay" (Serres 1984, 238). The whole cannot as a whole itself become active. Every operation reproduces the unity of the system as well as its limits. Every operation reproduces closure and containment. There is nothing without an operation—no cognition, either. And every operation has to fulfill the condition of being one operation among many, since it cannot exist in any other form, cannot otherwise possibly be an operation.

As a result, for an observer the system is a paradox, a unity that is a unity only as a multiplicity, a *unitas multiplex*. Even when the system observes itself, one has what is true for every observation. If a system wants to know what makes it possible that it can know, it encounters this paradox. All theory of knowledge has to begin with the resolution of a paradox.

A further consequence is: No system can perform operations outside its own limits. If new operations are integrated, it means that the limits of the system have been extended. Consequently, the system cannot use its own operations to connect itself with its environment since this would require that the system operate half within and half without the system. The function of the boundaries is not to pave the way out of the system but to secure discontinuity. Whatever one wants to call cognition, if it is supposed to be an operation then the operation necessarily has to be one incapable of contact with the external world, one that, in this sense, acts blindly.

These ideas can be worked out further, and en route the foreseeable extensions of a theory of closed, self-referring systems-in-an-environment will doubtless come to have an influence on the theory of knowledge. But we will leave this question aside for the moment since we are now confronted with a fundamental question: Is it possible, and is it acceptable, to call what here becomes perceptible "knowledge" at all?

In the search for an answer to this question it is advisable to introduce a second distinction, between *operation* and *observation*. This distinction occupies the place that up to this point had been taken by the unity-seeking logic of reflection. (This means, therefore, a substitution of difference for unity.)

An operation that uses distinctions in order to designate something we will call "observation." We are caught once again, therefore, in a circle: the distinction between operation and observation appears itself as an element of observation. On the one hand, an observation is itself an operation; on the other hand, it is the employment of a distinction. An example would be that between operation and observation. A logic that would take its point of departure here could be established only as the unfolding of a circle, and it would have to make certain that the distinction can reenter into what it has distinguished. Spencer Brown provides explicitly for this "reentry" after deliberately ignoring it at the beginning with his instruction to an observer to "draw a distinction." (Among other things this means that time is employed for the resolution of self-referring circles and paradoxes.)

An observation leads to knowledge only insofar as it leads to reusable results in the system. One can also say: Observation is cognition insofar as it uses and produces redundancies—with "redundancy" here meaning limitations of observation that are internal to the system. In consequence, particular observations are more or less probable.[15]

The passage to "constructivism" follows from the insight that *it is not*

*only for negations that there are no correlates in the environment of the system
but even for distinctions and designations (therefore for observations).* This
does not mean (to say it once again) that the reality of the external world
is being called into doubt. It is also beyond doubt that an observer can observe that and how a system is influenced by its environment or deliberately and successfully acts upon its environment. Nonetheless, all distinctions and designations are purely internal recursive operations of a system
(that is, operations that form or disturb redundancies). These are operations that are not able to go beyond the system and, as if at a distant remove, pull something into it. As a result, all achievements following from
these operations, above all what is usually called "information," are purely
internal achievements. There is no information that moves from without
to within the system. For even the difference and the horizon of possibilities on the basis of which the information can be seen as a selection (that
is, information) does not exist in the external world, but is a construct—
that is, internal to the system. Does this mean, however—as is claimed in a
direct line from Maturana—that the cognitive system operates "blindly"?

The metaphor of seeing and blindness can be retained as an abbreviated mode of speech, although it does not correspond to the current level
of knowledge. One must also distinguish here. If every relation to the outer
world is being denied in such a metaphor, too much is being called into
question. On the other hand, it must be made clear that all observation (including the observing of observations) presupposes the operative deploy-
ment of a distinction that at the moment of its use must be employed
"blindly" (in the sense of "nonobservably"). If one wants to observe the
distinction in its turn, one has to employ a different distinction for which
the same is true.

There can be no doubt, therefore, that the external world exists or
that true contact with it is possible as a necessary condition of the reality of
the operations of the system itself. It is the differentiation of what exists
that is contributed by the observer's imagination, since, with the support
of the specification of distinctions, an immensely rich structure of combi-
nations can be obtained, which then serves the system for decisions about
its own operations.

Expressed in other words, the unity of a distinction employed for observation is constituted within the system. It is only in the observing system

that things distinguished are brought to the unity of being distinct. Cognition is neither the copying nor the mapping nor the representation of an external world in a system. Cognition is the realization of combinatorial gains on the basis of the differentiation of a system that is closed off from its environment (but nonetheless "contained" in that environment).[16] If a system is forced to cognize with the aid of distinctions and is unable to cognize in any other manner, it means further that everything that is for the system, and that therefore has reality, has to be constituted over distinctions. The "blind spot" of each observation, the distinction it employs at the moment, is at the same time its guarantee of a world. For example, social reality is what one, in observing a majority of observers, can observe to be uniform among them despite their differences.[17] Social reality exists only when an observer can distinguish a majority of observers (which may or may not include himself). By "world" is meant that which, for every system, has to be assumed to be the unity of the system/environment distinction (self-reference and external reference), when (and only when) this distinction is employed.

In conclusion we can say that knowing systems are real (empirical—that is, observable) systems in a real world. Without a world they could neither exist nor know. It is only cognitively that the world is unapproachable for them.

IV

The contribution of the systems that makes cognition possible at all and to which nothing in the environment corresponds consists in the act of distinguishing. This recognition, which (as a distinction itself) implies its own limitation, has helped us as far as it goes. This would seem to answer the question usually raised in controversies about constructivism. But the interesting analyses are still to come. They involve not the question of a real agreement between knowledge and reality but questions of *time*. Cognitive systems (at least the brain, consciousness, and the systems of communication called societies) operate on the basis of events that have only a momentary presence and that already begin to disappear at the moment of their emergence. Furthermore, these systems operate on the basis of events that cannot be repeated but that must be *replaced* by other events.

Their structures must, therefore, provide for the passage from event to event—something for which there are also no equivalents in the environment. It is neither the case that the environment changes itself with the same tempo and rhythm (and this can be spoken of only on the basis of cognitive acts), nor the case that one can find in the environment those autopoietic structures that suggest the one in the other. How then is the time relation between system and environment to be understood? The answer can only be: as *simultaneity*. The foundation for the reality of the system— whatever the contours of its own meaningful observations might be—is the simultaneity of its operation with the conditions of reality that sustain it. Whatever the system might contribute in the way of a nonpresent future and a nonpresent past—that is, of distinctions—the simultaneity of the environment and the eternally immediate present of the system is a condition that cannot be eliminated. Whatever is simultaneous cannot be influenced, cannot be integrated into the causal constellations of the system, cannot be synchronized, but is nonetheless the precondition for the application of distinctions in time. The system can place itself in relation to time between future and past, or as a moment in relation to duration or to eternity. Whatever might emerge from this, the system constructs time in relation to itself. What one does not have control over is the simultaneity that reemerges from moment to moment in all the operations of the system, the "common aging" in the sense of Alfred Schütz (Schütz 1932, III–12), or the splashing of the water on the bank of the Île de Saint Pierre, that "continuing noise that is, however, filled by intervals," which, in convergence with internal movements, is sufficient "to make me sense my existence with pleasure, without my having to think" (Rousseau 1959b, 1040ff. [1045]).

It is out of the unavoidable certainty of the simultaneity of the system and the environment that current time projections can arise. Examples of this can be found in the widespread "anticipatory reactions" in the plant and animal kingdoms, that is, in mere reactions to something assumed to be present on the basis of regularities that prove to be beneficial for the future, although they have not been perceived (i.e., have not been integrated into the processing of information).[18] Highly developed cognitive systems can, in addition, make prognoses, which does not mean that they can now perceive future present times. They are able to span this impossibility by means of constructions that organize their own information processing with the help of a distinction between what is past and what is to come that cannot appear in the external world as a *distinction*. Presumably, prognosis has to be understood as a product of our own imagination that can be evaluated by the memory,[19] that is, as the creation of an excess of individual possibilities that is then offered up for selection according to self-constructed criteria of "suitability." In other words, systems that make prognoses can prepare themselves for risks that they themselves have created and derive benefits from this.

Cognitive systems, therefore, have only a momentary existence, as a result of the burden of simultaneity that keeps them on the ground. This existence must reproduce itself autopoietically in order to attain stability, even if it is only a dynamic one. They experience the world, therefore, with future and past—that is, as *duration*—only in the form of *nonpresentness*. These systems can, therefore, consider their history to be finished insofar as they do not make present—as if in a dream—retrospective preferences. In the same way their future is full of enticing and threatening possibilities (although in reality there is no possibility at all, since everything is as it is). It is possible then to keep the nonpresent constant, which yields in turn the fascinating possibility of cognition's representing *changes* in the external world by terminological *constants* (instead of by changes in the system itself). As a result, such systems need records, which can, however, be accessed only currently; subsequently these systems help themselves with a kind of "vicarious learning," with observing observations of others that have the same limitation. The vast unfolding of the world materially, temporally, and socially is a construct[20] anchored in the simultaneity of the world, a world that, in this regard, never changes but is nonetheless inseparable from every realization.

On the other hand, the freedom of cognition in its constructions is founded on a radical "de-simultaneity" of the world, on the reduction of the contemporaneous to an instant almost devoid of meaning. What is gained by this is a terrifying plethora of possibilities in which cognition has to find its way by its own guidance. This existential moment is doubtlessly only a moment for an observer who can see the limits of this presentness and can call it "existence." Descartes was aware of this—and therefore made God responsible for continuity.

V

Not only does the refined constructivist theory of knowledge that has been presented here dissolve the traditional rationalistic continuum of being and thinking—which presupposed the possibility of an agreement between the two and had founded it upon such concepts as nature or creation. It also renounces the theoretical transcendental position that had been the first reaction to the dissolution of this rationalist continuum. Furthermore, our theory rejects the assumption of a subjective faculty of consciousness that can guarantee a priori the conditions of the possibilities of cognition. But then, it is not sufficient to replace this conception by the distinction between irritation (or perturbation) from without and self-determination from within, which simply gives the difference between inner and outer yet another formulation and weight.[21] What remains (and has to replace those assumptions) is the *recursivity* of observation and cognition.

A process is called "recursive" when it uses the results of its own operations as the basis for further operations—that is, what is undertaken is determined in part by what has occurred in earlier operations. In the language of systems theory (which is not quite suitable here) one often says that such a process uses its own outputs as inputs. In any case, recursivity requires a continuous testing of consistency, and it has been shown by investigations in perception and memory that this necessitates a binary schematization even on the neurophysiological level, which holds in readiness the possibilities of acceptance and rejection.[22] The states of the system that have been produced by its own operation serve then as criteria for the acceptance or rejection of further operations; stimuli from the environment that affect the system can play a role here also. Decisive, however, is the continuous self-evaluation of the system—which always operates in a state of irritation or agitation by means of a code that permits acceptance and rejection with regard to the adoption of further operations. The brain functions in this way. And the same will be true for psychic and social systems. The codification true/false gives this schematization only its final finish and a form that is used only under very special circumstances.

One can, therefore, think of binarily schematized recursivity as a continuous calculation of operations on the basis of the current states of the system. The pleasure/pain mechanism also seems to function in this manner. With regard to observations, this structure makes possible the observation of observations. This can mean, first of all, that one repeats the same operation in order to see whether its results are confirmed or not confirmed. This leads then to a "condensation" of units of meaning whose verification can no longer be obtained by a single operation. More or less clear deviations can be built into such a replication. One observes the same thing at different times in different situations, under different aspects, which leads to a further enrichment of the condensed meaning and finally to the abstraction of denotation for what seems identical in the different observations. Thus it can safely be assumed that the meaningful construction of the world comes about, gaining thereby a power no single operation can possibly dispose of. One speaks here, in the language of mathematics, of the "eigenvalues" of a system.[23] Again, no correspondence between system and environment is presupposed, but only the claim is made that it was possible to bring about these states.[24]

This theory provides a good explanation for the normal evolution of a knowledge that overcomes distance, so-called "distal knowledge," as Donald Campbell, following Egon Brunswik, has called it (Campbell 1970). If one takes into consideration the dependence of all observation on distinction, other possibilities of recursive observation emerge. The usual understanding of the observations of observation focuses above all on *what* an observer observes (distinguishing thereby between subject and object, but concentrating above all on the object). Constructivism describes an observation of observation that concentrates on *how* the observed observer observes. This constructivist turn makes possible a qualitative change, a radical transformation, in the style of recursive observation, since by this means one can also observe what and how an observed observer *is unable* to observe. In this case one is interested in his blind spot, that is, the means by which things become visible or nonvisible. One observes (distinguishes) the distinction used by the primary observer in his observing. Since this observer, in the midst of his observation, cannot distinguish this distinction, what is observed is something that remains unknown to him or incommunicable. In the terms of sociology one could also say that observation is directed now to the observed observer's *latent* structures and functions.

The kind of reality, the kind of "eigenvalue," produced by recursions of this type is still largely unknown, since the technique itself is no older than 200 years. It was probably first practiced in the novel, then in the

Counter-Enlightenment, and then in the critique of ideology that is always from a holier-than-thou perspective. The primary observer was placed into the domain of the harmless or the naive; or he was treated as someone who, without realizing it, had something to hide. This holier-than-thou perspective fed upon suspicion. And the generalization of the principle of suspicion made it possible for whole disciplines—from psychoanalysis to sociology—to establish themselves with additional credentials in a world in which everyone knows, or imagines he knows, the situation in which he acts and the reasons for his actions.

It does not seem a coincidence that this observation of latent structures developed parallel to transcendental theory—at first at the end of the eighteenth century and then with particular intensity a century later during the heyday of neo-Kantianism. Apparently, something had been lacking in transcendental philosophy. All the same, a constructivist theory of knowledge goes beyond this state of affairs (again a hundred years later). Its concept of recursive observation includes the observation of latency, freeing it from the prejudice that latent structures give a false picture of the world, as it really is and as science sees it. The assumption—to be found above all in the classical sociology of knowledge—that latent structures, functions, and interests lead to distortions of knowledge, if not to blatant errors, can and must be abandoned.[25] The impossibility of distinguishing the distinction that one distinguishes with is an unavoidable precondition of cognition. The question of whether a given choice of distinction suits one's latent interests arises only on the level of second-order observation. The claim of ideological distortion can then be observed in the person making the claim (for which he has to be observed as observer, that is, in relation to what he is observing).[26]

The important question after all this is what "eigenvalues" a system is converging toward when it extends the recursivity of its observations in this direction—that is, when it continually turns its observations toward things other observers *cannot* observe. For the results of this method of observing we have, in the absence of anything better, a variety of different names: Gotthard Günther speaks of "polycontexturality," others of "pluralism," and still others of the postmodern arbitrariness in the emergence and passage of "discourses." For constructivism this is, above all, an epistemological question and a kind of compensation for the limitations inherent in every act of cognition as a consequence of its dependence upon a distinction. From the theory one cannot draw the conclusion that now special "eigenvalues" of the social system will emerge that will be resistant to enlightenment, for there is no guarantee that under all conditions such "eigenvalues" can be found and become stabilized. Still, the question can at least be raised and observation directed accordingly.

VI

If one takes seriously the endeavor to set up a constructivist theory of knowledge, an important question becomes shifted: that of the paradoxes. By a paradox is meant a permissible and meaningful statement that leads nonetheless to antinomies or undecidability (or, more strictly, a demonstrable proposition that has such consequences). Two possibilities for dealing with such a problem should be rejected. The first is used in the construction of formal systems and consists of an ad hoc procedure of exclusion. The paradoxes are eliminated by suitable precautionary measures. Structures that lead to paradoxes are forbidden—for example by the well-known but questionable theory of types. The epistemological questionability of such a procedure comes from its lack of justification; moreover, it usually has the consequence that it excludes more than just paradoxical possibilities for the construction of sentences.

As a result, philosophers have felt compelled to look for other means that would lead to a justifiable exclusion of paradoxes. MacKie, for example, suggests returning to a semantic theory of truth that would make it possible to say that the supposed objects designated by meaningful paradoxical propositions do not exist![27] It is, however, not possible for a constructivist theory of knowledge to accept this way out, since what is claimed here as being nonexistent does not exist for constructivism anyway. Given that paradoxes reemerge despite all the attempts to eliminate them, MacKie finally even calls for a "construction" of the paradoxical by adopting self-referring propositions into the construction and (at least implicit) quantification (MacKie 1973, 273). This suggestion is grist for the constructivist's mill: constructivism can view paradox as a problem in the machinery of the calculation of calculations, as a possible but nonetheless destructive construction. Should one look the Gorgon straight on—aware, however, that it is not the deadly Medusa one has before one but her immortal sisters, Sthenno (the Mighty) or Euryale (the Far Springer)?

We suggest instead a view from the side, the observing of observation. This enables one, when one includes observation of latency, to observe how other observers render invisible the paradoxes that get in their way, for example the paradox of each of our binary codes.[28] It is, therefore, not a psychoanalytical infection or a critical socio-ideological frivolity that brings us to include observation of the blind spot of the observer in the theory of knowledge. It is furthermore not simply an encouragement to propound values that are, in any case, irrational, as William James and Max Weber had thought. To see what others cannot see (and to accept that they cannot see what they cannot see) is, in a way, the systematic keystone of epistemology—taking the place of its a priori foundation.

It is, therefore, of importance that every observer involves himself in a paradox because he has to found his observing on a distinction. As a result, he is unable to observe either the beginning or the ending of his observing—unless it be by means of another distinction that he has already begun to make or by continuing with a new distinction after having ended.[29] This is why every projection, every setting of a goal, every formation of an episode necessitates recursive observation and why, furthermore, recursive observation makes possible not so much the elimination of paradoxes as their temporal and social distribution onto different operations. A consensual integration of systems of communication is, given such conditions, something that should sooner be feared than sought. For such integration can only result in the paradoxes' becoming invisible to all and remaining that way for an indefinite future.

This remedy solves, as it were, the problem of the paradoxes by reference to a concrete theory: the theory of autopoietic systems, which by means of recursive operations produce and reproduce a network of such operations as the condition for the very possibility of this reproduction (a solution logicians will hardly find satisfying). In such systems (one of which is science) there is no operation without reference to other operations of the system. Even when one forms universal propositions that refer to all the operations of the system, and also when one exposes these universal propositions, on the basis of the classic Cretan pattern, to self-reference, one only produces an operation that is a point of departure for other operations. We simply claim: it is this way; and logicians who attempt to dispute this are, in consequence, punished by paradoxes.

VII

Given all that has been said, what understanding of reality does constructivism have?

It may be useful here to review classical responses once again. As far as visual metaphors were used, two solutions were offered. Objectivists said that reality was manifold, which meant that there was no single observational point from which it could be seen in toto: what one sees conceals what one does not see. This deficiency can be countered only by changing the point of observation, that is, by working sequentially or by a division of labor. Subjectivists could speak instead of a multiplicity of perspectives each of which makes possible a conditioned seeing, but which at the same time makes impossible or difficult the perception of the perspective one sees with.[30] More eyes—and therefore more emotions: that was Nietzsche's postulate in *The Genealogy of Morals*. Constructivism goes beyond these positions by radicalizing the relationship between cognition and reality. It is no longer a question of the difficulties that arise from a multiplicity of sides or perspectives, and the problem is no longer how one arrives, given this situation, at unity. This multiplicity, regardless of whether it is a multiplicity of sides or of perspectives, is itself a product of cognition, resulting from certain types of distinctions, which, as distinctions, are instruments of cognition. It is precisely by means of distinguishing that cognition separates itself from everything that is not cognition. Nonetheless, one is always dealing with concretely determined operations—even in the case of knowledge. Without water the jellyfish goes limp. But in order to recognize that, distinctions are necessary: with/without water; not-limp / limp. These distinctions are codifications specific to cognition, which function independently of the environment (i.e., of stimuli), because there are not and cannot be any equivalents for them in the external world.

Cognitively all reality must be constructed by means of distinctions and, as a result, remains construction. The constructed reality is, therefore, not the reality referred to. This, too, can be recognized, but recognized only by means of precisely this distinction. For cognition, only what serves in a given case as a distinction is a guarantee of reality, an equivalent of reality. One could say more precisely: The source of a distinction's ability to guarantee reality lies in its own operative unity. It is, however, precisely as this unity that the distinction cannot be observed—except by means of another distinction that then assumes the function of a guarantor of reality. Another way of expressing this is to say that the operation emerges simultaneously with the world, which as a result remains cognitively unapproachable to the operation.

The conclusion to be drawn from this is that the connection with the reality of the external world is established by the blind spot of the cognitive operation. Reality is what one does not perceive when one perceives it. In no way does this mean, however, that somewhere in the world there are states of affairs one cannot know, above all not in the old sense that the essence of nature is secret. All that is meant is that the fruits of the concrete operation of cognition, which issue from the use of distinctions—that is, the proliferation of combinatorial possibilities—are due to an instrument requiring an operational closure specific for the given system. To attain this closure, no "similarities" with the environment can be tolerated. If cognition demands meaning and meaning demands distinctions, then the final reality must be thought of as devoid of meaning.

VIII

If one compares this result with what has traditionally been called "idealism," one can recognize an important change. It affects the basic question to which an answer is sought and, therefore, the whole theoretical structure.

One had proceeded from the distinction between knowledge and object and, as a result, had been forced to face the problem that could not be answered by means of this distinction: How does knowledge arrive at its object? In the final analysis, then, the problem lay in the unity of the difference between knowledge and object. One answer was provided by the claim of a dialectical relationship. Dialectical theories proved to be the adequate form here and required hardly any further argument. If one accepts the argument suggested above, however, the distinction between knowledge and object is itself only a distinction, that is, a construction used to wound, dissect, observe the world. The unity of this distinction is simply the blind spot used by someone who, by means of this distinction, produces observations and descriptions.

However, if one starts—as constructivism does—from the assumption that this is always a real process in a real environment, which is always subject to limitations coming from the environment, what might the problem be then?

The problem could reside in the question of how a system is able to transform such *limitations* into *conditions for increasing its own complexity*. The *nonarbitrariness* of knowledge would then be nothing other than the evolutionarily controlled *selectivity* of this process of change. It assumes no operations of the system that project into the environment, that is, no knowledge in the traditional sense. One has to postulate instead: Everything issuing from this process of a transformation of limitations into conditions for the increase of complexity is, for the system in question, knowledge.

In contrast with idealism, constructivist cognition neither seeks nor finds a ground. It reflects (when it reflects) the change in world-orientation from unity to difference. It begins and ends with distinctions, well aware that this is its own affair and not forced to this recognition by an unapproachable outer world. As the unity of the drawing of a distinction, it can conceive of itself as a symbolic processing. The unity of the separated, the mutual suitability of the differentiated, is what serves as a symbol here. Francisco Varela, too, has considered this to be an operation or a value and called it "self-indication."[31] We must leave the question open as to whether this leads to an effective calculus. On the other hand, it is easy to recognize that we are living in the world after the Fall. We have eaten of the tree of the knowledge of good and evil. "Distinctions" can be employed only by using "indications." The symbol can be employed only diabolically; only what has been distinguished is integrable.

IX

A few further thoughts on the matter will be given only cursorily. The concept of observing has been defined extremely formally as a distinguishing description. We reject, nonetheless, founding this formality "transcendentally." With observing, distinguishing, designating we always mean an empirical operation that changes the system executing it—which means an operation that, in its own turn, is observable. No observer can avoid being observed, not even in its quality as "subject."

On the other hand the formality of the concept leaves open which empirical operations are meant. Which organ—to speak in these terms— carries out the observation?

The abstractness of the concept is not meant to conduct one to a ground. This already results from the fact that the operation of observing can lead to both true and false knowledge, as an observer can determine who observes observing by means of the distinction between true and false. The abstractness of the concept is, therefore, intended not to provide a grounding for knowledge but only to keep open the possibility of observation operations being carried out by very different empirical systems—living systems, systems of consciousness, systems of communication. The abstraction makes allowances for the very wide domain of the "cognitive sciences," above all for the differentiation into disciplines in biology, psychology, and sociology. Observation takes place when living systems (cells, immune systems, brain, etc.) discriminate and react to their own discrimination. Observation occurs when thoughts that have been processed through consciousness fix and distinguish something.[32] It occurs as well when a communicable, integrable understanding of conveyed information—be it linguistic or nonlinguistic—is attained (whatever psychic processes might occur in the minds of the participating individuals).

Given the state of research today one cannot get around taking into account the differences between these empirical realizations of distinguishing and designation (or should one perhaps for once say here: of discriminative focusing?). With this, the traditional attribution of cognition to "man" has been done away with. It is clear here, if anywhere, that "constructivism" is a completely new theory of knowledge, a posthumanistic one. This is intended not maliciously but only to make clear that the concept "man" (in the singular!), as a designation for the bearer and guarantor of the unity of knowledge, must be renounced. The reality of cognition is to be found in the current operations of the various autopoietic systems. The unity of a structure of cognition (or the "system" in the sense of transcendental theory) can lie only in the unity of an autopoietic system that reproduces itself with its boundaries, its structures, and its elements.

In this way the significance of psychological epistemologies is considerably reduced, but they are relieved at the same time of the unreasonable expectation that they should provide more than individual-psychological knowledge. There is no such thing as "man"; no one has ever seen him; and if one is interested in the system of observation that organizes its distinctions by means of this word or concept, one discovers the communication-system called society. There are now approximately five billion psychological systems. It has to be asked which of these five billion is intended when a theory of knowledge employing a psychological reference system relates concepts such as observation and cognition to consciousness. If no answer is forthcoming, such a theory has to be characterized as practicing socio-communicative observation. And the suggestion would have to be made that it would be better if this practice were reflected upon.

Up to now, constructivism has profited mainly from research in biology, neurophysiology, and psychology (Maturana, Varela, Piaget, von Glasersfeld), although it actually favors development of a sociological theory of knowledge. What we know as cognition is the product of the system of communication called society, where consciousness plays a permanent but always only fractional role. It is only in extreme exceptions that one has to know individual persons in order to know what is known—and these are typical instances (for example, statements by witnesses in court) in which direct perception plays a central role. Neither in its claim to validity nor in the evaluation of its possibilities for development is the fund of knowledge of modern society approachable through processes of consciousness. It is an artifact of communication—and what is amazing here is not so much that the world is as it is constructed by modern science, as that it is still possible to pursue communication under the conditions of this construction. It is obvious that this cannot be explained by some capacity of consciousness (which one?!) but can be explained by the possibilities of storage made available originally by printing and, more recently, by electronic data processing.[33]

This preference for society as a referential system (that is, as the choice of a system from the perspective of which something else is environment) becomes absolutely unavoidable when one takes into consideration the difference between everyday knowledge and scientific knowledge. Whatever this distinction might mean and whatever theory might offer it, it cannot be presented convincingly as a distinction between different psychic types of knowledge. The distinction is a consequence of the differentiation of the social system of society. And it is only from here that psychical systems can be influenced. No further argument is necessary when one recalls the well-known phenomena of exponential growth, increasing differentiation, and specialization or the problems of the pace of change.

It is, finally, only in a sociological context that the ideas about recursive observation and second-order observation (i.e., the observation of observation) acquire their full significance. But why would an observer observe another observer as observer, as another psychical system? Why isn't the other system seen simply as a normal object in the external world, that is, why isn't it simply observed directly instead of as a pathway for the observing of its observing?

It is usually assumed that this is made possible by a sudden, intuitive analogy: the other is experienced as an alter ego, as operating like another I.[34] But we question, how does this occur? And further, is this phenomenon culturally invariant, independent of social structure? The usual answer describes only the result, is only another formulation of the problem and does not explain how it occurs.

Maturana avoids this problem by shifting to the mutually coordinating interaction of two organisms that interreact with each other in a sufficiently comparable area of interaction.[35] This makes it possible for him to explain the origin of language as a possibility of consensual coordination of the coordination of these interactions despite closure of the mode of operation of the participating systems. This still does not provide, however, a satisfying explanation of how the observation of observing emerges, that is, how observers construct the objects they have constructed as other observers.

A third theoretical suggestion (which draws on sociology, since psychology and biology have not sufficed) can begin with the assumption that the construction of the other observer is a necessary consequence of communication.[36] For communication is possible only when an observer is able, in his sphere of perception, to distinguish between the act of communication and information, that is, to understand communicative acts as the conveying of information (and not simply as behavior).[37] Out of this distinction—which remains stable only evolutionarily and reproduces itself as a communication system only when it is able to maintain itself—there emerges then a second one: that of subject and object. That communication can be continued requires no more than a kind of black-box concept for the subject and for the object, as far as the distinction operates. As a participant, one can make use of one's own constructions, which can then be evaluated during the course of one's participation in the communication. One does not need to know what is going on "inside" the subject (and of course, could never know this) and also does not need to know the "essence" of things (which is of itself infinite): the filling necessary for the continuation of communication suffices. However, to the degree that systems of communication, in the course of their own evolution, become more sophisticated, differentiated, and complex, more demanding concepts for subject and object are called for. It is in the course of this that one finally also learns to observe others as observers (even during the times they are not communicating) and finally even to observe that others do not observe what they do not observe while observing. Society, finally, makes even latent observation of latent structures possible.

The question still has not been answered of why communication together with its resulting achievements progresses. The answer can only be that the evolutionary force of a particular distinction—that between communication and information—has proven itself. This can, of course, be claimed of everything that exists, and is still not an explanation. Important, however, in the constructivist context outlined above is that this claim has been made for a *distinction*. With this, another distinction has been added to those already used—system/environment and operation/observation: that of communication/information, which is of special importance for the analysis of social systems. The familiar distinction between ego and alter ego can be dealt with as derivative, and with it the whole theory of knowledge founded on the concept of intersubjectivity.

X

The above has made it abundantly clear, we believe, that constructivism does not question the existence and reality of the world—but only constructs. But even after one has seen this, one can, as a sociologist, still ask why this happens, and why precisely today, after both ancient skepticism and idealism have been overcome, this constructivistic world-construction is of value. If a philosopher were to ask this question, he would be faced with the difficult problem of a deeper analysis of Hegelian logic, which is the most profound scheme so far developed for the processing of distinctions and of what is implied in them with regard to the identical and its contrary. For a sociologist the matter is simpler. He can take a theory of social evolution as his point of departure, a theory, obviously, that itself is founded on a relevant distinction—for example, constructed on a Darwinian scheme of variation and selection. It is then possible to understand constructivism as an epistemology suitable for a society with a highly differentiated system of the sciences.[38] In other words, in a society that can produce science in the modern sense, conceptual problems arise that can be solved only constructivistically, whatever one in this society might normally think about the world in which he lives, works, rides the bus, and smokes cigarettes.

It should not be very difficult to recognize that progress in science (whatever "progress" might mean here) is tied to even more sophisticated distinctions. This is, above all, the case for what Donald Campbell has called development in the direction of "distal knowledge"—that is, for the distinction between knowledge and the knower himself.[39] Divorce of the perspectives of comparison from the interests of the one doing the comparing also belongs here. Moreover, one need only think of the use of rigorously formal cognitive instruments—of logic, mathematics, quantification—as a form of representation of distinction in reality. This could still be dealt with under the concept of "idealism," and it is in this context that Husserl makes his criticism of modern, "Galilean" science.[40] Today the "cognitive sciences" and the theory of self-referential systems add a new perspective that cannot be subsumed under "idealism" or criticized as "idealism," that is, insight into the operative closure of self-referential systems. A theory of knowledge today that is to be compatible with the latest developments in science must be able to bear this new perspective. It is not surprising, therefore, that after a period of open and rather irresolute epistemological pragmatism and a period in which highly formalized methodology was presented as epistemology—after James and Dewey, Baldwin, Rescher, Popper, and others—epistemological constructivism is beginning to come into its own. Quantum physics, cytochemistry, and neurophysiology, as well as historic-sociological relativism, make this convergence necessary. If the task of epistemology is to analyze science as a social cognitive undertaking, one will not be able simply to ignore scientific results. Constructivism is the form assumed in reflection on the system of science facing its own extravagances; it is the form in which an increasingly improbable distinguishing is finally recognized as the contribution of cognition. But it is also the form that can no longer mislead one to conclude it has nothing to do with reality.

A society that increasingly differentiates its most important subsystems in relation to specific functions intensifies to a highly improbable degree its cognitive output in the area of science. If one then reflects on this situation, one arrives at theories that themselves seem improbable. For this reason epistemology cannot provide a foundation for the sciences. It cannot offer basic principles, arguments, or even certainty. It can no longer be understood as a theory of the founding of knowledge. The opposite is true: it analyzes the uncertainty of knowledge and gives reasons for it. It therefore should come as no surprise that no theory of knowledge today can attain the degree of certainty to be found in quantum physics or biochemistry.

It is perhaps not the least important function of constructivist epistemology to make society irritatingly aware of the fact that it produces science.

PART III

COMMUNICATION

7

What Is Communication?

*We no longer have a knowledge of psychological
and social systems that can be integrated.*

My goal is to criticize the current understanding of communication
and to place a qualitatively different variant alongside it. Before I begin,
some remarks on the scientific context in which this maneuver is to be per-
formed are called for.

First of all, I proceed from an indisputable state of affairs. The differentiation of the disciplines of psychology and sociology, with which we are
all familiar, and more than one hundred years of disciplinarily separated research have led to a knowledge of psychological and social systems that can
no longer be integrated. In neither of the disciplines does any one researcher
have an overview of the entire state of knowledge, but this much is clear: that
in each case it is a matter of highly complex, structured systems, whose internal dynamics are nontransparent and nonregulable for any observer. In
spite of this, there are still concepts and even theories that are unaware of
this state of affairs or that even systematically obscure it. In sociology, the
concepts of action and communication are part of this residue. They are
normative when used with reference to a subject. That is, they presuppose
an author, designated as individual or subject, to whom action or communication can be attributed. But the concepts of subject or individual function therein only as empty formulas for a state of affairs that is in itself highly
complex, one that falls under the domain for which psychology is responsible and does not further interest sociologists.

Only communication can communicate.

If one calls this conceptual disposition into question, as I want to do, one usually hears the following: In the end, it is always people, individuals, subjects who act or communicate. I would like to assert in the face of this that only communication can communicate and that what we understand as "action" can be generated only in such a network of communication.

My second prefatory remark concerns fascinating new developments in the field of general systems theory and the cybernetics of self-referential systems, developments that earlier bore the title "self-organization" and today bear that of "autopoiesis." The state of research is for the moment impossible to survey and controversial even in the formation of concepts. Nonetheless, a clearly recognizable restructuring of the theoretical tools extends as far as epistemology, and this in a way that covers biology, psychology, and sociology. Anyone who likes a multileveled architecture can observe a restructuring of theory that is taking place on multiple levels simultaneously and that thereby calls into question the distinction between levels that is immediately apparent for logical reasons.

Self-reference is not a special property of thought.

Contrary to fundamental assumptions of the philosophical tradition, self-reference (or "reflection") is in no way a special property of thought or consciousness, but rather a very general principle of system formation with particular consequences regarding evolution and the construction of complexity. The consequence that there are many ways of observing the world, according to which system-reference each is based on, should then be inevitable. Or, to rephrase it, evolution has led to a world that has very many different possibilities of observing itself without marking one of these possibilities as the best or only correct one. Every theory that measures up to this state of affairs must therefore be located on the level of the observation of observations, on the level of second-order cybernetics in the sense of Heinz von Foerster.

My question, then, is the following: what does a sociological theory of social systems look like when it seriously attempts to face these theoretical developments? And my supposition is that one must begin in this respect not with the concept of action but with the concept of communication. For not action, but communication is an unavoidably social operation and at the same time an operation that is necessarily set in motion whenever social situations are formed.

In the main part of my lecture, therefore, I would like to attempt to present a corresponding concept of communication, namely a concept that strictly avoids any reference to consciousness or to life, that is, to other levels of the realization of autopoietic systems. It should be noted only as a precaution that this naturally does not mean that communication is possible without life and consciousness. It is also impossible without carbon, without moderate temperatures, without the earth's magnetic field, without the atomic bonding of matter. Faced with the complexity of the world, one cannot take all of the conditions of the possibility of a state of affairs into the concept of this state of affairs, for the concept would thereby lose all of its contours and any technical applicability to theory construction.

Communication comes about through
a synthesis of three different selections.

Like life and consciousness, communication is also an emergent reality, a self-generated state of affairs. It comes about through a synthesis of three different selections, namely the selection of *information*, the selection of the *utterance* [*Mitteilung*] of this information, and selective *understanding or misunderstanding* of this utterance and its information.

None of these components can appear on its own. Only together do they generate communication. Only together: that means, only when their selectivity can be brought to congruence. Communication therefore takes place only when a difference of utterance and information is first understood. This distinguishes it from a mere perception of others' behavior. By understanding, communication grasps a difference between the information value of its content and the reasons for which the content is being uttered. It can thereby accentuate one side or the other and thus pay more attention to the information itself or to the expressive behavior. It is, however, always dependent on experiencing both sides as selection and *thereby* distinguishing them. In other words, we must presuppose that the information does not understand itself and that a particular decision is necessary in order for its utterance. And, of course, that also applies when the person speaking says something about him- or herself. If, and insofar as, this separation of selections is not carried out, it is a case of mere perception.

> *It is of paramount significance to maintain the*
> *distinction between perception and communication.*

It is of paramount significance to maintain this distinction between communication and perception even though, or precisely because, communication offers rich possibilities for an accompanying perception. But perception at first remains a psychological event without communicative existence. Inside the communicative occurrence, it is not connectable as it is. One can neither confirm nor refute, neither interrogate nor respond to what another has perceived. It remains locked up within consciousness and nontransparent to the system of communication as well as to every other consciousness. It can naturally become an external reason for a subsequent communication. Participants can bring into communication their own perceptions and the interpretations of the situation that are bound up with them, but only according to the autonomous laws of the system of communication, for instance, only in the form of language, only by claiming speaking time, only through imposing oneself, making oneself visible, exposing oneself—thus only under discouragingly difficult conditions.

> *Even understanding is itself a selection.*

Not only information and utterance but understanding [*das Verstehen*] is itself a selection. Understanding is never a mere duplication of the utterance in another consciousness but is, rather, in the system of communication itself, a precondition for connection onto further communication, thus a condition of the autopoiesis of the social system. Whatever the participants in their own respective self-referential, closed consciousnesses may think, the communication system works out its own understanding and creates processes of self-observation and self-inspection for this purpose.

*The participants cannot communicate
as simply as they would like about
understanding and misunderstanding.*

It is possible to communicate about understanding and misunderstanding or lack of understanding—though again only under the highly specific conditions of the autopoiesis of the system of communication and not as easily as the participants would like. The utterance "You don't understand me" therefore remains ambivalent and, at the same time, communicates this ambivalence. On the one hand, it means, "You are not ready to accept what I want to say to you," and attempts to provoke the admission of this fact. On the other hand, it is the utterance of the information that communication cannot be continued under this condition of not understanding. And, thirdly, it is a continuation of communication.

The normal technique of dealing with difficulties of understanding consists simply in questions and explanations, in normal, routine communication about communication without a special psychological charge. The person who tries to attribute this failure to communication through communication itself violates this normal routine: "You don't understand me" conceals the rigor of the problem of acceptance or rejection with a semantics that suggests that the problem can just as readily be solved by communication about communication.

What is new about this concept of communication?

What is new about this concept of communication? And what are the consequences of this innovation?

First of all, the distinction among the three components—information, utterance, and understanding—is new.

One finds a similar distinction in Karl Bühler from the point of view of different functions of linguistic communication. Anglo-American thinkers like Austin and Searle have augmented and rigidified this into a theory of types of acts or speech acts. To this theory, furthermore, Jürgen Habermas has annexed a typology of validity claims implicit in communication. All of this, however, still proceeds from an action-theoretical understanding of communication and therefore sees the procedure of communication as a successful or unsuccessful *transference* of news, information, or suppositions of agreement.

In light of this, a systems-theoretical approach emphasizes the *emergence of communication* itself. Nothing is transferred. Redundancy is produced in the sense that communication generates a memory to which many people can lay claim in many different ways. If *A* utters something to *B*, the subsequent communication can be addressed to *A* or *B*. The system pulsates, so to speak, with the constant generation of excess and selection. With the discovery of writing and printing, this process of system formation is once more immensely heightened, with consequences for social structure, semantics, indeed for language itself, consequences that are only now gradually entering the view of researchers.

> *With these three components, it is a matter*
> *of different selections.*

The three components—information, utterance, and understanding—must not, therefore, be interpreted as functions, as acts, or as horizons for validity claims (which is not to deny that these are also possible ways of applying the components). They are also not building blocks of communication that can exist independently and need only be put together by someone—by whom, the subject? Rather, it is a matter of different selections, whose selectivity and field of selection can be constituted only through communication. There is no information outside of communication; there is no utterance outside of communication; there is no understanding outside of communication. This is so not in a merely causal sense, according to which the information would have to be the cause of the utterance and the utterance the cause of understanding, but rather in the circular sense of mutual presupposition.

> *A system of communication is*
> *a completely closed system.*

A system of communication is therefore a fully closed system that generates the components of which it consists through communication itself. In this sense, a system of communication is an autopoietic system that produces and reproduces through the system everything that functions for the system as a unit. It is self-evident that this can occur only within an environment and under conditions of dependency on limitations set by that environment.

Formulated more concretely, this means that the system of communication itself specifies not only its own elements—what in each case is a unit of communication that cannot be further divided—but also its structures. What is not communicated cannot contribute to this. Only communication can influence communication; only communication can decompose units of communication (for example, by analyzing the horizon of selection of a piece of information or asking about the reasons for an utterance); and only communication can inspect and repair communication.

As one can easily see, the practice of such an execution of reflexive operations is a very strenuous process, one that can be held within bounds by the peculiarities of the autopoiesis of communication. One cannot reformulate more and more exactly. Sometime, and rather quickly, the useful limit of communication is reached or patience—that is, the load-bearing capacity of the psychological environment—is exhausted, or the interest in other themes or other partners prevails.

Communication has no goal.

This thesis of the circular, autopoietic closure of the system is not easy to accept. One must experiment with it quite a while in thought in order to gradually see what it yields. The same is true of another, closely related thesis. Communication has no goal [*Zweck*], no immanent entelechy. It happens, or not, and that is all that one can say on that point. In this regard, this theory follows no Aristotelian style but, rather, follows the theoretical style of Spinoza. Obviously, goal-oriented episodes can be formed inside of systems of communication, to the degree that autopoiesis functions, just as consciousness, too, can posit episodic goals for itself, without this positing of a goal being the goal of the system. Any other account would have to explain why the system lasts beyond the attainment of its goals, or one would have to say something not entirely novel: death is the goal of life.

*The theory of the rationality of communicative action
is simply false on empirical grounds alone.*

Often, it is more or less implicitly supposed that communication aims at consensus, that it seeks agreement. The theory of the rationality of communicative action developed by Habermas is built upon these premises. One can also communicate in order to mark dissent, one can desire to argue; and there is no compelling reason to hold the search for consensus to be more rational than the search for dissent. That depends entirely on themes and partners. Communication is obviously impossible without any consensus, but is also impossible without any dissent. What it necessarily requires is one's being able to leave aside the question of consensus or dissent in relation to themes that are not present at the moment. Even with present themes—even when one has finally found a parking lot and, after a long walk, has reached the café where they say the best coffee in Rome is served and then drinks the couple of drops—where is consensus or dissent in this case, as long as one does not spoil the fun through communication?

All communication is risky.

In place of a consensus-oriented entelechy, systems theory posits another thesis: Communication leads to the precise formulation of the question of whether the uttered and understood information should be accepted or rejected. One believes a piece of news or not. Communication creates at first only this alternative and thereby creates the risk of rejection. It forces a situation of decision that would not exist at all without communication. To this extent, all communication is risky. This risk is one of the most important morphogenetic factors. It leads to the building of institutions that secure a disposition of acceptance even toward improbable communications.

But, inversely, although this seems valid only for Far Eastern cultures, risk also seems able to sensitize. One avoids communication with probabilities of rejection; one seeks to fulfill wishes before they are expressed and thereby indicates boundaries; and one participates in communication without disagreeing and without disturbing communication by registering one's acceptance or rejection of it.

Communication duplicates reality.

Therefore, to repeat this important point once more in other words, communication duplicates reality. It creates two versions, a yes-version and a no-version, and thereby compels selection. Something must now occur (even if it is an explicit breaking off of communication); precisely therein lies the autopoiesis of the system, which guarantees to itself its own ability to continue.

The precise formulation of the alternatives of acceptance or rejection is thus nothing but the autopoiesis of communication itself. It differentiates the connecting position for the next communication, which must now be built on an attained consensus or must pursue dissent; or it can also attempt to conceal the problem and, in the future, to avoid the touchy point. Nothing that can be communicated evades this rigid bifurcation—with one sole exception: the world (in the phenomenological sense) as the final horizon of meaning in which all of this plays itself out and which can be neither positively nor negatively qualified, neither accepted nor rejected, but is co-produced in all sensible communication as the condition of access to further communication.

The value-reference of communication.

Allow me once more to try out this theoretical model in a specialized question: the problem of the value-reference of communication. We are trained on neo-Kantian foundations or, too, by Jürgen Habermas to detect validity claims right away here and to invite their testing. Reality is simpler—and at the same time more complicated.

What one can observe empirically is, at first glance, that values are brought into communication by implication. One presupposes them already. One alludes to them. One does not say directly, "I am for peace. I value my health." One avoids that for the already familiar reason that it would duplicate the possibilities for acceptance or rejection. Precisely that seems to be unnecessary in the case of values—or so one thinks, in any case.

One discusses not values but only preferences.

Consequently, values are valid because they are presupposed to be valid. The person who communicates with reference to values lays claim to a sort of values bonus. The other has to announce him- or herself if he or she does not agree. One operates, so to speak, under the protection of the beauty and goodness of values and profits thereby in that the person who wants to protest has to take complexity upon him- or herself. He or she has the burden of the argumentation. He or she runs the risk of thinking innovatively and having to isolate him- or herself. And since more and more values are implied than can be thematized in the next step, picking out, rejecting, or modifying is an almost hopeless task. One does not discuss values, only preferences, interests, prescriptions, programs. That does not mean that there is in fact a value system. That also does not mean—and this is of paramount importance—that it is a case of psychologically stable structures. On the contrary, psychologically, values seem to lead an extraordinarily labile existence. They are sometime used, sometimes not used, without one's being able to discover any kind of psychological deep structure. Their stability, as I would like to formulate it provocatively, is an exclusively communicative artifact, and the autopoietic system of consciousness uses this artifact as it pleases. Exactly because structures of the autopoiesis of the social system are at play here, the semantics of values is suitable for the representation of the foundations of the social system for one's own use. Their stability rests on a recursive supposition of the act of supposing and on a testing of the semantics with which this either functions or does not function. The "foundation of validity" is recursivity, hardened through the communicative disadvantaging of contradiction.

There is no self-realization of values.

What consciousness thinks of this is a completely different question. If it is well-versed, it will know that value consensus is as inevitable as it is harmful. For there is no self-realization of values, and one can allow everything that they seem to demand to go astray in their realization—in the name of values, naturally.

*Consequences for the field of the diagnosis
and therapy of system relations.*

Such a thoroughgoing revision of system- and communications-theoretical terminology will surely have consequences for the diagnosis and therapy of states of the system that are seen as pathological. I have no competence whatsoever in this field and, least of all, in the sort of automatic self-inspection that arises from a familiarity with this milieu. In spite of this, I would like to attempt to illuminate in a kind of summary several points that could perhaps allow the construction of known phenomena anew.

First of all, the model emphasizes the difference between psychological and social systems. The former operate on the basis of consciousness, the latter on the basis of communication. Both are circularly closed systems, each of which can apply only its own mode of autopoietic reproduction. A social system cannot think; a psychological system cannot communicate. Seen causally, there are nonetheless immense, highly complex interdependencies. Closure in no way means that there are no causal relations or that such relations cannot be observed or described by an observer. The initial situation of autopoietic closure must be subsumed under this description. This means that one must take account of the fact that effects can take place only through co-execution on the part of the system that undergoes these effects. And one must also be aware that the systems are opaque to each other and can therefore not steer each other.

From the consistency of this model, it follows that consciousness contributes only noise, interference, and disturbance to communication, and vice versa. In fact, when you observe a process of communication, you must know the preceding communication, perhaps also the themes, and what one can meaningfully say about it. Generally, you do not need to know the structures of the individuals' consciousness.

But this argumentation naturally needs refinement, since the systems of communication often thematize persons and since consciousness has grown accustomed to loving certain words, telling certain stories, and thus partially identifies itself with communication.

*One's own consciousness dances about
upon the words like a will-o'-the-wisp.*

An observer can therefore recognize a high degree of structural interdependency between psychological and social systems. Nonetheless, the psychological selectivity of communicative events in the experience of the participants is something entirely different from social selectivity, and by paying but little attention to what we ourselves say, we already become aware of how imprecisely we must select in order to say what one can say, how greatly the emitted word is already no longer what was thought and meant, and how greatly one's own consciousness dances about upon the words like a will-o'-the-wisp, uses and mocks them, at once means and does not mean them, has them surface and dive, does not have them ready at the right moment, genuinely wants to say them but, for no good reason, does not. If we were to make an effort to really observe our own consciousness in its operations from thought to thought, we would certainly discover a peculiar fascination with language, but also the noncommunicative, purely internal use of linguistic symbols and a peculiar, background depth of the actuality of consciousness, a depth on which words swim like ships chained in a row but without being consciousness itself, somehow illuminated, but not light itself.

This superiority of consciousness to communication (which, of course, corresponds in inverted system-reference to a superiority of communication over consciousness) becomes fully clear if one realizes that consciousness is occupied not only with words or with vague word-and-sentence ideas, but additionally and often more importantly with perception and with the imaginative construction and dismantling of images. Even during speech, consciousness is ceaselessly occupied with perception, and it often seems to me as if I see the written images of the words in formulating them (a fact that has not been noticed in investigations of the "scriptification" [*Verschriftlichung*] of civilization, as far as I am familiar with them). The degree to which one allows one's own speaking to distract one from the perceptual observation of others, or how far one still has a capacity for the simultaneous processing of perceived impressions in spite of one's attentiveness to the sequence of speech, also varies from individual to individual.

*It is inevitable to adapt communication
to the will-o'-the-wisp of consciousness.*

Changing the system-reference and coming back to the social system of communication, all of this makes it inevitable that communication will be adapted to the will-o'-the-wisp of consciousness. Of course, communication cannot transport bits of consciousness. Rather, consciousness, no matter what it itself thinks to itself, is maneuvered by communication into a situation of forced choice—or so it appears at least from the point of view of communication. Communication can be accepted or rejected in a way that is communicatively comprehensible (and, of course, this constellation of themes can be factored in such a way that the decision is decomposed into many decisions). The autopoietic autonomy of consciousness, one could say, is represented and compensated in communication by binarization.

*Communication can be interfered
with by consciousness.*

A decision treatable within communication takes the place of the incomprehensibly noisy consciousness-environment of the system of communication: yes or no, questioning, perhaps delay, postponement, withdrawal. To put it another way, communication can be interfered with by consciousness and even anticipates this, but only in forms that are connectable in further communication and that can thus be treated communicatively. In this way, a mixing of the autopoiesis of the two systems never comes about, yet a high degree of co-evolution and practiced reactivity does.

I am fully aware that this analysis is by no means sufficient to describe what we experience as a pathological state of the system. Indeed, seen from the point of view of this theory, the noise, interference, disturbance from both sides is precisely the normal case, for which a normal capacity of reception and absorption stands ready, psychologically as well as socially. Apparently, the impression of the pathological arises only if certain thresholds of tolerance are exceeded, or perhaps one could also say: if the memories of the system are hereby called into action and record, accumulate, and present again experiences of interference, reinforcing them through the reinforcement of deviance and hypercorrection and demanding more and more capacity for them. Be that as it may, from the theoretical position that I have tried to sketch out, one would have clearly to distinguish psychological from social pathologies and above all be cautious if one wanted to see one as an indicator or even a cause of the other.

Translated by Joseph O'Neil and Elliott Schreiber

8

How Can the Mind Participate
in Communication?

I

Within the communication system we call society, it is conventional to assume that humans can communicate. Even clever analysts have been fooled by this convention. It is relatively easy to see that this statement is false and that it functions only as a convention and only within communication. The convention is necessary because communication necessarily addresses its operations to those who are required to continue communication. Humans cannot communicate; not even their brains can communicate; not even their conscious minds can communicate. Only communication can communicate.

I would like to counter any and all doubts with the following: we have absolutely no idea how to comprehend that conscious minds can bring about communication. Neurophysiological studies, difficult enough in themselves, are not very helpful in terms of the mind. We no longer assume, as did the ancient Indians, that we can alter conditions by concentrating. The more common idea that the mind effects physical behavior or even communication is equally mysterious. The assumption that this occurs is nothing more than an observer's causal attribution. We have to start any clarification with the observer.

Once this is recognized, what follows is the question whether and—if the answer to that is affirmative—how the mind participates in communication. The fact that the mind does participate is undisputed, since communication could not exist without the mind, just as life could not exist without a molecular organization of matter. But what is participation?

Humans are living organisms developed on the basis of living cells. Even cells, as an indispensable foundation of life, are operationally isolated; that is to say, they are "autopoietically" organized.[1] The same is true of autopoietic systems of higher orders, that is, of organisms that are capable of exchanging cells in their own autopoiesis. This very isolation can be demonstrated in the brain. The brain can be stimulated by an extremely small amount of external impulses, but only internal changes are available for its own operations, and it cannot initiate any contacts with its environment through nerve impulses, whether as input or output. (There are no nerves in its environment that could take up and transmit such impulses.) Countless independent systems are at work within humans that determine, through their own structures, what operations will be carried out. They are, however, interdependent.

In the same way, what we experience as our own mind operates as an isolated autopoietic system.[2] There is no conscious link between one mind and another. There is no operational unity of more than one mind as a system, and whatever appears as a "consensus" is the construct of an observer, that is, his own achievement.[3] Even contemporaneous alertness or contemporaneous transformation of thoughts into thoughts is available only in the form of an operation internal to the mind and is based on the isolation of the system, an indispensable condition of its possibility, its autonomy, and its structural complexity. The mind cannot consciously communicate. It can imagine that it is communicating, but this remains an imagination of its own system, an internal operation that allows the continuation of its own thought process. This is not communication.

I hope to have made clear that my argument rests on the level of factually actualized operations. The initial (system-transcending) assumption is that *cognition* must be understood as a recursive processing of symbols (however they are materialized) in systems isolated by the conditions of the connectability of their own operations (be they machines, in the sense of artificial intelligence; cells; brains; consciously operating systems; or communication systems).[4] The question of what an observer observes and with what causal assumptions he calculates effects on causations is a completely different matter. This can be answered only by an investigation of the observer.

Aside from the idiosyncrasies of certain observers and aside from society's determination of who can be made responsible for what, who can demand consideration for his sensitivities, and how turn-taking can be managed, aside from all these special assignations of communication on something that can be dealt with as a "person," independently of an interior organization it is absolutely necessary in a theoretical explanation to distinguish clearly between systems of the mind and communicative (social) systems. We are dealing in both cases with structurally determined systems, that is to say, systems that orient each reproduction of their own operations, whatever the external causes may be, on their own structures. In both cases, we are dealing with systems that create differentiations through the realization of their own operations, create boundaries, accumulate their own history (as an observer can verify), and with all this define their own environment. This does not mean that the mind and communication have nothing in common. It is necessary to formulate more precisely how their relationship is to be understood in light of their irrefutable difference.

II

Once it has come into existence, a system of consciousness can be active even without communication. It experiences this and that within itself, observes something, feels itself thinking,[5] and even talks to itself. Communication, on the other hand, can hardly come into being without the participation of the mind. In this sense, the relationship is asymmetrical, however problems of indirect communication, unintentionally one-sided communication, communication with nonlinguistic gestures, and so on, are conceptually assigned. There is no communication without the mind; but: can there be communication without the mind's communicating?

We are faced with the following question: How is communication possible if it has such a fluid, constantly changing foundation? How can communication reproduce itself if it must rely on a multitude of nervously vibrating brains and agitated minds? How can it rely on systems that will realize their own production only through a constant change of conditions, that is, through creating other structures from one moment to the next in order to actualize the next condition?

The initial answer is a postulate: The continuation of communication obviously requires the maintenance of an organization that can cope with this material. It might actually be possible to describe everything that is communicated on the level of mental states (as are all life processes on the level of biochemical changes), with one exception: the autopoiesis of the emerging system; that is, with the exception of what alone can describe what communication (or life) is.

As a consequence of this hypothesis, we can transfer Humberto R. Maturana's concept of the "conservation of adaptation" from biology to sociology.[6] This concept does not contradict the concept of the structurally determined system but is considered complementary to such a system. Only when a system, in its autopoietic reproduction, adapts itself to the field in which it operates can it determine itself through its own structures. And only when it is in contact with its environment through its own structure can it continue its own operations. Reproduction either does or does not take place. Communication either is or is not continued. Whenever it does continue, it remains adapted, no matter how self-dynamically it proceeds. It is not the goal of communication to adapt itself to the respective mind. On the contrary, communication fascinates and occupies the mind whenever, and as long as, it continues. This is not its purpose, not its meaning, not its function. Only, if it doesn't happen, then it doesn't happen.

It is apparently possible to link communication to communication and in so doing to activate the necessary and indispensable states of consciousness, even though the required environment, the systems of consciousness, is made up of highly unstable, self-dynamic, diffuse mental states that (aside from individual consciousness) cannot be hooked up directly to one another. In saying certain things, each communication therefore reduces the possibilities of linkage, but still leaves open, by means of meanings, a wide spectrum of connected communication, including the possibility of negating or reinterpreting the received information or declaring it untrue or unwelcome. The autopoiesis of social systems is nothing more than this constant process of reduction and opening of connective possibilities. It can be continued only if it is already in progress. It can create episodes with a contemplated ending that serve only as a transition to another possibility of communication. Episodes can be determined by purposes (*télé*). Society is purposeless and must be treated in communication as untreatable through communication. It is possible to say: Stop! But the end of society can be brought about only by the end of its nonsocial conditions. Systems of consciousness and systems of communication end when their operations can no longer be continued. Only an observer can talk about a beginning and an end. The observer observes through the use of a distinction. In this case, he distinguishes beginning and non-beginning, or ending and non-ending. A system that observes itself can proceed only in this way. It must make use of a distinction in order to distinguish the end of its distinction. It is possible to stop only in an operative sense. In observation, the end of observation remains a paradox—a reentry of a distinction into itself.[7] It is all the more important that, on the basis of its own operations, a system is able to observe when another begins or ends, free of paradox.

The evolution of social communication is possible only in a constantly operative link with states of consciousness. This link was first achieved through language, then more effectively through writing, and finally through printing. Decisive in this process is not the symbolic character so often claimed for these developments but rather the differentiation of special experiential objects that are either extraordinary or fascinating. They have no similarity to anything else that can be experienced and are constantly in motion or (as in reading) usable only in motion. Language and script fascinate and preoccupy the mind and thereby secure its participation, even though this is in no way required by the internal dynamics of the mind and diversions are always held at the ready. It is possible to describe language and script as symbolic arrangements within this link as long as "symbol" means only that the link of what is separated can be presented within what is separated.[8]

In other words, language and script, along with all their technical developments, guarantee for the communication system what Maturana calls the conservation of adaptation: the constant accommodation of communication to the mind. They define the free space of autopoiesis within the social communication system. Thus the evolution of societal communication has built up an incredibly complex network of contemporaneous communication processes that is completely nontransparent for every communication that takes place within the system. This is also true for every mind that observes communication, whether it participates in it or not. Developments that make this observation easier, such as the "public opinion" created by the mass media or "markets" created by prices, do little to affect the basics of this process. They make one thing possible: a more effective recursivity in the observation of the observation of others.

The relationship of the accommodation of communication to the mind and the unavoidable internal dynamics and evolution of society is also evident in the fact that changes in the forms in which language becomes comprehensible to the mind, from simple sounds to pictorial scripts to phonetic scripts and finally to print, mark thresholds of societal evolution that, once crossed, trigger immense impulses of complexity in a very short time. It took only a few centuries for the effects of the alphabet to become apparent (Havelock 1982). The same is true for the introduction of printing in Europe,[9] and an equally radical change was accomplished with the transmission of printing to other cultures in less than a hundred years (Wood 1985).

In the classical Darwinistic evolutionary scheme, these kinds of radical breaks in continuity are difficult to explain when compared with relatively long periods of only slight structural change. The theory of autopoietic systems provides the foundation for new possibilities.[10] The possibilities for complexity in autopoietic systems are subject to quick and abrupt change when the conditions of their operative and structural linkage with the required environment change; or in our case, when communication's formation of the mind creates new possibilities for itself.

III

The mind thinks what it thinks and nothing else. From the perspective of an observer—either another mind or a communication system that communicates about the observed mind—the mind can be seen as a medium that could accept and transmit a myriad of conditions.[11] The observer can imagine a mind (doing what it does) as freedom, above all as the freedom to allow itself to be influenced. Or it could imagine possible states that the mind could accept or possible processes that it could complete. As a medium, as a freedom, as a modality, as a conjuncture—whatever label is placed on a mind, it is done so by an observer. In doing so, the observer abstracts the fact, either a little or a lot, that the mind in all its states and in all its operations is determined by its own structures. Instead of certain internal links that change from one minute to the next, the observer assumes a more or less loose linkage. In order to assume this, he himself must operate as an internally dynamic and structurally determined system. And this takes time.

The observer can also be identical to the observed system. Another type of observation, one that presumes nonobservation, must be distinguished from states of observation that presume intent for conscious observation, on the one hand, and for communication as an extremely painstaking thematization of the observed object, on the other. Just as visual and auditory perception use light and air precisely because these cannot be seen or heard as media,[12] so communication uses the mind as a medium precisely because communication does not thematize the mind in question. Metaphorically speaking, the mind in question remains invisible to communication. When it becomes visible, it becomes disruptive, just as the strong whoosh and whistle of the air inside a car traveling at high speed disrupt words of communication. The mind functions as a medium when it is assumed that it could take in everything that is said. It is a loosely linked mass of elements with practically no self-determination, a mass that can be impressed with whatever is said or read. In the convergence of loosely and rigidly linked elemental masses the rigid link wins out, just as a foot leaves behind traces in the soft ground. What the mind hears or reads almost necessarily makes an impression at that very moment. Whether it is taken up in memory is another question that presumes a consistency test within the context of a self-determination of the system of the mind and its brain. It is sufficient for the communication process to understand that the mind, virtually helpless, must participate. This leads to the question: How can the mind be a structurally determined system and a medium at the same time? The answer lies in the evolutionary acquisition of language.

In order to work through to this answer, it must be made clear that the concepts of a (loosely linked) medium and a (rigidly linked) form are correlative concepts. This distinction forms the basis for an observation: A medium is a medium only for a form, seen only from a form (Luhmann 1986b). Mind is no more a medium "in itself" than are light and air. It only allows for the evolution of language (whether it already exists or not and in whatever form), just as language is again a medium in which the mind can imprint concrete expressions by putting together words into sentences and eventually producing a corresponding communication in a way that does not use up the medium.

The law of medium and form states that the more rigid form prevails over the softer medium. This would lead, if it were unconditionally true, to the rapid rigidification of material. For the same reason, forms such as language offer an evolutionary advantage, forms that can also serve as media and that can, on the basis of their considerable discipline (specification of sounds that can be expressed as words, grammatical rules, etc.), de-link elements and be freed for an immense variation of possible links, so that other forms (*prágmata*, complexes of ideas, theories, etc.) can impress themselves. This requires a temporalization of the elements. Sentences that are thought and spoken are only parts of a process that disappear at the moment of their generation. They are constitutively unstable. Their accumulation would very quickly lead to uncontrolled complexity, that is, chaos. Just imagine the noise that would result if spoken words did not fade away but remained audible! A counterselection that prevents forgetting and creates the effects of "time binding" (Korzybski 1958) can take place only because elements are temporalized and reduced to events. This is supported by the neurophysiological device of constant consistency proofs. Finally, after the invention of writing, it can be described and honored with terms like *mnemosýne* and *a-letheia*.

IV

Communication is possible only as an autopoietic system. With the help of language, it reproduces communication from communication while using this structural requisite of its own reproduction to employ the mind as a medium. The mind therefore participates in communication as a structurally determined system and as a medium. This is possible only because the mind and communication, psychic systems and social systems, never fuse or even partially overlap but are completely separate, self-referentially closed, autopoietic-reproductive systems. As I said: humans cannot communicate.

Only with this premise is it possible to determine the specific relevance of the mind for communication in a way that is compatible with other insights of cognitive science. We can then say that the mind has the privileged position of being able to disturb, stimulate, and irritate communication. The mind cannot instruct communication, because communication constructs itself. But the mind is a constant source of impulses for the one or the other turn of the operative process inherent in communication. Only the mind is capable of perception (including the perception of communication). Perceptions remain locked up in the activated mind and cannot be communicated. Reports about perceptions are possible, and, in this way, perceptions can stimulate communication without ever becoming communication, and can suggest the choice of one theme or another. Reports of perception are not perceptions themselves; thus communication operates blindly (the neurophysiology of perception, not to mention the mind, also works constructively and can be stimulated but not instructed by the environment).

Remarkable is the fact that communication can be stimulated only by the mind and not by physical, chemical, biochemical, or neurophysiological operations as such. Radioactivity, smog, and diseases of all sorts may increase or decrease. Such a fact can have no effect on communication if it is not perceived, measured, and made conscious; only then can the fact stimulate the attempt to communicate about it according to the rules of communication. Even in an airplane that is about to crash, it becomes possible to communicate about the impending crash only if it is perceived. The crash itself cannot influence communication; it can only end it.

Systems of the mind and systems of communication exist completely independently of each other. At the same time, however, they form a relationship of structural complementarity. They can actualize and specify only their own structures and thus can change only themselves. They use each other for a reciprocal initiation of these structural changes. Systems of communication can be stimulated only by systems of the mind, and these in turn are extremely attracted to what is conspicuously communicated by language. My argument is as follows: the independence of each closed system is a requirement for structural complementarity, that is, for the reciprocal initiation (but not determination) of the actualized choice of structure.

We see that communication systems exist (for an observer) in a highly complex environment, but this environment, to use the neurophysiological analogy, can effectively stimulate, and thereby influence, only a very small part of its possibilities. Apparently, then, no system could observe its environment (or more generally, develop cognition) if it had to ward off every event in its environment with an internal state. The lack of connectability between operations assumes a distinct limitation of sensibility toward outside events (Roth 1986). It is possible to recognize a double filter, a double structural selectivity of autopoietic systems. Their sensibility is limited to a narrow spectrum of possible stimuli, and it is precisely in this area that their own operations are organized in a manner that is unspecific as to stimuli. Communication operates with an unspecific reference to the participating state of mind; it is especially unspecific as to perception. It cannot copy states of mind, cannot imitate them, cannot represent them. This is the basis for the possibility of communication's building up a complexity of its own and refining itself to such an extreme that it would be highly unlikely to reproduce itself without being adapted to an environment it cannot know.

It is now worth considering to what extent this theory is accurate, a consideration that leads back to an evolutionary-theoretical mode of observation. There certainly exists (at least among beings capable of speech) a communication based on speechless, mutual experience, that is to say, based on a representation understood by all participants. Such communication is experienced in this way; for example, when pedestrians move out of each other's way, and everyone can see that the other sees that the situation requires such a move. Maturana might already have called this "language" (1982, 258ff.). There is still a very close bond to the reciprocal-reflexive perception of perceptions. Important evolutionary steps take place from here to oral communication and to writing, to alphabetic scripts, and to printing, steps that differentiate the social communication system more and more regarding the simultaneous processes of the mind's perception and deduction. Communication is made all the more possible if we are not in the position of simultaneously perceiving what others are perceiving, and in this way we are independent of others' perceptions or failures to perceive that we perceive what we perceive. This progress in no way replaces older forms of oral or even speechless communication. Evolution allows for the side-by-side existence of early and late and also allows a refinement and functional specification of older forms of communication. We are certainly more adroit in questions of sexuality than our ancestors were before the invention of language and writing, even though we solve the related coordination problems in a nonwritten way.[13]

V

The interaction between systems of the mind and systems of communication is not realized in the creation of a supersystem that could accomplish operations integrating the conscious and communicative operations according to the structural determinations of both systems.[14] Instead, systems of the mind are capable of observing communicative systems, and communicative systems are able to observe systems of the mind. In order to be able to say this, we need a concept of observation that is not psychically conceived, that is, related exclusively to systems of the mind.

Observation is introduced here as a theoretical concept of difference. Observation is making a distinction.[15] An operative foundation, whether of the mind or of communication, is not crucial for this definition, but it does assume that observation can be accomplished as an operation and as such is itself an operation (that is, it can observe itself only with the help of another operation).

Operations of the mind and of communication proceed blindly. They do what they do. They reproduce the system. Meaning comes into play only on the level of observation, with all the provisions demonstrated by logic and hermeneutics: with the ability to negate (as distinguished from the ability to affirm); with the ability for logical modalization, for a simultaneous presentation of other possibilities and, building on this, for modalities such as necessity, impossibility, and contingency; with temporal orientations that can describe, with the help of the distinction between future and past, what happens in the operative present and what differentiates the system from its contemporary environment; and last but not least, with concepts of causality. All this does not exist if an observing system does not give these to itself. Everything that functions as a unity functions in this way only through its observer. Whenever we think or say, "There is 'a' . . . , there is a thing, there is a world," and in so doing mean more than simply, "There is something that is the way it is," an observer is involved, and the next question is not "What is there?" but rather "How does an observer construct what he constructs in order to be able to connect further observations?"

The consequences for cognitive theory that can be deduced from this distinction between operations and observations cannot be pursued further here.[16] Of importance for the analysis of the relationship between the mind and communication is the fact that the separation of these systems apparently assumes a reintegration on the level of observation, whereby observations necessarily remain separate empirical operations that can proceed either consciously or communicatively but are logically powerful enough to be able to reintroduce this distinction in the form of a reentry into their own system (Spencer Brown 1979).

What could be called "meaning," namely, a contemporaneously available excess of references within the operations that force selection, seems to be evaluated from a rudimentary ability to observe (Luhmann 1995b, 55ff.; Luhmann 1987a). Meaning pulls a net of possibilities over current operations and allows it to understand itself as a selection of . . . , both for conscious and for communicative operations. Without a meaningful ability to distinguish (something that in every operation includes a concurrent negation of others), the autopoietic systems of the mind and of communication would not have been able to exclude each other, because they would not have been able to distinguish themselves from each other. For this reason, the possibility of self-observation remains a component of the autopoiesis of psychic and social systems that cannot be eliminated. It is carried from thought to thought and from communication to communication and in the process prevents any overlapping of operations and constitutes both systems as closed in themselves.

VI

The more radically the mind is understood as the subject, the more difficult it becomes to understand how another subject, an "alter ego," can be constituted. In itself, so to speak, as the center of its own thought processes, the mind finds only itself, but no other mind. How then can it arrive at the idea that there are similar phenomena outside itself?

The Kantian solution is based on a *petitio principii*. We recognize the similarity of our own mind to other minds and then proceed from there. This solution has been taken up in "radical constructivism." The recognitive subject constructs an analog to itself with slightly altered structures and perspectives and thereby creates the chance for a double proof of reality from its own and from a foreign perspective (Glasersfeld 1985, 22ff.). But how can a mind arrive at such an idea except by perceiving an analog to itself by itself? How can it arrive at the idea that an "interior" exists within the other that is similar to one's own "interior," and that this "interior" is different from other systems? How can a completely different perspective be incorporated into this analogy? Finally, how is it that this has been going on for thousands of years with a stupendous regularity in all "normal" people?

I would like to replace this analogy theory with a construction founded in difference theory. The mind does not arrive at an analogy through another, similar case. It can take part in communication only if it can distinguish between utterance and information. An utterance is chosen from various behaviors; information is chosen from various facts; and communication combines the two into one event (Luhmann 1995b, 137ff.). The distinction between utterance and information is constitutive for all communication (as opposed to simple perception) and is therefore a requirement for participation. For example, it is necessary to address one's own utterances to the person sending utterances and not to the information. This can certainly be done, and mastery of this distinction can be achieved without knowing any details about the person for whom the utterance is intended. This distinction becomes important in actual participation in communication. The distinction between persons and things or subjects and objects condenses from this primary distinction. Only with the mastery of this semantic is it possible to arrive at the idea of an analogy between one's own and foreign minds. As long as mastery is not attained (or at least not with today's precision), then the boundaries of the social communication system will be drawn differently than they are today. They might include plants and animals, the deceased, ghosts, and gods and might exclude more distant humans, depending on the extent to which socialization can suggest possibilities of communication to the mind.

There is no doubt that direct perception, including the perception of the perceptions of others, plays a part in this matter. It is impossible, however, to perceive how others perceive; one can perceive only the fact that they do so. We have no access to biochemical or neurophysiological processes or to processes of the minds of others, except in the construction of an observer. A difference between persons and objects must always be constituted first, and for this to occur, participation in communication becomes indispensable.

The detour via communication, the participation in a completely different operating system, and the attractiveness of the constitutive difference of this system are all critical for the constitution of an alter ego. The theory offered here is based on distinctions and not on unity or similarities. This is compatible with the theory of self-referential and closed systems on the level of systems theory and with a constructivist approach on the level of cognitive theory. In social theory, both the primacy of language theory and the concept of intersubjectivity must be abandoned and replaced with the concept of a self-referential and closed system of social communication.

VII

Finally, it remains to be explained how it is that the social communication system is pervaded by the idea that humans can communicate or even that the individual can communicate with society.

My point of departure is the same: no system can effect its own operations outside its own boundaries. Every expansion of the operative possibilities, every increase in complexity, therefore means *eo ipso* the expansion of the system. We can postulate that no system is able to use its own operations to establish contact with its environment. This would require that operations take place at least in part, with one end, so to speak, outside the system. No brain can use nerve impulses to search for other nerve impulses outside the brain. No mind can operatively think outside itself, although it can certainly think of something else within itself. No societal system can communicate with its environment.[17]

For the classical theme of "individual and society," a concept must be found that does not rely on any internal operations of the system in question, that is, neither on conscious thought nor on communication. I have suggested designating this operative and structural link an interpenetration—not a terribly fortunate terminological choice, and one that still requires some explanation.[18] "Interpenetration" does not refer to a comprehensive system of coordination or to an operative process of exchange (something that would require being able to talk about inputs and outputs in this sense). "Interpenetration" can only mean: the unity and complexity (as opposed to specific conditions and operations) of the one is given a function within the system of the other. The way in which this occurs can be demonstrated only in the structures and operations of each individual system; it could not occur otherwise. Interpenetration therefore takes a different form in systems of the mind than in systems of communication.

Systems of the mind are socialized by interpenetrations with social systems. This concept requires a fundamental rethinking of the classical sociological theory of socialization, all the way from foreign socialization to self-socialization, but remains to be taken up elsewhere.[19] Communication systems experience interpenetration by considering the personal dynamics of humans in their physical and mental (including the mind) dimensions. I call this (again with reference to Parsons) "inclusion." The terminology and the valid rules of attribution vary with the evolution of each social system. Even simple societies form ideas (in some cases with a very restrictive execution, in other cases with a very broad one) about people or analogous communication partners (Cazeneuve 1958; Hallowell 1960). Very early on, concepts like that of the soul existed to identify people before and after death. Up until the early modern period, personhood remained an attribute mostly for legal relationships (but also relevant for existence as *civis* in a society). As an attribute, it assumes the power to control; that is, it assumes property and freedom. Subjects are spoken of to define the self-referential foundation of the cognitions of the mind by the mind and thus (in a doctrine that rapidly became problematic) to mark the social extraterritoriality of knowledge as distinct from what could for some time still be called *opinio* or common sense.[20] Only in the eighteenth century was the concept of the individual tailored to persons, a refinement that transformed the concept of person at the same time. These kinds of semantic changes allow us to see a clear reaction to structural changes in society and to a consequence of printing, the new societal relevance of a "reading public." Here we can do no more than point out conceptual prerequisites for an investigation of the structural and societal foundations of changes within the terminology of inclusion.

Everyone knows, of course, that the word "human being" is not a human being. We must also learn that there is nothing in the unity of an object that corresponds to the word. Words such as "human being," "soul," "person," "subject," and "individual" are nothing more than what they effect in communication. They are cognitive operators insofar as they enable the calculation of continued communication. They have limited connectability and therefore have a potential for distinction and definition. The unity that they represent owes its existence to communication. This is not to say, of course, that there is nothing else but communication. However, the cognitive style of "What?" questions must be changed to that of

"How?" questions. The unity of what is to be asked with a "What?" question is always a product of the system that asks the question. It is therefore necessary to know first how it is that the question came to be asked. The system, whether a psychic or social one, asks how it asks about what is as it is. But even this statement is naturally nothing more than a communicative maneuver of redirecting communication. I don't know if I mean what I say. And if I knew, I would have to keep it to myself.

Translated by William Whobrey

PART IV

CODA: "NOT IN FRANKFURT"

I See Something You Don't See

The topic of this conference, the relevance of the Frankfurt School, is understood by most participants as a summons to dissect this school's texts—regardless of whether they constitute a living or an already dead body. I will not dispute the right to such a procedure, either directly or indirectly. My contribution, however, is grounded in another approach to the topic. My impression is that European habits of thought should be put to the test in a much more radical way than simply in the form that has found a very special expression in Frankfurt. It seems to me to be no coincidence that neither in Frankfurt nor elsewhere has an even moderately adequate understanding of modern society been attained, which could be attributed to certain remnants of the old- or new-European tradition that exert an influence even if one formulates one's thoughts from the position of a "critique of society." Above all, the usual academic epistemology, together with what has been rediscovered in approximately the last two decades under the name of "praxis," shares important premises with the European tradition. One may, especially in Frankfurt, affect stances that range from critical to desperate; but that could merely be a symptom of the fact that more radical interventions into received thought are necessary. A commentary solely upon the thought signed "Frankfurt School" would probably miss the level on which a critique should be mounted today. I will therefore begin with a critique of the ontological presuppositions of knowledge.

Ontology is here understood to mean that an observer operates with

the distinction being/nonbeing and with the help of this distinction designates what he deems relevant, connectable, in short: "being" [*seiend*]. To
designate being [*Sein*], such an observer has only one logical value at his
disposal, a designation value, to adopt Gotthard Günther's formulation.
He needs the second value only to control his observations, to reflect, to
unmask errors. Bivalent logic consequently comprises an apparatus that is
specific to observation; that is to say, for such an observer, the negative has
no correlate in reality. The possibility of negation serves merely to disavow
his own operations of observation, operations that factually run as they do
regardless of whether they lead to true or false results.

As long as there is one such observer, several observers are in the same
situation. They can point out errors to each other; that is to say, they can
break through the operative indistinguishablity of recognition and error.
They can learn with one another because they all have only one value at
their disposal to designate reality, and they stand, as it were, under com-
pulsion to agree. Accordingly, ontology limits the observation of observers
to two functions: critique and learning. There is only one world for the observers, even if they observe one another—and hence there is perpetual
conflict among them.

In the late phase of this ontological thought, this presupposition was
once again split by the distinction objective/subjective. Knowledge is objective if all observers agree about it. One can hence ignore the differences
among the observers. One need observe not the observers but rather only
reality itself, in order to recognize what the observers are observing. This
does not hold for subjective knowledge. Here, one must observe the observer to recognize what he can and cannot observe. As is known, Hegel already found such a "diremption" [*Entzweiung*] to be unsatisfactory and attempted to overcome it through a historical logic. The neocybernetics of
the theory of observing systems solves the problem in another way, namely
by transferring all knowledge onto the level of the observation of observers.

Now, whether one prosecutes ontology partially or fully, whether,
with the help of the distinction objective/subjective, one grants its validity
only on one side of this distinction or grants it no validity at all, this tradition is in any case recognizable today as a specific historical "form."

What Jürgen Habermas views as the philosophy of modernity has
not freed itself from those premises, despite his insistence on "postmetaphysical thought." It has only proceduralized those premises. The observ-

ers develop methods and procedures in order to come to an agreement. They restrict their conflict of opinions to argumentation. They subordinate themselves to the norm of insight that is to be reached jointly. That defines rational communication for them. And if they do not in practice reach their goal of agreement, they nevertheless have to want to reach it—otherwise, they do not conduct the kind of discourse demanded from them by a normative concept of rationality. They act, I would now say, under the assumption that they live in one and the same world and that it is a matter of reporting in accord about this world. Thereby, however, they are nothing but victims of the bivalence of their apparatus, the ontological structure of their primary distinction. Only for this reason is nonconflictual agreement a condition of rationality for them.

Must that be so? And must we think in this way in modern society at the end of this century?

Jean-François Lyotard has already protested against this way of thinking. In his view, there is no unified account, but rather each account produces a difference. It is merely unfortunate that he has labeled this insight "postmodern," when it presumably indicates precisely the epistemology that enables modern society to describe itself.

Already in the eighteenth century, a century of the incipient self-description of modern society, one finds starting points for a very different style of observation, first in the novel. The novel enables the reader to observe something that the heroes of the novel—consider *Pamela*—cannot observe. Romanticism thereupon devises a style that relies on the reader's *not* believing what the immediate description sets before him. With Marx, this technique of observation is transposed to social-scientific analysis. Marx sees through the delusive coherence of capitalism and makes this insight the basis of a critique of political economy. One need only mention Freud in order to recognize the breadth and explosive force of this way of observing. However, the problem is still not envisioned with sufficient clarity, and is dampened down in part through dialectics, in part through therapeutics, in part quite simply through sociological arrogance. Social class, therapist, free-floating intelligentsia—one continues to search for a position of observation that explains to oneself and to others their inability to see and that thereby places within reach knowledge of the world about which one can ultimately agree. And how else is one to get up the courage needed to revolutionize society or to therapeutically heal people? The practical interests inhibit the observation and description of the new way of observing; and William James alone drew attention to precisely this fact in a little-noticed lecture, "On a Certain Blindness in Human Beings" (James 1995 [1912]).

If the official academic epistemology takes no notice at all, up to this very day, of what is taking shape here, this is to be attributed not least of all to the insufficiencies of the formulation of this alternative project that is "critical of ideology." In the meantime, however, neocybernetic systems theory is working on a theoretical design with a much more radical starting point. The overall problematic is transferred by authors such as Heinz von Foerster, Humberto Maturana, and Ranulph Glanville onto the level of observing systems. Reality is only what is observed. But in contrast to the subjective deviation of idealism, the empirical observation of empirical observers is essential for what is ultimately accepted as reality.

In this context, an abstraction of the concept of observation is first presupposed. Observation is the use of a distinction to designate one and not the other side. To draw a distinction is to mark a border, with the consequence that one can reach one side from the other only by crossing the border. Spencer Brown calls this "form." Since the use of a distinction is the presupposition of every observation, this distinction is itself not distinguishable in its operative use (although, on logical grounds that have yet to be clarified, there is also discussion of distinctions that distinguish themselves or that designate themselves). The distinction that is operatively used in observation but not observable is the observer's blind spot. Formulated in logical terms, the observer is the excluded middle of his observation; he is not the "subject" but rather the "parasite" (Serres) of his observation.[1] One can accordingly see what he cannot see if one merely asks about which distinction he is using—hence, for the ontologist, the distinction between being and nonbeing; for the moralist, the distinction between good and bad; or for Habermas, the distinction between technology and interaction, system and lifeworld, and so on. However, the difference between systems theory and the Marx/Freud-syndrome [critique of ideology] lies in the fact that the concept of observation is used universally and includes itself. Even distinctions such as operation/observation or system/environment function, when used, as the blind spot of the knowledge built upon them; and the question is only which theoretical apparatus can, not eliminate, but endure this insight into its own blindness.

As long as an epistemology only takes account of the immediate, simple observer, and also makes no exception for itself, the world remains the condensate of experiences that can be repeated. The reflection of this experience takes the form of ontology. It reckons with a univalent reality; additionally, though, on the level of recognition, it reckons with the possibility of exposing deceptions, of correcting errors. Appearance and deception are consequently aspects of an ontologically conceived world. That does not exclude an observation of other observers, but it can only serve to confirm them or convict them of an error. One then demands of them that they correct their (false) opinions, if necessary supported by the normative claim that the knower should bow to the correct knowledge and see his mistakes.

Second-order cybernetics, the cybernetics of observing observers, leads to a thorough shifting of this disposition. It grasps all observation, even its own, as being dependent upon distinction. It must withhold forcing its own distinctions upon the observed observer. It therefore does not normalize its behavior with regard to a truth that is to be "intersubjectively" ascertained or with regard to ultimately rational grounds for judging actions. It instead reckons with the fact that, in a society that continually enables an observation of observations, ultimately stable "eigenvalues" (David Hilbert, Heinz von Foerster) arise that are no longer varied with further observation. How this concept, taken from mathematical logic, functions in the area of cognition has not been sufficiently clarified theoretically; at any rate, during the perception of others' perceptions, such eigen-states continually arise—otherwise, the coordination of human behavior would constantly fail.

With the help of this second-order cybernetics one can also understand how the distinction between subject and object comes about, namely, not on the basis of ontic, exceptional qualities of human consciousness, not on the basis of corresponding empathy and analogical inferences, but rather by sheer virtue of the fact that operations of "subjects" are often best understood if one takes them to be induced by observation, that is, unleashed by the observed object itself functioning as observer. The distinction subject/object is consequently introduced neither naturally nor through transcendental theory by way of the self-reflection of consciousness; rather, it is a distinction that proves itself in observational praxis, a distinction that can be applied not only to people but also to animals, as well as to social systems,

perhaps even to electronic machines, *if the complicated, two-termed opera-*
tion of observing observers succeeds.

If one inquires after this concept's forerunners, one has to search not
in epistemology but rather in theology. For Nicholas of Cusa, for instance,
the unity that does not distinguish itself, the unity that even transcends the
distinction between being-distinguished and not-being-distinguished, carries the name of God. But that was already then a rather marginal theology, and Nicholas himself was of the opinion that one should expect it not
of all believers but rather only of specially prepared spirits. Besides, God
was naturally a term of unity, though one that could only be grasped with
terms of difference from below, as it were. By contrast, neocybernetics suggests that one renounce ultimately foundational unities and that one grasp
cognition (or action, design, control, etc.) as a processing of differences.

If one takes such considerations as a basis—and I naturally cannot
fully elaborate them here, but merely present them—what consequences
are there for judging the so-called Frankfurt School and also Jürgen Habermas's theory of communicative action that follows upon it?

First, it is simply necessary to contest that they represent the philosophical discourse of modernity at all. This contestation does not rely on
the absurd thesis of a postmodern age. Disputes of this sort are the product of literary inbreeding. One need only cast a glance at the structural continuities of modern society, at the dependence of the economy upon money,
at the intensity of scientific research, at the positivity of law that remains
indispensable, at the differentiation of intimate relations, at state-related
politics, at the so-called mass media, to see that there can be no talk of a
transition to a postmodern society. What has been concluded appears instead to be a transitional semantics that had to leave behind the old world
of aristocratic societies but could not yet observe and describe modern society; rather, out of this inability, it had to create a project of the future. I
mean the semantics of the Enlightenment, the ideas of the French Revolution, as well as the technical-economic optimism of progress of the nineteenth century. This transitory semantics is obviously exhausted, as can be
clearly gathered precisely from the convulsions, but also from the counterfactual obstinacy, of the Frankfurt School. The occupation with its own
history or the rediscovery of marginal classical authors such as Sorel, in
short, the occupation with texts rather than with realities, the description of

others' descriptions—all of this fits into the picture of a tradition of thought unable to see what possibilities today's society offers for self-description.

The distinction, above all, between affirmative and critical, a distinction so beloved in Frankfurt, misses the connection to what offers itself to observation. It is a specific case of blindness, for it excludes the possibility that what has become realized as society gives cause *for the worst fears, but cannot be rejected*. This holds if one considers the evolutionary improbability of supporting structures—to name but a few: the autonomy and reciprocal dependence (carried to an extreme) of function systems; grave ecological problems; the short-term nature of tenable perspectives in the economy and in politics.

Finally, one will be allowed to inquire as to the foundations of the emphasis that, if no longer subject-theoretical, is at least humanist. Apparently one requires this engagement in order to make normative claims plausible. The theory sides with the human to join the latter in battle against enemy forces. But isn't this human merely an invention of this theory, merely a veiling of this theory's self-reference? If he or she were meant as an empirical object (with the name of subject), the theory would have to declare who, then, is meant, for obviously it cannot send five billion humans, who at the same time are living and acting, on a discursive search for good grounds. Not only the length of this process of searching, and the conditions of "bounded rationality," but already the sheer simultaneity of behavior would doom such a project. One cannot idealize sociality without taking account of time.

These are very rough arguments whose details certainly need fine-tuning. But a rough survey of the possible positions suffices if one is interested in the question of whether, and how, modern society at the end of this century can achieve a representation of itself in itself (where else?). And, all things considered, my verdict is: not in Frankfurt.

Translated by Joseph O'Neil and Elliott Schreiber

REFERENCE MATTER

Notes

Introduction: The Self-Positing Society

1. The language of "world picture" and "Being" is, of course, taken from Heidegger. See esp. Heidegger 1977.

2. Just as Fichte notes the paradox of counterpositing (his "Second Principle"), so too does he for positing (his "First Principle"). See Fichte 1982, 107.

3. Sklar 1992, 115–16. See also Lyotard 1993, 120–21, and Serres 1982, esp. 76–77.

4. Wittgenstein 1974, 1.1–1.11. All references to Wittgenstein are to paragraph numbers, not page numbers.

5. Upon republishing the essay in 1917, Russell added the following footnote: "Cantor was not guilty of a fallacy on this point. His proof that there is no greatest number is valid. The solution of the puzzle is complicated and depends upon the theory of types, which is explained in *Principia Mathematica*, Vol 1. (Camb. Univ. Press, 1910)" (Russell 1981, 69). On the theory of types, see below.

6. On logicism, see Kline 1980, 216–30. On formalism (and its difference from logicism), see Kline 1980, 245–57. On Hilbert, see Reid 1996.

7. If the barber shaves himself, then he does not shave only those who do not shave themselves; and if he does not shave himself, then he does not shave all those who do not shave themselves. If all rules have exceptions, including the rule that states that all rules have exceptions, then there must be at least one rule that has no exception. On these and similar paradoxes, see Kline 1980, 204–7.

8. Spencer Brown reports that Russell felt the theory of types to have been "the most arbitrary thing he and Whitehead had ever had to do, not really a theory but a stopgap" (Spencer Brown 1979, xiv). Spencer Brown "solves" the problem of paradox by analogy to mathematics. The equation $x^2 + 1 = 0$ produces the paradoxical solution $-1 = +1$ (or, conversely, $+1 = -1$). To avoid this result, the concept of an imaginary number (i) is used, such that the solution to the equation above would be $\pm i$, "where i is a new kind of unity that consists of a square root of minus one." Thus, in math, numbers can be either positive, negative, zero, or imaginary. Spencer

Brown extends this mathematical figure to the domain of logic by stating that "a valid argument may contain not just three classes of statements, but four: true, false, meaningless, and imaginary" (xv). The virtue of imaginary numbers consists in the fact that one can operate with them and solve concrete problems. The same virtue is postulated for imaginary statements in logic (xiii). Ultimately, Spencer Brown equates this imaginary function with time (58–59), which leads to Luhmann's contention that unavoidable, originary paradoxes cannot be solved but are "unfolded" over time. It is the unique task of the social theorist to observe these "unfoldings" within the domain of social systems.

9. Kline, however, sees both the logicist ambition and Gödel's demonstration of the impossibility of that ambition as having been disastrous, for both have separated mathematics from its roots in "nature." See, for instance, Kline's introduction, where words like "tragedy," "disaster," and "intellectual calamity" are sprinkled liberally on nearly every page, and his concluding chapters (Kline 1980, 3–8, 307–54).

10. For Grim on the Liar Paradox, see Grim 1991, 5–47, and on the Paradox of the Knower, 49–69. The Paradox of the Knower states that it can be logically demonstrated that for any system Q', the following three statements, taken together, are inconsistent:

> If something is known to be so, it is so. (4)
>
> (4) is known to be so. (5)
>
> If B is derivable from A in Q', then if A is known to be so, then B is known to be so. (6) (Grim 1991, 51)

11. See also Luhmann's two essays "The Paradox of Form" and "Sign as Form" in Baecker 1999, 15–26, 46–63.

1. The Modern Sciences and Phenomenology

1. ["Die neuzeitlichen Wissenschaften und die Phänomenologie" is a lecture delivered by Luhmann in Vienna on May 25, 1995. The occasion commemorated Husserl's Vienna lectures of May 7 and 10, 1935, entitled "Philosophy and the Crisis of European Humanity" (German text in Husserl 1954a). We follow David Carr's translation (Husserl 1970b) of passages cited by Luhmann from Husserl's lecture, with modifications where noted.—Trans.]

2. Concerning methodological points of view, see de Berg 1994 and de Berg and Prangel 1993.

3. See Parsons 1942a; Parsons 1942b; Parsons 1942c; Gerhardt 1992; Gerhardt 1993.

4. See Parsons 1971, 11.

5. See Lutz 1994.

6. [Luhmann refers here to the designation of "royal and imperial" Austro-

Hungarian institutions as "k.u.k."—"kaiserlich und königlich." This may also be an allusion to Robert Musil's mordant reference to Austria as "Kakanien" in *The Man Without Qualities.*—Trans.]

7. To cite only one book title: Gerhart Schröder, *Logos und List* [Logos and cunning] (Schröder 1985).

8. In contrast to the *Crisis* book, the Vienna lectures only allude to this. See Husserl 1970a, ca. 270ff., esp. 271: "The result of the consistent development of the exact sciences in the modern period was a true revolution in the technical control of nature."

9. This is similar to Lyotard's answer to his own question, "Pouvons-nous aujourd'hui continuer à organiser la foule des évenements qui nous viennent du monde, humains et non-humains, en les subsumant sous l'Idée d'une histoire universelle de l'humanité?" ("Can we today continue to organize the swarm of events, human and inhuman, that come to us from the world by subsuming them under the Idea of a universal history of humanity?") (Lyotard 1985). Cf. also Vattimo 1991, 132.

10. See, above all, Ritter 1969.

11. The drastic character of these formulations is only heightened by the casualness with which they were presented.

12. Thus in Günther 1976.

13. On this, see Winograd and Flores 1987, 7.

14. On this latter point, see the correspondence edited by Richard Grathoff (Grathoff 1978).

15. See Spencer Brown 1979.

16. ["Draw a distinction" is in English in Luhmann's original, as are, in the next paragraph, "marked space" and "unmarked space," terms taken from Spencer Brown.—Trans.]

17. Husserl 1998, 94; for the original, see Husserl 1950 [1913]. Husserl's emphasis.

18. Compare the continuation of these analyses in Husserl 1948 and Merleau-Ponty 1945.

19. Derrida claims to be able to find a similar state of affairs in Kant, and not accidentally in the Third Critique, which completes the transcendental system. The figure of disinterested pleasure is broken down into the bracketing of existential questions (*epoché*), *auto-affection*, *hétéro-affection*, and, for the sake of this difference, *jugement*. See Derrida 1978, 54ff.

20. See Husserl 1928.

21. This is not so new as it might seem here. In Augustinian speculation, too, the present first arises in the reflection of the difference between past and future as something that must first be sought and can then be found in God. See, above all, Book 11 of the *Confessiones*.

22. See the famous footnote 2 on Aristotle and Hegel in *Sein und Zeit* (Heidegger 1949, 432).

23. [Luhmann here refers to Heidegger's notoriously slippery *Holzwege*. Literally, a *Holzweg* is a timber track. Idiomatically, however, to be on a *Holzweg* means to be on the wrong track.—Trans.]

24. On this point, see the review of George Spencer Brown by Heinz von Foerster 1993b, 9–11.

25. Or with regard to objects in general, as Ranulph Glanville seeks to prove (Glanville 1988, esp. 24ff.)

26. ["Cognitive science" is in English in the original.—Trans.]

27. Ruesch and Bateson 1968, 238.

28. It will become evident that, and why, this concept is already being used in the psychiatric sense here.

29. See, as one example among many, Ruesch and Bateson 1968, 253ff.

30. See Bloor 1976 and Barnes 1977. ["Strong programme" is in English in the original.—Trans.]

31. See Günther 1976.

32. Namely, Wasserman 1959. The analyses deal with the shift in the time between Dryden and Shelley from a still cosmologically linked form of mimesis/imitation to a form that is oriented only by self-reference and hetero-reference.

33. See Spencer Brown 1979; von Foerster 1981; Maturana 1982; von Glasersfeld 1987; Glanville 1988; and a good amount of secondary literature in between.

34. [The "angry fairy" (*die böse Fee*), an allusion to the Grimms' "Sleeping Beauty," is the thirteenth "wise woman" who was excluded from the celebration of the birth of the princess and therefore cursed her to prick her finger on a spindle and die.—Trans.]

35. Parsons had already been tinkering with a replacement in order to predict the personal system as a necessary, but not sufficient, component of the coming about of action. In any case, his suggestion of proceeding from the properly formed concept of action, rather than from "facts of consciousness," is also problematic itself. Yet this hardly justifies a return from Parsons to Weber or even to Kant, that is, to the subject. For one would thereby fall into familiar difficulties that one had believed to be long since overcome.

36. For such an attempt, see Luhmann 1995b. Also see von Foerster 1993a, with the thesis "Communication is recursivity," which establishes everything that comes after.

37. George Spencer Brown, referring to the reliably calculable operations of arithmetic and algebra, speaks of "unresolvable indeterminacy" (Spencer Brown 1979, 57).

38. As an application to a current problem, see Luhmann 1986c. See also Luhmann and De Giorgi 1992.

39. See Lawson 1985. See also Deleuze 1969, where Deleuze replaces the unity of the transcendental subject with the paradox of the unity of two or more rows,

wherein the row "subject" and the row "object" would be only one example among many.

40. See Smithson 1989.

41. See "Deconstruction as Second-Order Observing," Chapter 4 in this volume.

42. Cf. Herbst 1976, 88, which supposes mutual implications of primary distinctions of this kind.

43. See Schütz 1932.

44. To take a formulation from Jean Paul's "Kampanertal." See Jean Paul 1924.

45. ["Without the attitude" is in English in the original.—Trans.]

46. See the excursus on the metaphorics of theoretical explanations in Hesse 1966, 157ff.

47. This example and more from the field of modern art are in Baldwin, Harrison, and Ramsden 1994.

2. The Modernity of Science

This essay originally appeared as "Die Modernität der Wissenschaft," chapter 10 of Niklas Luhmann, *Die Wissenschaft der Gesellschaft* (Frankfurt a.M., 1990), 702–19.

1. These discussions are not without converging judgments. On this issue, see Berger 1988.

2. See Münch 1984. Münch explicitly discusses the modernity of "occidental" science (see especially 200ff.), but he does so, on the one hand, in terms of the generic concept of culture and, on the other hand, without any reference to the modernity of the social system. What is mentioned here remains nevertheless quotable: "What distinguishes modern occidental science from all other forms of thinking, verifying, experimenting, and solving technical problems, is that it unites, in a way unique only to itself, abstract constructions of concepts and theories, deductive-logical evidence, rational-empirical experiments, and practical technology" (200). However: one can speak of "deductive-logical" only with regard to postulates of the theory of science, not in view of the practice of scientific research itself.

3. Cf. Folkers 1987.

4. [In the entire volume of *Die Wissenschaft der Gesellschaft*.—Ed.]

5. A recent overview can be found in Fuller 1988, 65ff.

6. We are leaving aside the complication in the text and are noting it only in the footnote: even observing is itself an operation; it therefore always enacts something that it is unable to distinguish and to designate, unable to "objectify," namely itself. We are calling to mind the thesis of the "blind spot" of all observation.

7. See, for example, Bürger and Bürger 1988; also Hahn 1989.

8. See Günther 1968—which appeared at the beginning of the new excitement.

9. See Luhmann 1990c, 259–67. [See also Chapter 1 of this volume.—Ed.]

10. Husserl 1970a.

11. See in particular Gadamer 1986, especially 337–38. See also Gadamer 1977.

12. See Luhmann 1989b, 70–71.

13. Cf. Habermas 1968.

14. See again Spencer Brown 1979, 56ff., 69ff. Cf. also Miermont 1989.

15. Here we have a problem of the distinction between science and art, which Hegel in his lectures on aesthetics had to tackle as well. As we know, Hegel found a solution in the self-reflection of the distinction between the general and the particular. In our theoretical framework, one would have to take into account various ways of realizing (materializing, imagining) forms.

3. The Paradox of Observing Systems

1. See Löfgren 1988.

2. On this, see Lloyd 1979, esp. 72ff., about the emergence of paradoxes (Zeno) as the by-product of the elaboration of the right way to describe the world. Lloyd's "sociological" explanation points to the Greek culture of public debates and the political need for consensus—and not so much to the phonetic writing that also existed in other countries without leading to science based on observing how observers observe.

3. For references, see Probst 1989.

4. See, for instance, Lando 1545.

5. Munday 1969, A. 3. He adds: "Let no manne thinke then, that I or any other would be so sencelesse, as to hold directly any of these vaine reasons."

6. Even for officers, as recommended by La Noue 1967, 355ff.

7. As in, for instance, "sentences ou propositions qui repugnant aux opinion [*sic*] communes" ("sentences or propositions that are repugnant to popular opinion") (La Noue 1967, 355), or "inopinatam atque alienam à communi sensu, vulgataque consuetudine sententiam" ("An unexpected opinion which is different from what is commonly believed and from what is popular custom") (Lemnius 1574, 416).

8. This may remind the reader of Derrida's analysis of the "parergon" in Kant's *Kritik der Urteilskraft*. And in fact, there are close similarities between parerga and paradoxa, both being forms that dissolve the distinction between inside and outside by indicating that a form (be it an aesthetic form or a cognitive or conceptual form) has to include the exclusion of the outside. See Derrida 1978, for example: "Il y a du cadre mais le cadre *n'existe pas*" ("There was a frame but it no longer exists") (93).

9. See Bernard 1759, Morellet 1778, and Schkommodau 1972.

10. See Ruesch and Bateson 1968 for an early statement of what now seems to be the common sense of the therapeutic profession. The therapeutic profession would then distinguish between normal and pathological confusion of levels and see a

need for therapeutic intervention only in pathological cases. But this again is a frame that makes sense as long as there are limits to what people or insurance companies are willing to pay for.

11. We may also think of Derrida's *différance*. See Luhmann, "Deconstruction as Second-Order Observing," in this volume (Chapter 4).

12. See, among others, the contributions to the section on "Meaningfulness and Confirmation" in Feigl and Sellars 1949.

13. See Hahn 1987.

14. See Spencer Brown 1979 and Kauffman 1987.

15. This is a generalization and formalization of Fritz Heider's distinction, restricted to the field of perception, between medium and thing. A very similar distinction, used by cyberneticians and information theorists, would be variety and redundancy.

16. See Luhmann et al. 1990.

17. See Meyer 1990.

18. So, at the end of his text, Spencer Brown comes to the conclusion that was implied (but not explicable) at the beginning: "An observer, since he distinguishes the space he occupies, is also a mark" (Spencer Brown 1979, 78). And "is also a mark" means "can be observed."

19. In the sense that Hobbes explained in his *Leviathan*, chap. 16: "So that a *Person*, is the same that an *Actor* is, both on the Stage and in common Conversation; and to *Personate*, is to *Act*, or *Represent* himselfe, or an other" (Hobbes 1968, 217).

20. See Derrida 1978 again, and also Dünkelsbühler 1991.

21. See Colie 1966, Malloch 1956, McCanles 1966, and Schulz-Buschhaus 1991.

22. See Lawson 1985.

23. "Polycontextural" in the sense used by Günther 1979a. The term "contexture" corresponds to a transclassical logic that admits transjunctional operations that can surpass "tertium non datur."

24. See "Deconstruction as Second-Order Observing," in this volume (Chapter 4).

25. This is the organizing idea of the lexicon *Geschichtliche Grundbegriffe* (Brunner, Conze, and Koselleck 1972–92).

26. For the very different Jewish tradition, see Atlan 1993.

27. Or a second-order semantics in the sense of MacCannel and MacCannel 1982.

28. See Esposito 1993.

4. Deconstruction as Second-Order Observing

This essay is a revised version of a paper presented at the Commonwealth Center seminar "Cultural Change and Environmental Issues."

1. See Dumont 1966, 107–8; Dumont 1983, 214–15, 243–44 and passim.

2. See Derrida 1972b, 56–57.

3. The sociocultural *influence* on sexual inclinations of bodies is, of course, a well-known fact. See Schelsky 1955.

4. For a recent discussion see Rorty 1980.

5. Recent feminist readings of Freud suggest indeed that women have a less imposing and more complete sexuality, that they are less in need of maintaining a visible superiority—and therefore less in danger of deconstruction. See Mitchell 1975; Kofman 1980; and also Cixous 1975 for a Derridean approach that finds the solution in the undeconstructible bisexuality of women. Feminist observers might even go on, by *différance*, and insinuate that the protection against homosexual stimulation is needed for maintaining the hierarchical opposition of male and female.

6. But see also the purely technical advice given by Hogarth 1955 to reconstruct the "inner eye" of an object by surface lines (preferring serpentine-like lines) and to match the internal surface and the external surface. See Glanville 1988, a collection of papers originally published in English but available only in book form in German.

7. See Wellbery 1992.

8. Derrida 1985, 7.

9. Derrida 1972a, 77; here and elsewhere, unless stated otherwise, all translations are my own.

10. See Gumbrecht 1997.

11. See Bateson 1971, 271–72, 315, 489.

12. See Spencer Brown 1979.

13. As deconstruction has to do as well, "depuis un certain dehors, par elle inqualifiable, innommable" ("from a certain outside, unqualifiable and nameless in itself"), referring to philosophy by distinguishing it from what it has dissimulated. See Derrida 1972b, 15. See also Derrida's remarks on the possible future of a non-phonetic mathematical notation, published originally in 1968, which could almost be read as a prognosis of Spencer Brown's *Laws of Form* (1979), originally published in 1969: "Le progrès effectif de la notation mathématique va donc de pair avec la déconstruction de la métaphysique" ("the effective progress of mathematical notation goes together with the deconstruction of metaphysics") (Derrida 1972b, 47–48).

14. For the possibility of improving on Derrida by using the ideas of Spencer Brown, see Roberts 1992.

15. Some of the papers in question, and more recent papers, are available in German translation. See von Foerster 1993c.

16. See Günther 1976, 249–328.

17. In deconstruction theory, this reads as follows: "An opposition that is deconstructed is not destroyed or abandoned but reinscribed." See Culler 1982, 133.

18. See Derrida 1967, 41.

19. See Derrida 1972b, 11.

20. See Margolis 1985, 146.

21. I use "frame" in the sense of Erving Goffman. See Goffman 1974.

22. See Spencer Brown 1979, 105.

23. See Erasmus, *In Praise of Folly*, or Thomas More, *Utopia*; then Ortensio Lando, John Donne, and many others. A monographical account is given by Colie 1966.

24. See Holmes 1987 on the political liberalism of the eighteenth century.

25. The time-length of an event in the sense of its specious present remains, of course, an open question. But this has to be decided by an observer or by observing the observer. If the observer concedes enough time for changes (e.g., observing the German reunification), he is in fact observing not an event but a structure (which includes a structured process).

26. See the collection of papers published in German in Maturana 1982, and also Maturana and Varela 1984.

27. This comes very close to an unorthodox theory of decision making, proposed by Shackle 1979.

28. We presuppose here without further ado that "the human being" (in the singular) has been deconstructed anyway.

29. The combination specific/universal refers to the pattern variable of the action theory of Talcott Parsons, and shows up, within this theory, as a distinctly modern type of framing of observations. See Parsons 1960.

30. I underline *empirical* to insist that it is not a transcendental a priori in Kant's sense, based on the distinction (always distinctions!) between the empirical and the transcendental, the realm of causality and the realm of freedom. But it is a *condition of possibility* in Kant's sense, a condition of the possibility of observations.

31. See Luhmann 1990a, 175–90.

32. See Culler 1982, 8; and Culler 1988, 15.

33. See Lawson 1985.

5. Identity—What or How?

1. See Heinz von Foerster's tellingly titled *Observing Systems* (1981).

2. This is also the case with respect to an unproductive debate about "constructivism." See, for instance, Wendel 1989. Whatever its adherents may say, constructivism is obviously a realistic epistemology that uses empirical arguments. Its main thrust is directed only against epistemology's old claim to self-grounding and its forms of externalization: God or the subject. And the result is the thesis of the dependence of all knowledge upon systems with the correlate of a second-order observation, of an observation of observing systems that is likewise always empirically and systematically intended. This does not in any way dispute the relevance of a logical treatment of the problems of self-reference and of paradox *for empirical studies*.

See, for example, Miermont 1989. They exceed only the possibilities of the present study.

3. Here, too, one can refer to Heinz von Foerster. See for example von Foerster 1984, 3ff. A corresponding term first arose to describe the necessity of speaking about language in linguistics. See, for example, Löfgren 1981 and Löfgren 1988.

4. Michel Serres, *Der Parasit*, quoted from the German translation (Serres 1981, 365). Another version of the same matter is the injunctive form in which George Spencer Brown introduces the decisive presupposition of his calculus, namely the instruction "Draw a distinction." He does not write, "Distinguish a distinction," for that would only postpone the problem of beginning. See Spencer Brown 1979, 3.

5. An alternative that has received more recognition lies in distinguishing between being (*Sein*) and what is (*Seiendes*) (things, essences [*Wesen*], species and genera). In this way, however, one cannot arrive at a clear, mutually exclusive relationship between the two sides, and thus one cannot arrive at a form of being (*Form des Seins*), either. Almost necessarily, the distinction between being and what is has to be thought of as a relation of emanation in which being releases what is from itself and in so doing gives being to what is.

6. See Spencer Brown 1979, 3.

7. In order to concretize this, consider certain techniques of meditation.

8. Nicholas of Cusa 1964, 536. It becomes clear at this point that Nicholas meant that this theology was not for unprepared, insecure spirits.

9. See Günther 1980, 140ff.

10. Günther 1979a. One might add many other objections, especially the fact that there is a large number of systems of consciousness, such that the unity of "the" subject cannot be determined (or can be so only in an extraworldly way, or only transcendentally, or only as a regulative usage).

11. In this context see several case studies in Luhmann and Fuchs 1989.

12. As will be easily surmised, we are entering upon a path that Husserl also explored, especially in Husserl 1948. The Husserlian theme refers, however, to the (pre-predicative) *judgment* as an element of logic. We are pursuing the more abstract question of the production of meaningful *identity*.

13. Fritz B. Simon, with reference to Heinz von Foerster, also understands identity as the result of calculating the "eigenvalues" of a system. We wish only to add that the observation and description of this result is dependent upon the distinction identical/nonidentical. See Simon 1988, 99ff.

14. Spencer Brown 1979, 10. Here, $\daleth\daleth \to \daleth$ (condensation) and $\daleth \to \daleth\daleth$ (confirmation) are defined.

15. See Luhmann 1995b, 59ff.

16. See Grice 1975.

17. See Günther 1976–80, especially the contribution "Life as Poly-Contexturality" (Günther 1979a). It should be noted that Günther gives the concept of ontology a meaning different from ours.

18. Spencer Brown 1979, 2 and 5. Notation: ⌐ =

19. This is true most properly for external (sociological) descriptions of this phenomenon via analyses of the function and differentiation of religion. See Luhmann 1977 and Luhmann 1989a.

20. For a more detailed discussion, see Luhmann 1986c, esp. 75ff.

21. Jurists and especially legal philosophers tend to doubt that the code right/wrong has also in this sense to be posited as morally indifferent. But precisely this was the sense of determining law through the function of securing freedom, namely freedom to act irrationally and immorally insofar as this was not prohibited by law itself. And the practitioners of civil disobedience are even of the opinion that acting illegally under certain conditions is a form of gaining moral recognition.

22. Concerning this discussion, see Parsons 1960.

23. See Luhmann 1988a.

24. The metaphor, as is well known, comes from Alfred Korzybski, and is situated in the context of an interest in non-Aristotelian logic. See Korzybski 1958.

25. In this connection (with corresponding claims to a logic suited to describe such systems) see Varela 1979.

26. For clues as to how this could be further elaborated, see Luhmann 1985b, Luhmann 1987b, and Luhmann 1988b.

27. See also Steve Fuller's objections in Fuller 1988, 124ff.

28. Cf. Ashby 1962.

6. The Cognitive Program of Constructivism and the Reality That Remains Unknown

1. As a typical solution, the distinguishing of several levels of language or of cognition has been suggested, with the possibility of "autological" relationships on the higher level. See Löfgren 1988. But this is a transparently stopgap solution, since a level derives its identity only from the fact that there are other levels that can be reached from it.

2. See Bloor 1983, esp. 119ff. This "conventionalism," going back to Poincaré, has become a tradition; it meets with little opposition today since it has become almost a reflex.

3. See Bloor 1983, passim, for example, p. 95.

4. This can be found in the recent publication by Chalmers (1988). The argument presented, however, shows no progress.

5. See Watzlawick 1981; Gumin and Mohler 1985; Schmidt 1987; von Glasersfeld 1987.

6. See Plato, *Thaetetus*, 208C.

7. See, for example, Buffier 1971, 800ff., where this concept is dealt with at length in the "Traité des vérités de conséquences" (not in the "Traité des première vérités").

8. See in this regard, as well as for the limiting cases of universal distinction (nothing is excluded) and elementary distinction (nothing is included), Glanville and Varela 1981. Following Spencer Brown, the authors distinguish inclusion and exclusion by using the concept of form in order to distinguish the act of distinguishing. Their argument corresponds, moreover, exactly to the idea Nicholas of Cusa used to found the *coincidentia oppositorum* and upon it his concept of God beyond all distinctions.

9. See, for example, the "object-psychological" epistemology of Naess 1936, in particular 103ff., where the author demands that all epistemology should be limited to description "of the process in the internal functional space" of an organism. See also p. 105: "The common distinction between 'situation' and 'behavior' is, viewed psychologically, a distinction between two kinds of 'behavior.'"

10. See Maturana 1982, esp. 32ff.; Maturana and Varela 1987, esp. 31ff. See the critical discussion in Roth 1987a on precisely this connection between biological systems theory and epistemology.

11. See Roth 1987b, 419–20.

12. See the contributions of von Foerster 1985b. See also Varela 1984; Roth 1986, esp. 168ff.; Roth 1987c.

13. "The natural world has a small or non-existent role in the construction of scientific knowledge" is claimed, e.g., by Collins 1981, 3. See also Collins 1985. There would be far less controversy if one read the latter work in conjunction with works on brain research and not as an alternative to them. The question is not whether brains *or* language construct the world; the claim is that if it is brains, then it must be language, and vice versa.

14. See, for example, Campbell 1977.

15. With regard to this systems-theoretic use of the concept of redundancy, see Atlan 1979 or Atlan 1984.

16. On closure as "enclosure," see von Foerster 1985a.

17. Subtle analyses of this question are to be found in Tenbruck 1986, esp. 175ff.

18. Of course, these are always the statements of an observation that itself sees more time than the observed system does. An extensive analysis of these questions can be found in Rosen 1985.

19. The same is true for language, and this similarity points to a close evolutionary and even neurophysiological association. On this question see Jerison 1973, esp. 426–27.

20. For greater detail see Luhmann 1995b, 74–75.

21. This is the formulation of von Glasersfeld in his presentation of "radical constructivism" (1987). Maturana also uses such formulations to explain his constructivist position (1982).

22. See von Foerster 1969.

23. See von Foerster 1985a, esp. 205ff.

24. In Maturana's theory the corresponding concept is "conservation of adaptation." See Maturana and Varela 1987, 113–14, or, for greater detail, Maturana 1986a. It is crucial that adaptation can be only preserved, not improved. A system is adapted for the processing of its autopoiesis in its environment or it isn't, and is destroyed. There is no "more or less" in this regard, just as the operations of the system either can take place or cannot take place. Every other judgment is the affair of an observer and can be observed only in an observer.

25. And has been given up today. See, for example, Barnes 1974; Bloor 1976.

26. Quite consistently, Marxists learn about the critique of political economy from Marx; they do not turn to political economy for this. But the result is that the common views of the political economy of Marx's day are discussed with reference to Marx's works, that Marx himself seems like a political economist (not completely without this being his own fault), and that changes in the critique that have occurred over the last 150 years are not sufficiently taken into account.

27. See MacKie 1973, chap. 6, in association with chap. 2.

28. For case studies in this question, see Luhmann 1988b.

29. See Glanville 1984.

30. Rescher 1985, 187, expresses this perspective on perspectivity: "Perspectives are diaphanous, and one tends not to see them as such."

31. See Varela 1975.

32. In this regard, see Luhmann 1987a.

33. Furthermore, what is offered as epistemology in the context of the cognitive sciences is inconceivable without computers—with respect to both research technology and the stimulus of theory. See Varela 1986. This is also true of logical theories and their truth procedures.

34. This is also held by strict constructivists. See, for example, von Glasersfeld 1985, 20–21.

35. See Maturana 1982, 52ff. The literature that follows Maturana uses "parallelion" or "parallelizing," instead of "analogy." See, for example, Hejl 1987.

36. Related to this, but nonetheless to be distinguished from it, are the wellknown attempts of Quine to use the process of learning a language for the elucidation of epistemological questions. See, for example, Quine 1960. See also the less well known ideas of Campbell 1973. The only question dealt with here, however, is the claim that the learning of language is not possible without reference to things of the external world, which means that language can never completely construct reality out of itself.

37. See Luhmann 1995b, 137ff.

38. Here see also Luhmann 1986a.

39. See, for example, Campbell 1970.

40. See Husserl 1954b. See also Whitehead 1954.

8. How Can the Mind Participate in Communication?

1. See Maturana 1982, 138ff., 157ff., 170ff; Varela 1979; Maturana and Varela 1987.

2. See Luhmann 1985a.

3. This is also true when communication communicates, as communication, the observation that consensus is a fact. "Using a metalanguage which is a restriction of his language, L, an observer can say: 'it is a fact that A and B *agree* over T,' and other *observers* may *agree*, in this metalanguage, that 'this *is* a fact.'" This is how Gordon Pask (1981, 1331) formulates the same fact from a somewhat different theoretical basis.

4. The related field of study is now called cognitive science(s). Along with the already cited works of Maturana and Varela, see, above all, McCulloch 1965 and von Foerster 1981. I am concerned in the text with only a small part of this immense field of study of an operative cognitive theory.

5. See Pothast 1987.

6. See Maturana 1986a; Maturana 1986b.

7. See Spencer Brown 1979; Glanville 1984.

8. As in the case of the *symbolon*, the sign of hospitality, *in the hands of the guest.*

9. See Eisenstein 1979; for a rather cursory view, see Ong 1971.

10. See Roth 1982; Maturana 1982; Maturana 1986b.

11. "Medium" here is used in the sense of Heider 1959. One might also think of Plato's well-known wax metaphor in *Theaetetus* 191C and 194C–D, although it is still not clear what else the soul might be (that is, what else besides a container) when the wax inside it is like its heart (a play on the words *kaér/kerós*). The better soul in this case consists of the purer wax, which is better suited to take up forms (194–195).

12. The example is from Heider 1959.

13. Even the use of printed letters or copies of printed originals for sending declarations of love is suspect, but only as a result of the invention of printing and only since about the middle of the seventeenth century. A certain irony lies in relying on printed originals in matters of sexuality, for example, in the "erotic supersystem" as described by Weck-Erlen 1978.

14. This rejects a demanding concept of "spirit," and also rejects what might have been called "intuition" in the Middle Ages.

15. The term is used by Spencer Brown 1979 to denote a beginning: "Draw a distinction." Spencer Brown is very much aware of the immanent duality of this basic operation and differentiates between distinctions and indications.

16. In order to show that things have changed since the advent of classical cognitive theories (including those with a transcendental bent), we now speak of "constructivism," or, with the increased application of artificially supported analyses of empirical conditions, of cognitive sciences.

17. This is, of course, not true for social systems that differentiate themselves

within the society. These systems are able to use their societal constitution to communicate with other social systems (provided they are capable of collective action). For the exceptional theological problems that result from this theory, see Luhmann 1985a.

18. See Luhmann 1995b, 218ff. Historically, this term comes from the theory of general action systems by Talcott Parsons. He discusses the same problem but in the context of a completely different theoretical architecture. See Luhmann 1978.

19. See Gilgenmann 1986.

20. The fusion of these terms was a concern of the eighteenth century. This is especially the case with Buffier 1724.

9. I See Something You Don't See

1. In discussing this lecture, it was pointed out that the manner of observation of a Marx or of a Freud does not proceed arbitrarily but instead feels itself committed to "immanent critique." In the terminology suggested here, that means that the observer is called upon to incorporate himself into the schema of his observation, to include himself as the excluded middle. However, it is surely no coincidence that this figure of inclusion ruins the concept of the subject. In the meantime, this figure has also been much discussed in its logical problematic. What one had hoped for as emancipation toward rational self-determination appears then only as concurrent self-reference, as "self-indication" (Varela 1975), as "reentry" (Spencer Brown 1979). The consequence will thus be less an experience of plenitude than a shifting to transformed distinctions for the further processing of distinctions.

Works Cited

Ashby, W. Ross. 1962. "Principles of the Self-Organizing System." In Heinz von Foerster and George W. Zopf, Jr., eds., *Principles of Self-Organization*, 255–78. New York. (Also in Walter Buckley, ed., *Modern Systems Research for the Behavioral Scientist: A Sourcebook*, 108–18. Chicago, 1968.)

Atlan, Henri. 1979. *Entre le cristal et la fumée*. Paris.

———. 1984. "Disorder, Complexity and Meaning." In Livingston 1984, 109–28.

———. 1993. *Enlightenment to Enlightenment: Intercritique of Science and Myth*. Albany, N.Y.

Baecker, Dirk, ed. 1993. *Kalkül der Form*. Frankfurt.

———. 1999. *Problems of Form*. Trans. Michael Irmscher, with Leah Edwards. Stanford, Calif.

Baecker, Dirk, et al., eds. 1987. *Theorie als Passion*. Frankfurt.

Baldwin, Michael; Charles Harrison; and Mel Ramsden. 1994. "On Conceptual Art and Painting and Speaking and Seeing: Three Corrected Transcripts." *Art-Language*, n.s., 1: 30–69.

Barnes, Barry. 1974. *Scientific Knowledge and Sociological Theory*. London.

———. 1977. *Interests and the Growth of Knowledge*. London.

Bateson, Gregory. 1971. *Steps to an Ecology of Mind*. New York.

Berger, Johannes. 1988. "Modernitätsbegriffe und Modernitätskritik in der Soziologie." *Soziale Welt* 3: 224–36.

Bernard, Jean-Fréderic. 1759. *Eloge d'Enfer: Ouvrage critique, historique et moral*. 2 vols. The Hague.

Bloor, D. 1976. *Knowledge and Social Imagery*. London.

———. 1983. *Wittgenstein: A Social Theory of Knowledge*. London.

Bohr, Niels. 1961. *Atomic Theory and the Description of Nature*. Cambridge, Eng.

Brunner, Otto; Werner Conze; and Reinhart Koselleck, eds. 1972–92. *Geschichtliche Grundbegriffe: Historisches Lexikon zur politisch-sozialen Sprache in Deutschland*. 7 vols. Stuttgart.

Buffier, C. 1724. *Traité des premieres véritéz et de la source de nos jugemens*. Paris.

———. 1971 [1732]. *Cours de sciences sur des principes nouveaux et simples*. Reprint. Geneva.

Bürger, Peter, and Christa Bürger. 1988. *Prosa der Moderne*. Frankfurt.

Campbell, Donald T. 1970. "Natural Selection as an Epistemological Model." In R. Navoll and R. Cohen, eds., *A Handbook of Method in Cultural Anthropology*, 51–85. Garden City, N.Y.

———. 1973. "Ostensive Instances and Entitativity in Language Learning." In W. Gray and N. D. Rizzo, eds., *Unity Through Diversity: A Festschrift for Ludwig von Bertelanffy*, 2: 1043–57. New York.

———. 1977. "Descriptive Epistemology: Psychological, Sociological and Evolutionary." William James Lectures at Harvard University. Manuscript.

Cazeneuve, J. 1958. "La connaissance d'autrui dans les sociétés archaïques." *Cahiers internationaux de sociologie* 25: 75–99.

Chalmers, A. 1988. "The Sociology of Knowledge and the Epistemological Status of Science." *Thesis Eleven* 21: 81–102.

Cixous, Hélène. 1975. "Sorties." In Hélène Cixous and Catherine Clement, *La jeune née*, 114–246. Paris.

Colie, Rosalie. 1966. *Paradoxia Epidemica: The Renaissance Tradition of Paradox*. Princeton, N.J.

Collins, H. 1981. "Stages in the Empirical Programme of Relativism." *Social Studies of Science* 11: 3–10.

———. 1985. *Changing Order*. London.

Culler, Jonathan. 1982. *On Deconstruction: Theory and Criticism After Structuralism*. Ithaca, N.Y.

———. 1988. *Framing the Sign: Criticism and Its Institutions*. Oxford.

Dauben, Joseph Warren. 1990. *Georg Cantor: His Mathematics and Philosophy of the Infinite*. Princeton, N.J.

da Vinci, Leonardo. 1954. *The Notebooks of Leonardo da Vinci*. Trans. Edward MacCurdy. New York.

de Berg, Henk. 1994. *Kontext und Kontingenz: Kommunikationstheoretische Überlegungen zur Literaturhistoriographie mit einer Fallstudie zur Goethe-Rezeption des Jungen Deutschland*. Ph.D. diss., University of Leiden.

de Berg, Henk, and Matthias Prangel, eds. 1993. *Kommunikation und Differenz: Systemtheoretische Ansätze in der Literatur- und Kunstwissenschaft*. Opladen.

Deleuze, Gilles. 1969. *Logique du sens*. Paris.

Derrida, Jacques. 1967. *L'écriture et la différence*. Paris.

———. 1972a. *Marges de la philosophie*. Paris.

———. 1972b. *Positions*. Paris.

———. 1978. *La vérité en peinture*. Paris.

———. 1985. "Letter to a Japanese Friend." In David Wood and Robert Bernasconi, eds., *Derrida and Différance*, 1–5. Coventry.

Dumont, Louis. 1966. *Homo Hierarchicus: Essai sur le systeme des castes*. Paris.

———. 1983. *Essais sur l'individualism*. Paris.

Dünkelsbühler, Ulrike. 1991. "Rahmen-Gesetze und Parergon-Paradox: Eine Übersetzungsaufgabe." In Gumbrecht and Pfeiffer 1991, 207–23.

Eisenstein, E. 1979. *The Printing Press as an Agent of Change: Communications and Cultural Transformations in Early-Modern Europe*. 2 vols. Cambridge, Eng.

Esposito, Elena. 1992. *L'operazione di osservazione: Costruttivismo e teoria dei sistemi sociali*. Milan.

———. 1993. "Ein zweiwertiger, nicht-selbstandiger Kalkül." In Baecker 1993, 96–111.

Feigl, Herbert, and Wilfried Sellars, eds. 1949. *Readings in Philosophical Analysis*. New York.

Fichte, J. G. 1982. *The Science of Knowledge*. Ed. and trans. Peter Heath and John Lachs. Cambridge, Eng.

Folkers, Horst. 1987. "Verabschiedete Vergangenheit: Ein Beitrag zur unaufhörlichen Selbstdeutung der Moderne." In Baecker et al. 1987, 46–83.

Fuller, Steve. 1988. *Social Epistemology*. Bloomington, Ind.

Gadamer, Hans-Georg. 1977. "Theorie, Technik, Praxis." In Hans-Georg Gadamer, *Kleine Schriften*, 4: 173–95. Tübingen.

———. 1986. "Text und Interpretation." In Hans-Georg Gadamer, *Gesammelte Werke*, 2: 330–60. Tübingen.

Gerhardt, Uta. 1992. "Die soziologische Erklärung des nationalsozialistischen Antisemitismus in den USA während des Zweiten Weltkriegs: Zur Faschismustheorie Talcott Parsons." *Jahrbuch für Antisemitismusforschung* 1: 253–73.

———, ed. 1993. *Talcott Parsons on National Socialism*. New York.

Gilgenmann, K. 1986. "Sozialisation als Evolution psychischer Systeme." In H.-J. Unverferth, ed., *System und Selbstproduktion: Zur Erschließung eines neuen Paradigmas in den Sozialwissenschaften*, 91–165. Frankfurt.

Glanville, Ranulph. 1984. "Distinguished and Exact Lies." In R. Trappl, ed., *Cybernetics and Systems Research 2*, 655–67. Amsterdam.

———. 1988. *Objekte*. Berlin.

Glanville, Ranulph, and F. J. Varela. 1981. "'Your Inside Is Out and Your Outside Is In' (Beatles 1968)." In G. E. Lasker, ed., *Applied Systems and Cybernetics*, 2: 638–41. New York.

Goffman, Erving. 1974. *Frame Analysis: An Essay on the Organization of Experience*. New York.

Grathoff, Richard, ed. 1978. *The Theory of Social Action: The Correspondence of Alfred Schütz and Talcott Parsons*. Bloomington, Ind.

Grice, H. Paul. 1975. "Logic and Conversation." In Peter Cole and Jerry L. Morgan, eds., *Syntax and Semantics*, 3: 41–58. New York.

Grim, Patrick. 1991. *The Incomplete Universe: Totality, Knowledge, and Truth*. Cambridge, Mass.

Gumbrecht, Hans Ulrich. 1997. *In 1926: Living at the Edge of Time.* Cambridge, Mass.

Gumbrecht, Hans Ulrich, and K. Ludwig Pfeiffer, eds. 1991. *Paradoxien, Dissonanzen, Zusammenbrüche: Situation offener Epistemologie.* Frankfurt.

Gumin, H., and A. Mohler, eds. 1985. *Einführung in den Konstruktivismus.* Munich.

Günther, Gotthard. 1968. "Kritische Bemerkungen zur gegenwärtigen Wissenschaftstheorie: Aus Anlaß von Jürgen Habermas: 'Zur Logik der Sozialwissenschaften.'" *Soziale Welt* 19: 328–41. (Reprinted in Günther 1976–80, 2: 157–70.)

———. 1976. "Cybernetic Ontology and Transjunctional Operations." In Günther 1976–80, 1: 249–328.

———. 1976–80. *Beiträge zur Grundlegung einer operationsfähigen Dialektik.* 3 vols. Hamburg.

———. 1979a. "Life as Poly-Contexturality." In Günther 1976–80, 2: 283–306.

———. 1979b. "Logistischer Grundriß und Intro-Semantik." In Günther 1976–80, 2: 1–115.

———. 1980. "Strukturelle Minimalbedingungen einer Theorie des objektiven Geistes als Einheit der Geschichte." In Günther 1976–80, 3: 136–82.

Habermas, Jürgen. 1968. *Technik und Wissenschaft als "Ideologie."* Frankfurt.

———. 1981. "Die Moderne—ein unvollendetes Project." In Jürgen Habermas, *Kleine politische Schriften,* 444–64. Frankfurt.

Hahn, Alois. 1987. "Sinn und Sinnlosigkeit." In Hans Haferkamp and Michael Schmid, eds., *Sinn, Kommunikation und soziale Differenzierung: Beiträge zu Luhmanns Theorie sozialer Systeme,* 155–64. Frankfurt.

———. 1989. "Das andere Ich: Selbstthematisierung bei Proust." In Volker Kapp, ed., *Marcel Proust: Geschmack und Neigung,* 127–41. Tübingen.

Hallowell, I. 1960. "Ojibwa Ontology: Behavior and World Views." In S. Diamond, ed., *Culture in History: Essays in Honor of Paul Radin,* 19–57. New York.

Havelock, E. A. 1982. *The Literate Revolution in Greece and Its Cultural Consequences.* Princeton, N.J.

Heidegger, Martin. 1949. *Sein und Zeit.* Sixth printing. Tübingen.

———. 1977. "The Age of the World Picture." In Martin Heidegger, *"The Question Concerning Technology" and Other Essays,* trans. William Lovitt, 115–54. New York.

Heider, F. 1959 [1926]. "Thing and Medium." Trans. Fritz Heider and Grace M. Heider. *Psychological Issues* 1/3: 1–34. (This article is an abridged translation of "Ding und Medium," *Symposium* 1 [1926]: 108–57.)

Hejl, P. M. 1987. "Konstruktion der sozialen Konstruktion: Grundlinien einer konstruktivistischen Sozialtheorie." In Schmidt 1987, 303–39.

Herbst, Phillip G. 1976. *Alternatives to Hierarchies.* Leiden.

Hesse, Mary. 1966. *Models and Analogies in Science.* Notre Dame.

Hobbes, Thomas. 1968 [1651]. *Leviathan.* Ed. C. B. MacPherson. Harmondsworth, Eng.

Hofstadter, Douglas R. 1979. *Gödel, Escher, Bach: An Eternal Golden Braid*. New York.

Hogarth, William. 1955 [1753]. *The Analysis of Beauty, Written With a View of Fixing the Fluctuating Ideas of Taste*. Ed. Joseph Burke. Oxford.

Holmes, Stephen. 1987. "Poesie der Indifferenz." Trans. Herbert Willems, Rainer Winter, and Hartmann Tyrell. In Baecker et al. 1987, 15–45.

Husserl, Edmund. 1928. *Vorlesungen zur Phänomenologie des inneren Zeitbewusstseins*. Ed. Martin Heidegger. *Jahrbuch für Philosophie und phänomenologische Forschung* 9: 367–496.

———. 1948. *Erfahrung und Urteil: Untersuchungen zur Genealogie der Logik*. Hamburg.

———. 1950 [1913]. *Ideen zu einer reinen Phänomenologie und phänomenologische Philosophie*. In Edmund Husserl, *Husserliana*, vol. 3, 1, ed. Karl Schuhmann. The Hague.

———. 1954a [1935]. "Die Krisis des europäischen Menschentums und die Philosophie." In Edmund Husserl, *Husserliana*, vol. 4, ed. Walter Biemel, 314–48. The Hague.

———. 1954b [1936]. *Die Krisis der europäischen Wissenschaften und die transzendentale Phänomenologie*. In Edmund Husserl, *Husserliana*, vol. 6, ed. Walter Biemel. The Hague.

———. 1970a. *The Crisis of European Sciences and Transcendental Phenomenology*. Trans. and intro. David Carr. Evanston, Ill.

———. 1970b [1935]. "Philosophy and the Crisis of European Humanity." In Husserl 1970a, 269–99.

———. 1998 [1913]. *Ideas Pertaining to a Pure Phenomenology and a Phenomenological Philosophy*. Book 1. Trans. F. Kersten. Dordrecht.

James, Mervyn. 1974. *Family, Lineage, and Civil Society: A Study of Society, Politics, and Mentality in the Durham Region 1500–1640*. Oxford.

James, William. 1995 [1912]. "On a Certain Blindness in Human Beings." In William James, *Selected Writings*, ed. G. H. Bird, 320–37. London.

Jean Paul [pseud.]. 1924. "Das Kampanertal oder über die Unsterblichkeit der Seele." In Jean Paul, *Jean Pauls Werke: Ausgabe in zwei Bänden*, 2: 170–229. Stuttgart.

Jerison, H. J. 1973. *Evolution of the Brain and Intelligence*. New York.

Johnson, Samuel. 1963. *The Idler and the Adventurer*. Ed. W. J. Bate, J. M. Bullit, and L. F. Powel. New Haven, Conn.

Kauffman, Louis H. 1987. "Self-Reference and Recursive Forms." *Journal of Social and Biological Structures* 10: 53–72.

Kline, Morris. 1980. *Mathematics: The Loss of Certainty*. Oxford.

Kofman, Sarah. 1980. *L'enigme de la femme: La femme dans les textes de Freud*. Paris.

Korzybski, Alfred. 1958 [1933]. *Science and Sanity: An Introduction to Non-Aristotelian Systems and General Semantics*. 4th ed. Lakeville, Mass.

Lando, Ortensio. N.d. *Confutatione del libro de paradossi nuovamente composta in tre orationi distinta.* N.p.

———. 1545. *Paradossi, cioe sententie fuori del commun parere.* N.p.: Venegia.

La Noue, François. 1967 [1587]. *Discours politiques et militaires.* Geneva.

Lawson, Hilary. 1985. *Reflexivity: The Postmodern Predicament.* London.

Lemnius, Levinus. 1574. *De miraculis occultis naturae libri IIII.* Antwerp.

Livingston, Paisley, ed. 1984. *Disorder and Order: Proceedings of the Stanford International Symposium* (Sept. 14–16, 1981). Saratoga, Calif.

Lloyd, G. E. R. 1979. *Magic, Reason and Experience: Studies in the Origin and Development of Greek Science.* Cambridge, Eng.

Löfgren, Lars. 1978. "Some Foundational Views on General Systems and the Hempel Paradox." *International Journal of General Systems* 4: 243–53.

———. 1981. "Life as an Autolinguistic Phenomenon." In Milan Zeleny, ed., *Autopoiesis: A Theory of Living Organization,* 236–49. New York.

———. 1988. "Towards System: From Computation to the Phenomenon of Language." In Marc Carvallo, ed., *Nature, Cognition and System I: Current Systems-Scientific Research on Natural and Cognitive Systems,* 129–55. Dordrecht.

Luhmann, Niklas. 1977. *Funktion der Religion.* Frankfurt.

———. 1978. "Interpenetration bei Parsons." *Zeitschrift für Soziologie* 7: 299–302.

———. 1980–95. *Gesellschaftsstruktur und Semantik: Studien zur Wissenssoziologie der modernen Gesellschaft.* 4 vols. Frankfurt.

———. 1985a. "Läßt unsere Gesellschaft Kommunikation mit Gott zu?" In Bogensberger and Kögeler, eds., *Grammatik des Glaubens,* 41–48. Vienna.

———. 1985b. "Society, Meaning, Religion—Based on Self-Reference." *Sociological Analysis* 45: 5–20.

———. 1986a. "Intersubjektivität oder Kommunikation: Unterschiedliche Ausgangspunkte soziologischer Theoriebildung." *Archivio di Filosofia* 54: 41–60.

———. 1986b. "Das Medium der Kunst." *Delfin* 7: 6–15.

———. 1986c. *Ökologische Kommunikation: Kann die moderne Gesellschaft sich auf ökologische Gefährdungen einstellen?* Opladen.

———. 1987a. "Die Autopoiesis des Bewußtseins." In A. Hahn and V. Kapp, eds., *Selbstthematisierung und Selbstzeugnis: Bekenntnis und Geständnis,* 25–94. Frankfurt.

———. 1987b. "Tautologie und Paradoxie in den Selbstbeschreibungen der modernen Gesellschaft." *Zeitschrift für Soziologie* 16: 161–74.

———. 1988a. *Erkenntnis als Konstruktion.* Bern.

———. 1988b. "The Third Question: The Creative Use of the Paradoxes in Law and Legal Theory." *Law and Society Review* 15: 153–65.

———. 1989a. "Die Ausdifferenzierung der Religion." In Luhmann 1980–95, 3: 259–357.

———. 1989b. "Staat und Staatsraison im Übergang von traditionaler Herrschaft zu moderner Politik." In Luhmann 1980–95, 3: 65–148.

————. 1990a. *Essays on Self-Reference*. New York.

————. 1990b. *Political Theory in the Welfare State*. Berlin.

————. 1990c. *Die Wissenschaft der Gesellschaft*. Frankfurt a.M.

————. 1995a. "Kultur als historischer Begriff." In Luhmann 1980–95, 4: 31–54.

————. 1995b. *Social Systems*. Trans. John Bednarz, Jr., with Dirk Baecker. Stanford, Calif.

————. 1997. *Die Gesellschaft der Gesellschaft*. Frankfurt.

Luhmann, Niklas, et al. 1990. *Beobachter. Konvergenz der Erkenntnistheorien?* Munich.

Luhmann, Niklas, and Raffaele De Giorgi. 1992. *Teoria della Società*. Milano.

Luhmann, Niklas, and Peter Fuchs. 1989. *Reden und Schweigen*. Frankfurt a.M.

Lutz, Burkhart. 1994. "Das 'Projekt Moderne' liegt noch vor uns! Zur Notwendigkeit einer neuen Makrotheorie moderner Gesellschaften." In *Festschrift Renate Mayntz*, 513–26. Baden-Baden.

Lyotard, Jean-François. 1985. "Histoire universelle et différences culturelles." *Critique* 456: 559–68.

————. 1993. "The Wall, the Gulf, and the Sun: A Fable." In Jean-François Lyotard, *Political Writings*, trans. Bill Readings and Kevin Paul Geiman, 112–23. Minneapolis.

McCanles, Michael. 1966. "Paradox in Donne." *Studies in the Renaissance* 13: 266–87.

MacCannel, Dean, and Juliet E. MacCannel. 1982. *The Time of the Sign: A Semiotic Interpretation of Modern Culture*. Bloomington, Ind.

McCulloch, W. S. 1965. *Embodiments of the Mind*. Cambridge, Mass.

MacKie, J. L. 1973. *Truth, Probability and Paradox: Studies in Philosophical Logic*. Oxford.

Malloch, A. E. 1956. "The Techniques and Function of the Renaissance Paradox." *Studies in Philology* 53: 191–203.

Margolis, Joseph. 1985. "Deconstruction; or, The Mystery of the Mystery of the Text." In Hugh J. Silverman and Don Ihde, eds., *Hermeneutics and Deconstruction*, 138–51. Albany, N.Y.

Maturana, Humberto R. 1982. *Erkennen: Die Organisation und Verkörperung von Wirklichkeit: Ausgewählte Arbeiten zur biologischen Epistemologie*. Trans. Wolfgang K. Köck. Braunschweig.

————. 1986a. "The Biological Foundations of Self-Consciousness and the Physical Domain of Existence." Manuscript.

————. 1986b. "Evolution: Phylogenetic Drift through the Conservation of Adaptation." Manuscript.

Maturana, Humberto, and Francisco Varela. 1984. *El árbol de conocimiento*. Santiago de Chile. (Published in English as *The Tree of Knowledge: The Biological Roots of Human Understanding*. Trans. R. Paolucci. Boston, 1992.)

————. 1987. *Der Baum der Erkenntnis: Die biologischen Wurzeln des menschlichen Erkennens*. Bern.

Merleau-Ponty, Maurice. 1945. *Phénoménologie de la Perception*. Paris.

Meyer, Eva. 1990. "Der Unterschied, der eine Umgebung schafft." In Ars Electronica, ed., *Netz der Systeme*, 110–22. Berlin.

Miermont, Jacques. 1989. "Les conditions formelles de l'état autonome." *Revue internationale de systématique* 3: 295–314.

Mitchell, Juliet. 1975. *Psychoanalysis and Feminism*. New York.

Morellet, André. 1778 [1775]. *Theorie des Paradoxen*. Leipzig. (This is a German translation of *Theorie du paradoxe*.)

Münch, Richard. 1984. *Die Struktur der Moderne: Grundmuster und differentielle Gestaltung des institutionellen Aufbaus der modernen Gesellschaften*. Frankfurt a.M.

Munday, Anthony. 1969 [1593]. *The Defence of Contraries*. Amsterdam and New York.

Naess, A. 1936. *Erkenntnis und wissenschaftliches Verhalten*. Oslo.

Nagel, Ernest, and James R. Newman. 1958. *Gödel's Proof*. New York.

Nicholas of Cusa. 1964. *Apologia Doctae Ignorantiae*. In Nicholas of Cusa, *Philosophisch-theologische Schriften*, ed. Leo Gabriel, vol. 1. Vienna.

Ong, W. J. 1971. *Rhetoric, Romance and Technology: Studies in the Interaction of Expression and Culture*. Ithaca, N.Y.

Parsons, Talcott. 1942a. "Democracy and the Social Structure in Pre-Nazi Germany." *Journal of Political and Legal Sociology* 1: 96–114.

————. 1942b. "Max Weber and the Contemporary Political Crisis." *Review of Politics* 4: 61–76, 155–72.

————. 1942c. "Some Sociological Aspects of the Fascist Movements." *Social Forces* 21: 138–47.

————. 1960. "Pattern Variables Revisited." *American Sociological Review* 25: 467–83. (Reprinted in Parsons 1967, 192–219.)

————. 1967. *Sociological Theory and Modern Society*. New York.

————. 1971. *The System of Modern Societies*. Englewood Cliffs, N.J.

Pask, G. 1981. "Developments in Conversation Theory: Actual and Potential Applications." In G. E. Lasker, ed., *Applied Systems and Cybernetics*, 3: 1326–38. New York.

Plato. 1990. *The Thaetetus of Plato*. Ed. M. Burnyeat. Indianapolis.

Pothast, U. 1987. "Etwas über 'Bewußtsein.'" In K. Cramer et al., eds., *Theorie der Subjektivität*. Frankfurt.

Probst, P. 1989. "Paradox." In Joachim Ritter and Karlfried Gründer, eds., *Historisches Wörterbuch der Philosophie*, 7: 81–90. Basel.

Quine, W. V. 1960. *Word and Object*. New York.

Reid, Constance. 1996. *Hilbert*. New York.

Rescher, N. 1985. *The Strife of Systems: An Essay on the Grounds and Implications of Philosophical Diversity.* Pittsburgh.

Ritter, Joachim. 1969. *Metaphysik und Politik: Studien zu Aristoteles und Hegel.* Frankfurt.

Roberts, David. 1992. "The Law of the Text of the Law: Derrida Before Kafka." Manuscript. Melbourne.

Rorty, Amélie O. 1980. "Self-Deception, Akrasia and Irrationality." *Social Science Information* 19: 905–22.

Rosen, R. 1985. *Anticipatory Systems. Philosophical, Mathematical and Methodological Foundations.* Oxford.

Roth, G. 1982. "Conditions of Evolution and Adaptation in Organisms as Autopoietic Systems." In D. Mossakowski and G. Roth, eds., *Environmental Adaptation and Evolution*, 37–48. Stuttgart.

———. 1986. "Selbstorganisation—Selbsterhaltung—Selbstreferentialität: Prinzipien der Organisation der Lebewesen und ihre Folgen für die Beziehungen zwischen Organismus und Umwelt." In A. Dress et al., eds., *Selbstorganisation: Die Entstehung von Ordnung in Natur und Gesellschaft*, 149–80. Munich.

———. 1987a. "Autopoiese und Kognition: Die Theorie H. R. Maturana, und die Notwendigkeit ihrer Weiterentwicklung." In Schmidt 1987, 256–86.

———. 1987b. "Die Entwicklung kognitiver Selbstreferentialität im menschlichen Gehirn." In Baecker et al. 1987, 394–422.

———. 1987c. "Erkenntnis und Realität: Das reale Gehirn und seine Wirklichkeit." In Schmidt 1987, 229–55.

Rousseau, Jean-Jacques. 1959a. *Oeuvres complètes.* Vol. 1. Paris.

———. 1959b. *Les rêveries du promeneur solitaire, Cinquième promenade.* In Rousseau 1959a, 995–1099.

Ruesch, Jürgen, and Gregory Bateson. 1968 [1951]. *Communication: The Social Matrix of Psychiatry.* New York.

Russell, Bertrand. 1981 [1901]. "Mathematics and the Metaphysicians." In Bertrand Russell, *Mysticism and Logic: And Other Essays*, 59–74. Totowa, N.J.

Schelsky, Helmut. 1955. *Soziologie der Sexualität: Über die Beziehungen zwischen Geschlecht, Moral und Gesellschaft.* Reinbek.

Schkommodau, Hans. 1972. *Thematik des Paradoxes in der Aufklärung.* Wiesbaden.

Schmidt, Siegfried J., ed. 1987. *Der Diskurs des radikalen Konstruktivismus.* Frankfurt.

Schröder, Gerhart. 1985. *Logos und List: Zur Entwicklung der Ästhetik in der frühen Neuzeit.* Königstein / Taunus.

Schulz-Buschhaus, Ulrich. 1991. "Vom Lob der Pest und vom Lob der Perfidie: Burleske und politische Paradoxographie in der italienischen Renaissance-Literatur." In Gumbrecht and Pfeiffer 1991, 259–73.

Schütz, A. 1932. *Der sinnhafte Aufbau der sozialen Welt. Eine Einleitung in die verstehende Soziologie.* Vienna.

Serres, Michel. 1980. *Le parasite.* Paris.

———. 1981. *Der Parasit.* Frankfurt.

———. 1982. "The Origin of Language: Biology, Information Theory, and Thermodynamics." In Michel Serres, *Hermes: Literature, Science, Philosophy,* ed. Josué V. Harari and David F. Bell, 71–83. Baltimore.

———. 1984. "Dream." In Livingston 1984, 225–39.

Shackle, George L. S. 1979. "Information, Formalism, and Choice." In Mario J. Rizzo, ed., *Time, Uncertainty, and Disequilibrium: Exploration on Austrian Themes,* 19–31. Lexington, Mass.

Simon, Fritz B. 1988. *Klinische Epistemologie: Grundlagen einer systemischen Psychiatrie und Psychosomatik.* Berlin.

Sklar, Lawrence. 1992. *Philosophy of Physics.* Boulder.

Smithson, Michael. 1989. *Ignorance and Uncertainty: Emerging Paradigms.* New York.

Spencer Brown, George. 1979 [1969]. *Laws of Form.* 2nd ed. New York.

Stone, Lawrence. 1965. *The Crisis of the Aristocracy 1558–1641.* Oxford.

Strauss, Leo. 1953. *Natural Right and History.* Chicago.

———. 1988. *"What Is Political Philosophy?" and Other Studies.* Chicago.

Tenbruck, F. H. 1986. *Geschichte und Gesellschaft.* Berlin.

Thom, René. 1975. *Structural Stability and Morphogenesis: An Outline of a General Theory of Models.* Trans. from the French edition, as updated by the author, by D. H. Fowler. Reading, Mass.

Thomas, Keith. 1988. *Vergangenheit, Zukunft, Lebensalter: Zeitvorstellungen im England der frühen Neuzeit.* Berlin.

Tiryakian, Edward A. 1985. "The Changing Centers of Modernity." In Erik Cohen et al., eds., *Comparative Social Dynamics: Essays in Honor of S. N. Eisenstadt,* 121–47. Boulder.

Ulrich, Hans, and Gilbert J. B. Probst, eds. 1984. *Self-Organization and Management of Social Systems: Insights, Promises, Doubts, and Questions.* Berlin.

Varela, Francisco J. 1975. "A Calculus for Self-Reference." *International Journal of General Systems* 2: 5–24.

———. 1979. *Principles of Biological Autonomy.* New York.

———. 1984. "Living Ways of Sense-Making: A Middle Path for Neuroscience." In Livingston 1984, 208–23.

———. 1986. *The Sciences and Technology of Cognition: Emerging Trends.* Manuscript. Paris.

Vattimo, Gianni. 1991. "The End of (Hi)story." In Ingeborg Hoesterey, ed., *Zeitgeist in Babel: The Postmodernist Controversy,* 132–41. Bloomington, Ind.

von Foerster, Heinz. 1969. "What Is Memory That It May Have Hindsight and

Foresight as Well?" In S. Bogoch, ed., *The Future of the Brain Sciences*, 19–64. New York.

———. 1981. *Observing Systems*. Seaside, Calif.

———. 1984. "Principles of Self-Organization in a Socio-Managerial Context." In Ulrich and Probst 1984, 2–24.

———. 1985a. "Entdecken oder Erfinden. Wie läßt sich Verstehen verstehen?" In Gumin and Mohler 1985, 27–68.

———. 1985b. *Sicht und Einsicht. Ausgewählte Arbeiten zu einer operativen Erkenntnistheorie*. Braunschweig.

———. 1993a. "Für Niklas Luhmann: Wie rekursiv ist Kommunikation?" *Teoria Sociologica* 1/2: 61–85.

———. 1993b. "Die Gesetze der Form." In Baecker 1993, 9–11.

———. 1993c. *Wissen und Gewissen: Versuch einer Brücke*. Frankfurt.

von Glasersfeld, Ernst. 1985. "Konstruktion der Wirklichkeit und des Begriffs der Objektivitäat." In Gumin and Mohler 1985, 1–26.

———. 1987. *Wissen, Sprache und Wirklichkeit: Arbeiten zum radikalen Konstruktivismus*. Braunschweig.

Wasserman, Earl R. 1959. *The Subtler Language: Critical Readings of Neo-Classical and Romantic Poems*. Baltimore.

Watzlawick, P., ed. 1981. *Die erfundene Wirklichkeit*. Munich.

Weber, Max. 1946. *From Max Weber: Essays in Sociology*. Trans. and ed. H. H. Geerth and C. Wright Mills. New York.

———. 1958. *The Protestant Ethic and the Spirit of Capitalism*. Trans. Talcott Parsons. New York.

Weck-Erlen, L. van der. 1978 [1907]. *Das goldene Buch der Liebe: Ein Eros-Kodex für beide Geschlechter*. Reprint. Reinbek.

Wellbery, David. 1992. "The Exteriority of Writing." *Stanford Literature Review* 9: 11–23.

Wendel, Hans Jürgen. 1989. "Wie erfunden ist die Wirklichkeit?" *Delfin* 12: 79–89.

Whitehead, A. N. 1954. *Science and the Modern World* (1925 Lowell Lectures). New York.

Williams, Raymond. 1958. *Culture and Society 1780–1950*. New York.

Winograd, Terry, and Fernando Flores. 1987. *Understanding Computers and Cognition: A New Foundation for Design*. Reading, Mass.

Wittgenstein, Ludwig. 1974. *Tractatus Logico-Philosophicus*. Trans. D. F. Pears and B. F. McGuinness. London.

Wood, A. E. 1985. *Knowledge Before Printing and After: The Indian Tradition in Changing Kerala*. Delhi.

Žižek, Slavoj. 1993. *Tarrying with the Negative: Kant, Hegel, and the Critique of Ideology*. Durham, N.C.

Index

Cultural Memory | *in the Present*

Richard Rand, ed., *Futures: Of Jacques Derrida*

William Rasch, *Niklas Luhmann's Modernity: The Paradoxes of Differentiation*

Jacques Derrida and Anne Dufourmantelle, *Of Hospitality*

Jean-François Lyotard, *The Confession of Augustine*

Kaja Silverman, *World Spectators*

Samuel Weber, *Institution and Interpretation: Expanded Edition*

Jeffrey S. Librett, *The Rhetoric of Cultural Dialogue: Jews and Germans in the Epoch of Emancipation*

Ulrich Baer, *Remnants of Song: Trauma and the Experience of Modernity in Charles Baudelaire and Paul Celan*

Samuel C. Wheeler III, *Deconstruction as Analytic Philosophy*

David S. Ferris, *Silent Urns: Romanticism, Hellenism, Modernity*

Rodolphe Gasché, *Of Minimal Things: Studies on the Notion of Relation*

Sarah Winter, *Freud and the Institution of Psychoanalytic Knowledge*

Samuel Weber, *The Legend of Freud: Expanded Edition*

Aris Fioretos, ed., *The Solid Letter: Readings of Friedrich Hölderlin*

J. Hillis Miller / Manuel Asensi, *Black Holes / J. Hillis Miller; or, Boustrophedonic Reading*

Miryam Sas, *Fault Lines: Cultural Memory and Japanese Surrealism*

Peter Schwenger, *Fantasm and Fiction: On Textual Envisioning*

Didier Maleuvre, *Museum Memories: History, Technology, Art*

Jacques Derrida, *Monolingualism of the Other; or, The Prosthesis of Origin*

Andrew Baruch Wachtel, *Making a Nation, Breaking a Nation: Literature and Cultural Politics in Yugoslavia*

Niklas Luhmann, *Love as Passion: The Codification of Intimacy*

Mieke Bal, ed., *The Practice of Cultural Analysis: Exposing Interdisciplinary Interpretation*

Jacques Derrida and Gianni Vattimo, eds., *Religion*